Churchill, America and Vietnam 1941 45

Also by T. O. Smith

BRITAIN AND THE ORIGINS OF THE VIETNAM WAR: UK POLICY IN
INDO-CHINA 1943–50

Churchill, America and Vietnam, 1941–45

T. O. Smith

Associate Professor of History, Huntington University, USA

First published 2011 by
PALGRAVE MACMILLAN

Palgrave Macmillan in the UK is an imprint of Macmillan Publishers Limited,
registered in England, company number 785998, of Houndmills, Basingstoke,
Hampshire RG21 6XS.

Palgrave Macmillan in the US is a division of St Martin's Press LLC,
175 Fifth Avenue, New York, NY 10010.

Palgrave Macmillan is the global academic imprint of the above companies
and has companies and representatives throughout the world.

Palgrave® and Macmillan® are registered trademarks in the United States,
the United Kingdom, Europe and other countries.

ISBN 978–0–230–29820–0 hardback
ISBN 978–0–230–29821–7 paperback

This book is printed on paper suitable for recycling and made from fully
managed and sustained forest sources. Logging, pulping and manufacturing
processes are expected to conform to the environmental regulations of the
country of origin.

A catalogue record for this book is available from the British Library.

Library of Congress Cataloging-in-Publication Data
Smith, T. O.
    Churchill, America and Vietnam, 1941–45 / T. O. Smith.
        p.   cm.
    Includes bibliographical references and index.
    ISBN 978–0–230–29821–7 (pbk.)
    1. Great Britain—Foreign relations—Indochina.   2. Indochina—Foreign
relations—Great Britain.   3. Great Britain—Foreign relations—United
States.   4. United States—Foreign relations—Great Britain.   5. Great
Britain—Foreign relations—1936–1945.   6. Vietnam War, 1961–1975—
Causes.   7. Churchill, Winston, 1874–1965.   I. Title.
DS546.5.G74S66 2011
940.53'597—dc23   2011021393

10   9   8   7   6   5   4   3   2   1
20   19   18   17   16   15   14   13   12   11

Printed and bound in Great Britain by
CPI Antony Rowe, Chippenham and Eastbourne

For Elizabeth Anne Smith
'Many women do noble things, but you surpass them all'.
Proverbs 31:29

Contents

Acknowledgements

In the course of researching and writing this volume I have incurred a number of debts which it is my pleasure to acknowledge. To all of the individuals and institutions cited here I would like to express an immense debt of gratitude, although the usual disclaimer applies that none bears any responsibility for the author's conclusions.

I am greatly indebted to Professor John Charmley, with whom many years ago I first discussed the idea of a book about the relationship between Churchill, America and Vietnam. Despite fierce competition for his time, he indulged me with advice and the opportunity to share ideas. Likewise I am immensely grateful to my dear friend Dr Larry Butler, not only for his helpful observations and encouragement during the evolution of this project but also for reading and commenting on large portions of the typescript.

As the bibliography reflects, I am obliged to many scholars for their previous research in similar fields. However, I am especially thankful to those scholars that have taken a personal interest in this project and been unsparing with their time when needed. To this end I am most grateful to Professor Ben Kiernan, Dr Thomas Otte, Dr David Roberts and Professor Martin Thomas. Likewise, I am indebted to my colleagues in the History Department at Huntington University – Professor Dwight Brautigam, Professor Paul Michelson and Professor Jeffrey Webb – for providing the conditions in which serious historical research can thrive and with whom I have had the opportunity to debate and share many ideas over several years. Equally, I am also grateful to my late teacher, Professor Ralph Smith, whose own pioneering research and generous support have been of great significance.

The history students at Huntington University also deserve special mention – especially those who over the last few years have taken my senior seminar 'Britain and the End of Empire' or an independent study. Their attitude of not taking anything that I have said for granted has been an immense source of encouragement and pleasure.

I owe a special debt to the staff, trustees and individual copyright holders of the following libraries and archives: The Cadbury Research Library, Birmingham University; the British Library; the Centre for the Archives of France Overseas, Aix en Provence; Churchill College,

Cambridge; the Franklin D. Roosevelt Library, Hyde Park, New York; the Harry S. Truman Library, Independence, Missouri; Huntington University Library; the Middle East Centre Archive, St Anthony's College, Oxford; the Mountbatten Archive, Southampton University Library; the National Archives, Public Record Office, London; the University of East Anglia Library. If I have inadvertently infringed any copyright, I trust that the owner will notify the publisher so that this may be corrected in any future editions. I would also like to thank Mr Philip Judge, of the School of Environmental Sciences at the University of East Anglia, for drawing the map of Southeast Asia.

I am indebted to the Lilly Foundation for funding my Huntington University Research Fellowship in 2010, thereby providing a significant teaching load reduction towards my research. Likewise Dr Norris Friesen, Academic Dean of Huntington University, generously provided additional financial assistance towards my study.

My publisher Michael Strang and his assistant Ruth Ireland have, yet again, demonstrated aid beyond the call of duty and have shown exemplary patience, understanding and support for which I am very grateful.

Finally, I must thank my family who have contributed through their encouragement to this study. The constant love, advice and support of my parents, Victor and Joan Smith, and my brother and his wife, Thomas and Helen Lyman Smith, have been invaluable. However, my greatest debt is to my wife Elizabeth, who has lived with this project from the beginning and who has accompanied me on many of the research trips. It is more than convention which makes me say that without her I could never have written this tome. Therefore, as a small token of thanks, this book is dedicated to her.

T. O. Smith

List of Abbreviations

CCS	Combined Chiefs of Staff
COS	Chiefs of Staff (British)
JIC	Joint Intelligence Committee
JSM	Joint Service Mission (Washington)
PM	Prime Minister
SEAC	Southeast Asia Command
SOE	Special Operations Executive
UN	United Nations

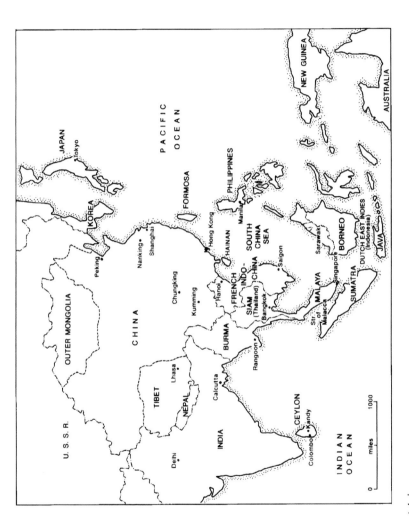

Map of Southeast Asia

Introduction

> In the beginning was the word, and the word was Churchill's
> and he pronounced it good.[1]

Since its inception during the Second World War, the Anglo-American
special relationship has remained a central feature of contemporary British foreign policy. Moreover it has been personified by its
chief architect – Winston Leonard Spencer Churchill. The strength of
Churchill's enchantment was to create a platform whereby subsequent
generations of Britons regarded the special relationship with increasing fondness and in ever more monolithic terms. Yet – as successive
historians have argued – the special relationship that Churchill sought
to construct, with the American President Franklin D. Roosevelt, was
neither monolithic nor harmonious. After all, American and British
war aims were very different; nowhere was this more evident than in
the Allied high-policy debate towards French Indo-China – modern
Cambodia, Laos and Vietnam.

The initial stages of Britain's association with French Indo-China
were orchestrated neither by Britain, nor France, nor Vietnam, but by
the United States. Britain owed its entanglement in the affairs of this
French colony to the musings of Roosevelt. Hitherto British high-policy
debate had been far less concerned with Indo-Chinese affairs. But in
the confines of Washington, Roosevelt had developed the notion that
he would like to detach Indo-China from French colonial control and
to place Indo-China into some form of post-war trusteeship. Although
this was not a plan for immediate autonomy, this trusteeship scheme
would evolve and the Indo-Chinese people would move towards sus-
tainable independence. Roosevelt did not care about the finer details
of his endeavour: one example being that Indo-China was a French

1

colonial possession rather than American and therefore not his to dispose. Roosevelt's war aims did not envisage the restoration of the European balance of power or the old world colonial order. He saw it as one of his primary objectives to fashion a new 'international order based on harmony'.[2] The management of this new system would naturally be in the hands of the American President.

Trusteeship was a dangerous concept. It set a perilous precedent for decolonisation. Roosevelt's open advocacy of Indo-Chinese trusteeship demonstrated the vehemence of his faith in national self-determination. This was an important anti-colonial 'test case' by an ardent anti-imperialist who had once quipped to Churchill that 'the British would take land anywhere in the world even if it were only a rock or a sand bar'.[3]

Roosevelt was not beyond using other nations to foster his trusteeship ideals. Indeed trusteeship occupied a special place in Sino-American relations, because Roosevelt visualised Nationalist China as being one of the four world policemen – with Britain, Russia and the United States – bound to protect post-war harmony and security.[4] Britain feared the rise of China as a Great Power. A strong China – backed by the United States – could exert undue pressure upon British colonial possessions in the Far East. Likewise, Britain doubted the lucidity of Chinese intentions for Southeast Asia, especially as a potential trustee.[5]

Churchill naturally sought to defend the future of the British Empire. When trusteeship discussions touched upon British possessions he advocated a strong anti-trusteeship line. This was shared by many members of Britain's coalition government and across the British political divide. For example, the Labour Home Secretary, Herbert Morrison, stated that trusteeship 'would be like giving a child of ten a latch-key, a bank account and a shotgun'.[6]

Nevertheless, when trusteeship deliberations focused upon other nations' imperial spheres, Churchill was short-sighted and absent-minded. While Whitehall attempted to develop a unified British policy towards Indo-Chinese trusteeship, Churchill continually rebuffed any actions that could potentially result in a conflict with Roosevelt and thereby produce a rift in the Anglo-American special relationship. Therefore, from the outset Churchill chose to regard Roosevelt's policy of trusteeship for Indo-China as 'an aberration'. As Churchill's 'instinct' was the prevailing factor in British wartime policy, he prevented Whitehall and the Dominions of Australia, Canada, New Zealand and South Africa from developing a more unified and co-ordinated approach.[7] Ultimately, as the war progressed and Churchill became more concerned about his legacy, he gradually turned his attention towards Indo-China and resolved his split with the rest of the British establishment and the Dominions. If the Foreign Office had directed British Indo-China policy from the beginning, then Anglo-American diplomacy would have definitely been more belligerent and the special relationship would have been developed in a more robust climate. For that reason Churchill saw it as his duty to step warily. He believed that he alone could be the pivot of Anglo-American relations. Churchill vainly believed that his Anglo-American pedigree would ensure that a balance could be maintained between American anti-imperialism and Foreign Office support for colonial spheres of influence. But in reality – in Indo-Chinese matters – the Prime Minister became a friendless and remote figure.

Roosevelt did not know how isolated Churchill eventually became concerning French Indo-China. But the President was well aware of the general operational constraints of his British ally. The pro-French nature of the Foreign Office had not escaped the attention of the American President. When the two leaders discussed Allied policy towards Italy in December 1943, Roosevelt pitied Churchill: 'I know what problems you have with your own Foreign Office', and he flattered the Prime Minister's ego that in reality they did not require any assistance.[8] However, despite a general appreciation for Churchill's circumstances, Roosevelt did not go out of his way to alleviate the universal sufferings of his special friend. Quite the opposite was actually the case. Any discussion of Indo-China tended to accelerate Roosevelt's strategy for colonial liberation and it gratified his desire to chastise the French.[9]

The Foreign Office and the Dominions were wise not to trust Roosevelt's apparent intention of only applying trusteeship to Indo-China. Roosevelt clearly had it in mind to use Indo-China as a precedent for old world decolonisation. He often revealed as much during some of his more abundant contemplations. On one such occasion, he turned his anti-colonial zeal upon the future of the British Empire when he expressed a desire to confiscate Hong Kong. At another juncture, Roosevelt toyed with the idea of encouraging Australia to purchase Timor from the Portuguese.[10] The American Secretary of State Cordell Hull naturally sought to downplay the President's soaring imagination. Hull guaranteed a nervous Britain that the United States would 'respect Portuguese sovereignty'.[11] But Roosevelt's ardent anti-colonialism could not be undone by his underlings; this was his personal flight of fancy. American foreign policy was the sole preserve of the President and with it the nature of the post-war world. Indeed Roosevelt was not embarrassed by any American territorial assurances, his trusteeship pronouncements were made in open contradiction of such assertions. The United States had already agreed to guarantee the 'territorial integrity' of the pre-war French Empire. Furthermore this was not an isolated declaration; after the Japanese attacked Pearl Harbor, the United States made a similar 'unqualified undertaking that they would support the return of Indo-China to France in all circumstances'.[12] Indo-China thus became an important political sideshow to Allied military policy. In such circumstances Britain needed to develop a coherent response that would protect its own interests and navigate unforeseen dilemmas.

The Anglo-American historiography of the origins of the Vietnam War has tended to place a lot of emphasis upon American President Harry S. Truman's 1945 'Lost Opportunity'. This 'Lost Opportunity' can be best defined by three questions about American foreign policy. Firstly, did American policy towards Vietnam fail at a critical moment because Truman did not understand his predecessor's (Roosevelt) vision for the post-war world? Secondly, what would have happened had Roosevelt lived? Finally, could America have actually forced trusteeship upon the European colonial powers during the post-war peace process? Within this historiography debate, Britain's role has naturally become minimised and obscured by the volume of literature dealing with Roosevelt's death and Truman's accession to the presidency. In doing so, the British role in the origins of the Vietnam War has been simplified and solely associated with the pro-imperial views of Churchill. As Churchill was a staunch defender of the British Empire it has erroneously been assumed that he always defended all of the European Empires against Roosevelt – lest trusteeship create a dangerous precedent for decolonisation.

In the 1970s the historians Christopher Thorne and William Roger Louis considered a broader history of Britain's response to trusteeship.[13] *Churchill, America and Vietnam, 1941–45* builds upon their work and considers Britain's response mainly through the lens of French Indo-China – the most important trusteeship case study. It reveals that although Churchill was content to be portrayed by his contemporaries as a unilateral defender of imperialism, he was also happy to sacrifice French Indo-China – especially if it threatened his special relationship with Roosevelt. On the other hand, the British Foreign Office and the Dominions Office both campaigned against what they regarded as Churchill's underhand policy because it set a dangerous precedent for decolonisation, undermined colonial development policy and post-hostilities planning, and threatened various post-war Anglo-European relationships.

Therefore, unlike the current historiography, this Anglo-centric study explores the multi-faceted nature of the British high-policy debate (between the War Cabinet, Colonial Office, Dominions Office, War Office, South East Asia Command and the Prime Minister) concerning Indo-China. It reveals the intensification of Asian nationalism, Britain's decline as a Great Power, the flow and ebb of Anglo-American relations, and the development of Britain's regional Southeast Asian policy for the post-war world. Moreover, because the formulation of British high-policy towards Vietnam cut across so many facets of British foreign policy, especially the Anglo-American special relationship, it was dominated by Churchill. As a result this book reflects a new perspective on Churchill's wartime leadership in relation to an issue that could have resulted in multiple British policy denouements, and it reveals that at times Churchill was prepared to sacrifice Vietnam for the sake of his special relationship with America – much to the chagrin of the rest of the British establishment. For these reasons, *Churchill, America and Vietnam, 1941–45* clarifies Britain's role in the origins of the Vietnam War, and it sets the scene for the post-war French return to Vietnam and the future American involvement in that country's troubled affairs.

1
Churchill's Conundrum

Late one night in 1943 one half-American British Prime Minister, Winston Churchill, asked another half-American (who would much later be British Prime Minister), Harold Macmillan, if Oliver Cromwell had been a great man. Macmillan immediately replied in the affirmative. Churchill, for whom the study of British history was an intellectual pastime, mocked his younger colleague's cocksure response. He said that Cromwell had after all 'made one terrible mistake. Obsessed in his youth by the fear of Spain, he failed to observe the rise of France. Will that be said of me?' Churchill's first official biographer, his son Randolph, suggested that this comment in 1943 was made by the Prime Minister reflecting upon his own anxiety with Germany vis-à-vis his failure to detect the rapid growth of Russia.[1] In this context Randolph's analysis certainly rings true and therefore the natural response to Churchill's rhetorical question should have been an unequivocal 'Yes'. Nevertheless an alternative interpretation is also possible. This would be to keep 'Germany' as the replacement for 'Spain' but to introduce 'America' as the substitution for Churchill's 'France' or Randolph's 'Russia'. In this context the analysis again would be correct. Churchill was obsessed with winning the war against Nazi Germany. The cost was that Britain would end the war severely weakened and with the future of the British Empire dependent upon the benevolence of the United States.

It was natural for Churchill to be an ardent Americanophile. His parentage guaranteed him an atypical insight into the transatlantic world. Yet in his vision of the United States, Churchill beheld the same difficulty as in his image of the British Empire. Both mental pictures were backwards looking to the triumphs of a high-Victorian past. Churchill was on balance a product of the late nineteenth century and Roosevelt would later quip that the Prime Minister was without a doubt 'mid-Victorian'.[2] For Churchill, the British Empire was characterised by ardent and dynamic imperialists such as Lord Curzon, Viceroy of India 1899–1905, and Joseph Chamberlain, Colonial Secretary 1895–1903. In addition, the United States was widely considered to be part of the English-speaking civilisation (alliance) that was benefiting the world. Known romantically as 'Anglo-Saxonism', this fashionable Victorian ideology advocated a shared Anglo-American racial superiority and civilising mission built upon a common heritage. It was a powerful vogue. Churchill's American mother, Lady Randolph Churchill, shared its sentiments and duly established *The Anglo-Saxon Review* to proselytise to those unfortunate enough not to believe.[3]

Under these circumstances, it is unsurprising that Churchill developed into the embodiment of a potent socio-political cocktail. Fervent imperialism mixed with zealous 'Anglo-Saxonism' was always going to produce a powerful brew. Therefore it was highly predictable that Churchill would carry his faith as a zealous Americanophile into public life. But whereas many similar brethren gradually began to fall by the wayside after the First World War, Churchill maintained his myth of an Anglo-American special relationship throughout his life. His often blind enthusiasm bordered upon fundamentalism. Yet Churchill appeared oblivious to the proverbial elephant in the room – did the United States wish to reciprocate his affections and upon his terms?

America, Roosevelt and anti-colonialism

The United States by its very nature, born out of a war of independence, could have been nothing other than an anti-colonial nation that advocated self-determination. But to say that the United States was fully anti-colonial would be erroneous. In the eighteenth and nineteenth centuries the United States had employed all of the tools of imperialism to establish itself. Known as Manifest Destiny, the United States formerly annexed Hawaii, Native American Indian territory, the Philippines, Puerto Rico and parts of Mexico. Informal imperial control was exerted over Cuba, Haiti, large swathes of mainland Central America and numerous Pacific islands.[4] America certainly knew how to create an empire. Indeed:

> In North America the problems of the indigenous inhabitants had been solved by the application of the sort of brutality which, had it been practised elsewhere, would have aroused fervent condemnation from Washington.[5]

The language that was used to describe America's new formal acquisitions was bereft of old world association. These were not colonies. The Native American Indians were 'wards of the United States'. Hawaii became a 'territory' and Puerto Rico a 'commonwealth'.[6]

It would be more appropriate, therefore, to state that although the United States practiced new world imperialism it also railed against old world colonialism. It was from old world colonialism that independence had been achieved. Moreover, it was the fear of domination by old European empires that had continued to haunt the young republic. American Manifest Destiny – new world colonialism mixed with a messianic zeal and a civilising mission – justified the American-led new world order in the Western hemisphere. The only alternative to American leadership was Haiti, which gained its independence in 1804. But Haiti was not a serious threat to American hegemony. To American observers at the time, Haiti's 'dark-skinned' people were no more worthy of their independence than American slaves.[7]

Like Churchill, Roosevelt was a creation of the late nineteenth century. He was the product of Hyde Park gentry and he had a Harvard education. Moreover, akin to Churchill, Roosevelt was strongly influenced by his mother. He was the fifth cousin of the Republican President Theodore Roosevelt – affectionately known in family circles as Uncle Ted. An eternal man of action, Uncle Ted had a colourful rise to high office. He had also gone to Harvard. Uncle Ted was a vibrant president with a strong foreign policy. Roosevelt visited Uncle Ted a number of times at the White House. He had clearly reserved a special place in his heart for the first Roosevelt to aspire to the presidency. He even married Uncle Ted's niece – Roosevelt's own fifth cousin once removed – Eleanor.[8]

Elected to the New York Senate in 1910, Roosevelt quickly rose onto the national stage to become the Assistant Secretary of the Navy under the Democrat President Woodrow Wilson. This appointment took him, as part of Wilson's administration, into the politics of the First World War. The result was that Roosevelt witnessed the vanity and failure of triumph in the armistice negotiations at Versailles. America had entered the war as an associate power rather than a full Allied nation. But Wilson hoped to use the peace process and American financial muscle to force Britain and France to adopt American values. The old world did not appreciate the moralising of the new.[9] On this occasion the Allies managed to snatch an incomplete victory from the jaws of success – a result Roosevelt endeavoured to rectify 25 years later as president.

The United States that Roosevelt inherited in 1933 had been greatly shaped by Wilson. Unsurprisingly, Roosevelt was also very much influenced by his former Commander in Chief. Wilson was a confident and dynamic leader who embodied American values and symbolised its coming of age – especially in foreign policy. The relationship between Wilson and Roosevelt was affable. Roosevelt was in many respects on the periphery of the administration. But Wilson genuinely liked his Assistant Secretary of the Navy and Roosevelt was an enthusiastic disciple.[10] Wilson articulated the belief that colonialism was out of date. Yet, under Wilson the United States garrisoned American troops in the Dominican Republic, Haiti, Mexico and Nicaragua. Force was justified to prepare the redeemed for self-government. Wilson thereby positioned the United States to take the lead towards the Promised Land.[11] Later at Versailles, Wilson articulated 'democracy, nationalism and the American way' upon the world stage.[12] This became known as Wilsonianism and every American president since Wilson has adopted this philosophy in foreign policy.[13]

The day-to-day workings of the Roosevelt White House, and the innermost organisation of his mysterious political regime, have for a long time held a certain fascination for historians. Lord Halifax, the British Ambassador in Washington, was able to study the internal workings of the Roosevelt administration at close quarters. The President certainly took less of a direct interest than Churchill in the everyday affairs of the Second World War. This left a considerable swathe of American policy solely in the hands of his apparatchiks – some of whom were vehemently against old world colonialism. As devotees of the type of America that Roosevelt envisioned, these administrators, generals and politicians did not have to worry about the President constantly looking over their shoulders. Roosevelt was not interested in detail. Halifax had observed how Roosevelt's 'mind was not at all confined to any beaten track, but both by the nature and choice enjoyed the liberty of exploration'. Roosevelt was a broad strategist who was prepared to think outside of the box. For Churchill – himself prone to the lure of academic rabbit trails – this added to the President's appeal.

Roosevelt also had a habit of using 'conversation as others of us use a first draft of paper'. This was his preferred method of 'trying out an idea'. If the conversation went badly, the idea could be modified later or dropped altogether.[14] At times this could be greatly frustrating as the President appeared to lack any clear direction. It left listeners groping for any inclination as to the President's actual feelings. It also had the disadvantage of creating contrasting and at times conflicting ideas as to the true nature of his policy in the minds of his officials. Henry Stimson, Secretary of War, concluded that Roosevelt was the 'poorest administrator' that he had ever worked with. But it would be a mistake to underestimate the President. Stimson, for one, was not taken in by the outward appearance of inefficiency. The President was in his experience a 'tough customer'.[15]

Multiple policies in fluid revision clearly had benefits for Roosevelt and often enabled the President to switch horses mid-race to achieve his preferred outcome. The problem was not that Roosevelt did not know what he wanted to achieve, but rather how he ought to achieve it. The goal was never in dispute, only the path to fruition. Roosevelt liked 'to play his cards so close to his chest that the ink rubbed off on to his shirt'.[16] Nonetheless, not everyone in Washington was brought to despair by the President's unconventional working practices. Harold Smith – whom Roosevelt made his Budget Director in 1939 – reported that the President was 'a real artist in government'.[17]

If American officials at times found Roosevelt difficult to fathom, the problem was magnified for the British. The British Foreign Secretary, Anthony Eden, was particularly sceptical about the workings of the American President. To Eden's eye Roosevelt was a 'conjuror, skilfully juggling with balls of dynamite whose nature he failed to understand'.[18] Yet Eden fell into Roosevelt's intended trap. His disbelief caused him to be blinded to the President's Machiavellian ways of achieving results.[19] The President was fully aware of just how frustrating he could be. During a conversation with his personal envoy Harry Hopkins, Roosevelt stated his full appreciation for the British who had behaved perfectly in all of their dealings with the United States, whereas Britain must have been 'mad' with him.[20]

In contrast to Britain, France represented all of the tribulations of old world colonialism. It had not behaved perfectly. France had prostituted itself upon Germany and capitulated to Japan. It embodied the worst excesses of old world colonialism. Immoderation had made it rotten to the core. The country of liberty, equality and fraternity had failed. To Roosevelt the Free French leader General Charles de Gaulle epitomised the ' "acute and unconquerable" nationalism' that had destroyed France as a Great Power. A view shared by other leading figures in Washington including the Secretary of State Cordell Hull.[21] The arrogant prima donnas of failed states did not deserve to shape the new world order.[22] In addition, de Gaulle's 'autocratic temperament' and his grave sin of 'playing Britain off against America' did not endear him to the President.[23] Roosevelt was the puppet master, not de Gaulle. Only one set of hands was going to pull the strings of the new world order.

Roosevelt was a devious political operative. His lithe approach towards issues enabled him to adopt supple attacks. But it would be a mistake to assume that the President did not possess a strong ideological tradition beneath the external facade. He was a fervent Wilsonian, an opponent of old world colonialism, and – above all else – an American. It was 'his dexterity, his command of a variety of roles, his skill in attack and defense, [and] above all his personal magnetism and *charisma* [*sic*]' that made him such a dazzling political operator.[24] These were the traits that Churchill fell for.

Roosevelt, then, was a brilliant tactician who had clear Wilsonian war aims. But the question remained as to whether the United States was ready for global leadership. General George Marshall, the Commander in Chief of the American Army, for one, had his doubts: 'there will have been no example in history of a nation as young as ours having responsibility thrust upon it. God only knows whether we shall be worthy of it'.[25] Roosevelt believed otherwise. In his mind the United States had finally come of age.

The Atlantic Charter, Washington and Casablanca

The Second World War had carried Churchill into power. He had held Britain together in its finest hour – the dark days of 1940 – when Britain had faced the Nazi menace alone. But Churchill was a gambler with 'a big bank running'. In 1940 he could not afford to 'look up from the table'.[26] By the time of the Prime Minister's first wartime meeting with Roosevelt in August 1941, the die was cast. Churchill took a great deal of personal interest in the direct day-to-day running of the war. But his new found American ally was less interested in such matters and saw the need to look up from the table to consider what the post-war world would look like.

The Atlantic Conference was the product of a careful courtship of Roosevelt by the Prime Minister. Although the United States had not as yet officially entered the war, the conference marked the beginning of a formal period of Anglo-American engagement. Churchill was aided in his wooing of Roosevelt by Halifax, who 'provided lubrication' for their relationship. Halifax also got on well with Hull and Hopkins, thus increasing his value to Churchill's enterprise. Although Halifax chaperoned the matchmaking, he was also well aware of the deficiencies of the intended union. From his perspective, Roosevelt was an 'adroit manipulator' and Churchill tended to idolise the American President.[27]

The clandestine series of conference meetings were held aboard the USS Augusta moored, in Placentia Bay, just off the Newfoundland coast from 9 to 14 August 1941. After the usual pre-conference formalities, the conference got down to the main business. The President received the Prime Minister and Sir Alexander Cadogan, the Permanent Under-Secretary of State at the Foreign Office, on 11 August – along with the American Under-Secretary of State Sumner Welles and Harry Hopkins – for a number of important discussions. The conference was wide ranging and included a full and frank exchange of views about Portuguese affairs, the deteriorating situation in the Far East and the issuance of a joint post-conference declaration of their deliberations. This latter item later became known as the Atlantic Charter.

During the discussions on the Far East, Churchill agreed to Roosevelt's proposal that the British Government would give an assurance that it had no territorial designs towards Siam or Indo-China.[28] Several weeks earlier, Roosevelt had asked Churchill not to commit Britain to any secret arrangements concerning post-war territorial transfers without the prior consent of the United States. Welles now reiterated this stand-point to Cadogan during the Atlantic Conference.[29] The implication was clear – America might not formally be at war but the United States was going to design the peace. This was to be the price of continued Anglo-American co-operation.

The first British draft of the Atlantic Charter envisioned a joint Anglo-American declaration which directly addressed the aggression of Nazi Germany. The British interpretation therefore started from a European perspective. Words such as 'freedom' and allusions to democracy and statehood were put forward only with this context in mind.[30] This initial draft contained only five specific commitments. Over the course of the conference the joint declaration was reworded by both sides and expanded to eight full pledges. The final declaration contained a lot of new world language. It was almost Wilsonian in nature. It envisioned a world built upon harmony rather than the old world balance of power. It alluded to vague concepts of freedom, democracy, peace and security, sovereignty, equality, and collaboration. In addition it acted as a Trojan horse, paving the way for American access to colonial markets.[31] This was an audacious statement. After all, the United States had not yet officially entered the war. The Japanese attack on Pearl Harbor did not take place until four months later.

After the conference had concluded, the press was free to report upon the proceedings. The media had certainly gained a favourable impression of the affairs. An *Associated Press* correspondent reported on Churchill's 'boyish' demeanour. The British *Daily Mail* correspondent was likewise full of praise. He quoted a senior American official who reported that during the conferences 'it was hard to tell which looked the happier – the President or Mr Churchill'. *International News* described Churchill's 'high spirits' and a general ambience of good-natured Anglo-American 'fraternization'.[32] The conference was a huge public relations success. It helped to strengthen Anglo-American liaison but – as yet – did not lead to full association.

Roosevelt left the Canadian coast to return to Washington. A week later, he wrote to Congress about his negotiations with Churchill. Roosevelt included in his report the actual wording of both the general press statement agreed by the President and the Prime Minister, and also the joint Atlantic Declaration. But in conclusion to everything that had been achieved, he informed Congress that it was for the 'whole freedom for which we strive'.[33] The American definition and connotations of freedom were very different from British ones.

Churchill came away from the Atlantic Conference in triumph. He was convinced that the Atlantic Charter applied only to Europe. The reaction in Washington was very different. Although not present at its inception, Hull was not as limited as the Prime Minister in his application of the Charter. The Secretary of State believed that the Charter encompassed a much more comprehensive outlook. It was to be 'universally applied to all nations and peoples – to all peoples, whatsoever their condition, and whatsoever shade of independence and freedom they might aspire to'.[34]

The British appreciated the ambiguity of the Atlantic Charter. After all, it was not a legally binding document. The vagueness that Churchill had created suited Britain's nebulous objectives. When conflict and contradiction with the United States arose, the indistinctness provided a diplomatic breathing space for British Government departments. American misinterpretation could therefore be attributed to a language barrier. Thus the subtle nuanced differences between American-English and British-English were used to good effect.[35]

Churchill was ruthless enough to renege on the American interpretation of the Atlantic Charter from the outset. He now sought to capitalise on his personal ties with Roosevelt by visiting Washington for a further conference with the President. Now that America had officially entered the war, the Prime Minister was more than willing to cross the Atlantic once more to develop further the fundamental mechanisms for a joint Anglo-American stratagem.[36] Churchill's hands-on approach towards Anglo-American relations meant that he was already well aware of the limitations of both the State Department and the Foreign Office as vehicles for his endeavours. This was confirmed to him in Washington. During Churchill's first meeting with Hull, the Prime

Minister quickly grasped the vulnerability of Hull's position within the American decision-making process. It was apparent to Churchill that the American Secretary of State had limited access to the President.[37] If the Anglo-American special relationship was to be the lynchpin of Churchill's wartime policies, the Prime Minister could not trust its development to others. Hull's inadequate contact with Roosevelt unwittingly confirmed to Churchill the importance of his personal relationship with the President, and it no doubt spurred Churchill into developing this intimacy even further.

It was during these idealistic days in Washington that Churchill resolved to bring his courtship of Roosevelt to fruition. The dowry that Churchill offered the President to settle the marriage was that the war would be run from Washington. It was a huge price to pay considering the length of Britain's wartime record and the current degree of equality within the Anglo-American relationship. But Churchill believed that the price was worth paying. The American share of the burden at that stage may have been limited, but the potential was colossal. In the meantime, Churchill believed that a close personable camaraderie with Roosevelt would smooth out 'every' difficulty. Furthermore, Churchill was confident that the dividends of their relationship would quickly materialise.[38]

Intimacy with the President was Churchill's chief desire. He worked liked a 'beaver' in Washington to achieve it and Roosevelt took the bait well. The President visited Churchill in his bedroom at 'any hour' and in one unfortunate incident became 'the only head of state whom he, Winston, has ever received in the nude'. The amount of time paid to the courtship did have its price. Churchill's passion prevented him from dealing with other urgent business. The British Embassy in Washington doubted whether Churchill actually took the time to read the telegrams related to the Lend-Lease Agreement or whether he would 'apply his mind to it'. On post-hostilities planning the Prime Minister was equally bored.[39]

Churchill was clearly enamoured with Roosevelt. A communiqué from the Prime Minister to London during his White House sojourn waxed lyrical concerning the President.[40] Indeed, confident of successful nuptials, Churchill informed King George VI that Britain and the United States 'were now "married" after many months of "walking out" '.[41] But was the same true for Roosevelt? Did the allusion of romance blind the Prime Minister to the fact that America was an independent country with its own war aims? Roosevelt was a shrewd political operator. He politely returned Churchill's lavish compliments and slyly encouraged the British Prime Minister to put his trust in an American president to the very last.[42]

The Foreign Office remained circumspect of Churchill's new bride. Oliver Harvey – Eden's Parliamentary Private Secretary – bluntly noted how 'determined' Roosevelt was to run the peace. The British Embassy in Washington was also in 'no doubt of his [Roosevelt's] ambition and determination to run the world'. The President had clearly given some thought to such issues and appeared more advanced in his designs than his closest confidants or the State Department.[43] Eden was equally unimpressed with the 'exaggeratedly moral' tone of American policy – presided over by Roosevelt – towards other nations' affairs.[44] There appeared just cause for the Foreign Secretary's concern. Dutch officials in London had already expressed their frustration and dissatisfaction at the direction of American policy towards their affairs. This was a charge made even more sober by the failure of the United States to consult with the Dutch.[45]

Mindful of Eden's concern, Churchill attempted to placate his Foreign Secretary's qualms about the future. Even though it would be impossible to predict the final post-war balance of power, Churchill believed that an alliance of the United States and the British Empire would eventually emerge as the strongest economic and military force in the world. Moreover, if any inconvenient problems arose – as wartime munitions difficulties had already demonstrated – these could be easily resolved by the excellent personal understanding between the Prime Minister and the President.[46]

Nonetheless, the honeymoon was brief. Britain suffered a number of military defeats during the spring of 1942. These culminated in the fall of Singapore – rapidly followed by Rangoon. Roosevelt was sympathetic to Britain's military defeats and he good-naturedly put pen to paper to comfort the Prime Minister: 'I want you to know that I think of you often and I know you will not hesitate to ask me if there is anything you think I can do'. Yet the President did not judge the circumstances too untimely to begin to press for Indian self-government.[47] The burden of leadership weighed heavily upon Churchill. He gratefully responded to Roosevelt's message of support that he did not enjoy 'these days of personal distress' and admitted to finding it difficult to concentrate on the task at hand.[48] Roosevelt could be supportive as well as charming, personable as well as ruthless. It was the President's personal diplomacy that appealed so much to Churchill. It increased the Prime Minister's faith in Roosevelt – their intimacy could cope with every crisis.

The fall of Singapore and the surrender of 85,000 British Empire troops 'stupefied' Churchill. He believed that it was an utter 'disgrace' for the British Empire to lose its most prestigious Asian base. Churchill found it hard to accept Britain's decline. Yet the portents of Britain's decay were evident for all to see. Roosevelt had previously pressed the issue of Indian self-government during the Prime Minister's visit to Washington. At that time, Churchill's vexed reaction had prompted no further discussion. But the issue had not gone away. Now in the safety of their transatlantic correspondence and Churchill's weakness, Roosevelt once again pressed the Prime Minister about the prospect of wartime self-government for India.[49] Roosevelt continued to raise the constitutional status of India with Churchill throughout the spring and summer of 1942.[50] Whereas the Prime Minister had been content to use the Atlantic Charter to snare Roosevelt, the President was now pre-pared to employ the Charter to gain moral ascendancy in the eyes of the colonial peoples.[51] The British failures at Singapore and Rangoon, and the Japanese use of French Indo-China to invade Java, had only served to undermine what little American faith there was in old world colonialism.[52]

Senior British officials continued to be under no illusions as to Roosevelt's dangerous political motives. Charles Peake, Counsellor at the British Embassy in Washington, reiterated that the President was determined to 'run the world'.[53] Similarly the Chief of the Imperial General Staff, General Sir Alan Brooke, foresaw that Roosevelt sought to use the war to break up the British Empire. However, Brooke also regarded Churchill as an equally 'grave danger'. Churchill was, after all, a politician and

> politicians still suffer from that little knowledge of military mat-ters which gives them unwarranted confidence that they are born strategists! As a result they confuse issues, affect decisions, and con-vert simple problems and plans into confused tangles and hopeless muddles.

Brooke was just as ruthless in his assessment of the President's lim-ited military knowledge as he was of the Prime Minister's. His opinion of Roosevelt's lieutenants was equally damning. Marshall's strategic ability did not impress Brooke and neither did the American Secre-tary of War, Stimson.[54] Brooke no doubt saw Stimson and Marshall's tactical weakness as further empowering Roosevelt's hard-nosed grand designs. However the South African Prime Minister Jan Smuts, who was also a military man, was less negative in his outlook. In spite of Roosevelt's anti-colonialism, Smuts perceived the emergent prime ministerial–presidential relationship as a blessing rather than a curse and he encouraged Churchill to develop it further: 'Your contacts with Roosevelt are now a most valuable war asset, and I hope that your weaker brethren with their purely domestic outlook will be made to realise this'.[55]

Nevertheless, despite the colonial powers' combined failures in the Far East, Churchill attempted to rebuff Roosevelt's Indian overtures.[56] In spite of everything, American entry into colonial affairs held menacing mercantile implications for the future of the British Empire. Churchill therefore endeavoured to play a subtle game with the evolution of British colonial development policy. Primarily this was concentrated on the West Indies. This location was chosen in order to appease Roosevelt.[57] A Memorial Day speech by Sumner Welles, Roosevelt's close friend and confidant, had ominously declared that Allied victory would result in the death of imperialism and the liberation of all peoples.[58] The subsequent use of the term 'partnership' by Macmillan during a House of Commons speech symbolised not only Britain's need to temper American criticism but also a genuine attempt at colonial readjustment that required social, economic and political progression.[59]

On 15 June, Churchill flew to the United States for further discussions with Roosevelt. These were to take place at the President's family home in Hyde Park, New York, and at the White House. Following the disappointments of early 1942, the nine-day whistle-stop tour was an attempt to rekindle personal relations and further co-ordinate war plans. It was Churchill's third meeting with Roosevelt in ten months, but this time fate would not be kind to the Prime Minister. It was during the dialogue between Roosevelt and Churchill at the White House that the blow came. The Prime Minister was passed a note which stated that Tobruk had fallen to the German advance upon the Egyptian border. 33,000 men had been taken prisoner. After a substantial silence, Roosevelt's response was both affectionate and genuine. The President asked Churchill how the United States could assist.[60]

Throughout 1942, the Colonial Office contemplated various post-war colonial modifications for the British Empire. In addition, despite Churchill's reluctance to address the future organization of the post-war world, the Foreign Office began to advocate detailed long-term planning concerning the future structure of the international order. Eden was weary of placing all of Britain's hopes into Churchill's Anglo-American abstract dream. Eden therefore sought to rejuvenate France as a Great

Power in order to counterbalance Churchill's grand Anglo-American alliance. In a July radio broadcast to France, Eden reiterated Anglo-French shared heritage and fraternity.[61] The inference that he articulated was that colonial nations should stick together.

Eden's problem however was – whose France did he wish to support? The State Department only wanted to do business with Marshal Henri Philippe Petain and the Vichy authorities. The Foreign Office sponsored support for de Gaulle and the Free French movement based in London. Churchill was inclined to keep both French horses in the race.[62] He was willing to appease Vichy on the one hand and maintain his turbulent relationship with de Gaulle on the other. This suited Churchill's flexible approach to post-war issues and avoided any confrontations with the State Department which might antagonise his union with Roosevelt. In fact, throughout both 1941 and 1942 there was little mention of de Gaulle in the wide-ranging correspondence between the Prime Minister and the President.[63]

In keeping with Brooke's healthy scepticism of politicians, the Chief of the Imperial General Staff was equally circumspect of the Foreign Office's unswerving support for de Gaulle, and Brooke was less than generous as to the Frenchman's general worthiness.[64] Eden not only faced opposition from Brooke. He also met with resistance to his post-war strategy from Clement Attlee, the Deputy Prime Minister. Attlee favoured the creation of an international system of colonial management. Eden was not against internationalised management systems. He wished to see defence and economic issues internationalised, but he believed that internal administration must be left to the colonial powers.[65] The Foreign Secretary recognised the sheer scale of the task that he faced, in trying to align the Colonial Office, the COS and Attlee with the Foreign Office vision, before taking on the Prime Minister.[66]

By October, the Foreign Office had created two policy papers dealing with post-war issues. The first paper proposed the adoption of the Foreign Office-inspired Four-Power Plan – the four powers being Britain, the United States, Russia and China. Under this proposal, these four powers would be responsible for the global management and administration of international affairs after the war. The second paper dealt with post-war colonial questions. It proposed the espousal of multinational regional councils for defence, economics and planning, whilst leaving internal administration in the hands of the individual colonial powers. Nonetheless, despite the rigorous planning being undertaken and confidence in Eden's grasp of post-war matters, Oliver Harvey disdainfully regarded Churchill as the 'chief obstacle' towards the implementation of any settled policy.

Eden hoped to broach the papers gently with Churchill. He wanted to be able to prepare the ground for an affable response by the Prime Minister towards the documents. Eden therefore intended to discuss the papers with Smuts and Churchill over the course of a weekend which they were spending together. Unfortunately, circumstances did not permit this to happen and Eden was only able to pass the Prime Minister copies of the policy papers for his consideration. Churchill was not amused with the documents. He considered them an irritant and instructed Eden that such topics were to be 'left to those who have nothing else to do'. Eden was aggrieved with the Prime Minister's scornful attitude and constant refusal to address post-war issues.[67]

Nonetheless, Churchill returned to post-war matters several days later. In a minute to Eden, the Prime Minister chastised his Foreign Secretary that post-war planning was a distraction to actual business of winning the war. In Churchill's eyes the former could not happen without the latter and therefore did not require his full attention. Harvey was not amused with the Prime Minister's criticism of his chief. The danger was evident. Roosevelt was bent upon dissolving the British Empire. It was important for the Foreign Office to gain Churchill's approval of the Four-Power Plan so that serious discussions could commence with the United States.[68] The longer that Churchill stalled the less prepared was the Foreign Office in comparison with Roosevelt. But Churchill was weary of the Foreign Office Four-Power Plan. As far as he was concerned the plan was flawed. This was because Churchill regarded China as nothing more than the 'faggot vote' of the United States. It was not a Great Power but rather an American vassal to assist with the dismemberment of the British Empire.[69]

Churchill would have been more mindful than normal of Roosevelt's post-war plans during the autumn. Eleanor Roosevelt, the President's wife, was due to arrive in Britain on 21 October 1942 as the guest of King George VI. During her three week sojourn, Eleanor resided at Buckingham Palace where she received numerous visitors including the Prime Minister, Smuts, Lord Mountbatten and Lord Woolton. Roosevelt's paralysis could not be a hindrance to wartime unity. As with the American electorate, Eleanor would be the President's personal envoy. Eleanor consequently became his eyes and ears in London, and Eleanor was no fool. She could be expected to hold her own in discussing international affairs with distinguished company.[70]

Post-war issues were raised again between the Prime Minister and the Foreign Secretary during a heated Cabinet meeting on 3 November 1942. Eden revealed Churchill's previous intransigence to the Cabinet. He informed them that the Prime Minister had for weeks been blockading his plans which required their consultation. Churchill was 'uneasy' with this revelation and the Cabinet naturally demanded to see the plans. Eden was livid with the Prime Minister and the Foreign Secretary half-heartedly threatened to resign. Harvey was furious. He was convinced that Churchill risked Britain winning the war but losing the peace.[71] Cadogan was more diplomatic preferring to record the Cabinet discussion as 'difficult'.[72] Foreign Office ire was evident for all to see.

Churchill was also clearly upset with the continuing discussions concerning the character of the post-war world. He returned to the issue seven days later. In a speech on 10 November 1942, at the Lord Mayor's luncheon banquet in the Mansion House of the City of London, the Prime Minister issued his truculent – and now infamous – battle cry. Churchill had not become Prime Minister to oversee the dismantling of the British Empire.[73] It was one of Churchill's great speeches of optimism and victory. But what was Churchill optimistic about? The Prime Minister was not interested in post-war planning, nor machinations about the future world organisation, nor Roosevelt's Machiavellian discourses about the independence for colonial peoples and end of the old world colonialism.

Eden was clearly upset about his contretemps with Churchill. The Foreign Secretary was equally annoyed with Kingsley Wood, the Chancellor of the Exchequer, for his foray into Foreign Office territory. Wood had instructed the Treasury to construct a policy paper in opposition to the Four-Power Plan. To the chagrin of the Foreign Office, the Prime Minister did not discourage the Treasury's venture into foreign policy.[74] Indeed it suited Churchill's purposes to keep government departments divided and the Four-Power Plan on the backburner until he was ready for further discussions with the Americans. The only problem with all of this was the urgency with which the Foreign Office treated such issues. Churchill was not convinced that they merited his immediate attention. Yet he did grasp the nature of the potential danger from across the Atlantic. Therefore, Churchill asked the War Cabinet to prepare a detailed record of Britain's past colonial policies and future aspirations.[75]

A subsequent speech by Sumner Welles allayed some of Churchill's fears about the Four-Power Plan. Thus, the Prime Minister agreed to the plan being brought before the Cabinet. He also approved that Eden should be dispatched to Washington for discussions with the

State Department.[76] The War Cabinet accepted the principles contained within the Four-Power Plan on 27 November 1942 – including China as one of the four Great Powers. The discussion of arrangements for regional councils was postponed to a later date.[77]

Notwithstanding the speech by Welles, the Foreign Office was becoming increasingly frustrated with America's conduct. It appeared to Harvey that the United States sponsored the most secretive policies, and insisted on running the war without consultation with the British, to the benefit of American commercial interests. The American General Dwight Eisenhower's local negotiations with the French in both North and West Africa – to the exclusion of the British – seemed to justify Foreign Office fears. The Americans were determined to compromise with the Vichy Vice President and Foreign Minister – Admiral Jean-Francois Darlan. For Harvey, American negotiation with Darlan and Petain was a step too far. It had the aroma of 'appeasement'. He feared that Britain would be powerless to avoid being dragged into 'blind self-effacement' in front of the United States. Churchill was also concerned with the general direction of Allied policy towards French affairs. He wrote to Roosevelt and complained at the growing rivalry between the different French factions – Darlan, General Henri-Honore Giraud, and de Gaulle. The Prime Minister was not impressed at having to do business with unhelpful French 'prima donnas' or the prospect of becoming entangled in a 'cat-fight' between Darlan and Giraud in relation to the command of French military forces.

Meanwhile Roosevelt indicated that he wanted to discuss the organization of the post-war world with Churchill in January 1943. Considering the Foreign Office's recent battles with the Prime Minister over such matters, Harvey was not overly optimistic about the nature of the meeting or its outcome. His reservations were compounded as 'the dictatorial tendencies of Winston are flattered and gratified by meeting these dictators [Roosevelt and Stalin] man to man, but as A.E. [Eden] says, we haven't a dictatorship here whatever the P.M. may imagine'. In comparison to Churchill, Roosevelt had constructed a presidential administration in which he held an enormous amount of power. He was the sole person who co-ordinated policy in Washington, because he alone held all of the 'strings'.

Roosevelt's blatant anti-colonialism appeared content to exclude Britain from North African issues. The success of the Allied Northern African campaign, Operation Torch, which had included British forces, flattered Roosevelt's perception that colonial North Africa was his to deal with at will. Moreover, even Churchill was 'peeved' with the

President's arrogant presumption that, because this operation was under an American Supreme Allied Commander, it was for Roosevelt alone to set Allied policy.

Roosevelt was no doubt weary of the British Foreign Office and its plans for the post-war world. When the President invited Churchill to attend a bilateral meeting with him in North Africa in January 1943, the invitation contained the specific request for Churchill not to bring any Foreign Office representatives. The Prime Minister naturally acquiesced to the President's wishes. But Churchill also agreed to Eden's counter-proposal that the Foreign Secretary should visit Washington as soon as possible after the Casablanca Conference.[78] After all, Roosevelt's veto on Foreign Office attendance was not a guarantee that the President's wide-ranging discussions with the Prime Minister would not touch upon post-war topics, and Churchill knew Roosevelt's mind well enough to consider that this would enter their discussions.

In the face of sustained pressure, War Cabinet unity concerning colonial matters continued to prevail. A Chinese request for the return of the New Territories – one of the three regions of Hong Kong – leased by Britain was raised in Cabinet. Churchill was in a melancholy mood that day, but the opportunity to give an impromptu speech cheered him. During the course of his refrain, the Prime Minister rounded on 'those people who got up each morning asking themselves how much of the empire they could give away'. Once again the United States appeared emboldened to pry into colonial affairs. Cadogan bitterly reflected that America needed to be stopped sooner rather than later, otherwise their continued meddling would prove even more dangerous for British interests.[79]

Churchill delayed going to Casablanca, because of inclement weather, and he therefore used the opportunity to ponder the future of the post-war world.[80] In Washington, Hull complained to the British Embassy that the British press was critical of American policy towards France. Roosevelt was unrelenting in his distrust of de Gaulle. It was readily acknowledged in Whitehall that Britain could not afford to rile its American ally. But previous American support for the former quisling Admiral Darlan and even now the less than promising General Giraud rather than de Gaulle represented a serious gulf in Anglo-American strategy towards French affairs. Churchill may have been weary of upsetting Roosevelt, but on this occasion he had no inclination to appease State Department underlings, whatever their stature. The Prime Minister issued a stoutly worded rebuff to Hull, in which he clinically reminded the Secretary of State that Britain currently possessed both 'a free press and parliament'.[81] Up to this point the Foreign Office, despite its pro-French leanings, had been cautious about publicly committing Britain to the restoration of the French Empire and instead limited pronouncements to the more general notion of restoring France. The American Government appeared less restrained in making much bolder pro-Empire restoration statements.[82] Eden suspected these statements as having been sent with the approval of Roosevelt – who advocated a very different agenda.[83]

Churchill flew to Casablanca in mid-January for discussions with Roosevelt. Operation Torch had successfully liberated North Africa and both leaders now appeared as emperors surveying the spoils of war. The Prime Minister was in his element at Casablanca – and sought to use the fruits of victory to renew his personal relationship with the President. Churchill wrote to Eden and informed him of the mutual intimacy that had been quickly re-established between the leaders. The Casablanca Conference, however, was rapidly hijacked by unresolved French affairs. Churchill uneasily informed the War Cabinet about the President's continued disquiet regarding de Gaulle.[84] For once, Cadogan would have found little grounds for disagreement with the President. De Gaulle's temperament had already caused the Foreign Office significant anxiety. To all intents and purposes, from Cadogan's viewpoint, the Frenchman had behaved like a 'mule' in his negotiations with the Allies.[85] Lord Moran, Churchill's personal physician, witnessed first hand de Gaulle's 'arrogance' and 'defiance' at Casablanca.

Britain and America needed to remedy French affairs at Casablanca and unify Free French forces under de Gaulle and Giraud. Churchill therefore made a personal endeavour to facilitate a resolution. The Prime Minister invited de Gaulle to his conference villa and attempted to bribe and cajole the Frenchman into doing business with Giraud. But to no avail. As de Gaulle confidently walked away from the villa, Churchill turned to Moran and ruefully observed:

> His country has given up fighting, he himself is a refugee, and if we turn him down he's finished. Well just look at him! Look at him!...He might be Stalin, with 200 divisions behind his words. I was pretty rough with him. I made it quite plain that if he could not be more helpful we were done with him.

De Gaulle was, according to Churchill, the 'quintessence of an inferiority complex'. It was a role that de Gaulle played to diplomatic perfection.

Harry Hopkins and Roosevelt providentially orchestrated a successful French Union. [86] Moreover, despite the Gallic distemper, Churchill actually enjoyed the Casablanca Conference. After the dejection following the defeats earlier in the year, the conference re-energised the Prime Minister. Macmillan, whom Churchill had appointed as the British Government's political representative in North Africa, observed that 'I have never seen him in better form. He ate and drank enormously all the time, settled huge problems, played bagatelle and bezique by the hour, and generally enjoyed himself'.[87] Similarly Brigadier Ian Jacob, the Assistant Secretary to the War Cabinet who himself was a man of 'tireless energy', described Churchill's bed at Casablanca as a constant hive of bureaucratic activity as the Prime Minister set about directing the day's affairs.[88] Moran, however, was less than enamoured with the way that business was conducted at Casablanca. In his opinion, the conference maintained a juvenile air as neither Churchill nor Roosevelt had really 'grown up'.[89] Brooke was also less than impressed with the conference proceedings. The attitude of the American military delegation was particularly irksome to the Chief of the Imperial General Staff. It appeared to Brooke that although the Americans were happy enough to criticise British military strategy and objections, they seemed to have none of their own to employ. Brooke was also irritated with the de Gaulle–Giraud sideshow. This diversion of precious conference time seemed to be at valuable military expense. Brooke therefore shared the Prime Minister's exasperation with de Gaulle who 'had the mentality of a dictator combined with the most objectionable personality'.[90] Nonetheless, Churchill experienced a good conference and the Prime Minister rekindled his liaison with Roosevelt. At the post-conference media forum, Churchill pointedly asked the assembled media to convey the unity that had been achieved.[91]

The reality was markedly different. The stage was thereby set for further conflict. The Americans had now experienced the wartime weaknesses and petty jealousies of old world colonialism. In early 1943 Roosevelt did not doubt that an Allied victory was ultimately possible. For this reason, the President began to ponder in earnest the price that he could extract from Britain for Churchill's grand alliance. Britain was after all a vagrant.[92] The Prime Minister's dependence upon Roosevelt would give the President the leverage that he required for the pursuit of America's broader war aims. These aims were naturally made in the American national interest. Roosevelt was, after all, a disciple of Wilson. The Atlantic Charter clearly demonstrated that the President sought to create a new international order based upon harmony, democracy and the end of old world empires. American values were being espoused for a new American-led world order.

The failure of France, in particular, and the opportunity that this accorded played upon the President's mind. Even before attending the Casablanca Conference, Roosevelt was showing his true colours. The President had already met with the American Joint Chiefs of Staff and expressed 'grave doubts' about restoring Indo-China to France after the war. Furthermore, Roosevelt had also pointed out to the Pacific War Council that Britain should refrain from making additional pledges about rejuvenating the French Empire. Based in Washington, the Pacific War Council was a favourable audience for Roosevelt's Asian ideas – Australian, Canadian, Chinese, New Zealand and Philippine members could all be relied upon for affable support vis-à-vis British and Dutch representatives.[93]

Churchill's conundrum was his special relationship with Roosevelt. Their personal liaison was the focal point of the Prime Minister's wartime strategy. But the strategy received little post-war enunciation above winning the war and preserving the British Empire. On the other hand, American post-war aims were very different and growing in substance. By comparison Churchill's amounted to little. The Foreign Office was well-aware of the danger. Churchill was not. The Prime Minister's romantic vision of his alliance with Roosevelt blinded him to the President's deeper motives. Churchill was having too much fun with directing the war and Foreign Office concerns for the post-war world were seen by him as an unnecessary distraction to the main business at hand. In addition, Foreign Office plans also threatened his special relationship with Roosevelt and therefore had to be rebuffed. The problem at the beginning of 1943 was that Roosevelt was narrowing his anti-colonial sights upon French Indo-China and that this would eventually become the President's model for ending old world imperialism. The Foreign Office was more than aware of the dangerous precedent being established for global old world decolonisation. Churchill was not.

2
Churchill's Conceit

Churchill and Roosevelt left Casablanca and journeyed to Marrakesh together. After the intense cauldron of the Casablanca Conference the Prime Minister and the President had a few moments respite before Roosevelt left the next day. The dinner party that evening was an 'affectionate' one for both men. Roosevelt departed the following morning, Churchill lingered a few hours longer, maintaining 'the illusion of a holiday' by indulging in painting the Atlas Mountains.[1] The respite proved to be short-lived. Attlee and Eden sent a joint telegram to Churchill on 27 January 1943. They expressed concern that Roosevelt's version of the Atlantic Charter encapsulated a broader and more enduring security system than Churchill had envisaged. 'Parent (or Trustee) states' would be required to ensure the protection and administration of their territories.[2] Harvey was less than diplomatic about the direction of Churchill's relationship with Roosevelt noting in his diary: 'Why can't PMs be content to use their foreign secretaries. They are all alike in fancying themselves'. To Harvey's dismay Churchill returned to London reinvigorated from his exchanges with Roosevelt, 'His encounters with Roosevelt always have a bad effect. He dominates the President and at the same time envies him for being untrammelled by a Cabinet'.[3]

From Washington Halifax gaily noted the differences between Roosevelt and Churchill over the handling of the French. Roosevelt appeared to be entangled because of statements made by his diplomatic envoy to North Africa, Robert Murphy, promising the restoration of French territory. Churchill and the State Department had allowed themselves greater room for manoeuvre by making much more general pledges.[4] But if Churchill believed that he was in the clear concerning such issues, another threat to his special relationship with Roosevelt was being conceived in Whitehall which, as yet unknown to him, would haunt Churchill in the months to come. Draft British plans for political warfare in Indo-China had been drawn up and approved by the Foreign Office.[5]

Washington and Quebec

On 4 February Halifax had the opportunity to question Hull regarding Roosevelt's statement – made at the January meeting of the Allied Pacific War Council – not to restore the French Empire. Hull conceded, with embarrassment, that the State Department was unaware of Roosevelt's commitments.[6] Roosevelt could expect opposition from the British, but his erratic relationship with the State Department resulted in a State Department sub-committee delivering a thesis which concluded that a strong France would be required to achieve security stability in Europe.[7] The possibility persisted of a joint Anglo-American declaration on colonial policy.[8] Churchill despatched Eden to Washington on the pretext of establishing closer relations between the Foreign Office and the State Department and for discussions on a number of other wide-ranging subjects.[9] Harvey suspected that Churchill had altered Eden's terms of reference to avoid any discussions on the post-war world. Harvey resented the way in which Churchill controlled and changed foreign policy without regard to the Foreign Office but noted rather dryly 'what he [Eden] talks about when he gets there [Washington] cannot be controlled from no.10'. Towards the end of February, Harvey's annoyance with the Prime Minister again surfaced, but this time it was tempered by Churchill's latest bout of illness: 'The PM is getting more and more reactionary and more dictator-minded. He is in a mood to defy the Cabinet and public opinion. Naturally this is increased by his illness'.[10]

The trusteeship debate spilt over into the press. An article in the *The Times* reiterated that the administration of British colonies was for Britain alone rather than jointly with the United States. Post-war economic collaboration could be a possibility but trusteeship was definitely not possible.[11] This was the same stance as that taken by the government's bulwarks of empire – Colonial Secretary Colonel Oliver Stanley and Dominions Secretary Lord Cranborne. Stanley regarded trusteeship as an ill-guided and blatant attempt to liquidate the British Empire.[12] The Viceroy of India, the Marquess of Linlithgow, wrote to his Secretary of State, Leo Amery, deploring American interference in Indian affairs.[13]

In Washington Eden met with the senior members of Roosevelt's Administration. His first official visit to the United States began well. Hopkins informed the Foreign Secretary that Roosevelt was 'eager for the fullest conversations'. He explained that Roosevelt 'loves Winston as a man for the war, but is horrified at his reactionary attitude for after the war'. Roosevelt believed that Churchill's time was passing and regarded Eden as the heir in waiting. Hopkins was a brilliant emissary 'earnest, ignorant, worried, determined [and] woolly'.[14] Those first few preliminary meetings flattered Eden and raised his expectations. Eden's primary meeting with Roosevelt was at dinner on 13 March. Hopkins and John Winant, the American Ambassador to Britain, were also present. Although the conversation was limited to generalities, Eden quickly gained the impression that Roosevelt would not let the United States return to pre-war isolation and would instead assume leadership at the forefront of the world powers.[15] Eden was, however, unimpressed with the unprofessional attitude to business adopted in Washington, the petty jealousies of Hull, Welles and Winant, and the resultant confusion. Harvey noted how disorganised the White House appeared and also the amount of alcohol consumed. Similarly, both Eden and Harvey discovered that just as Churchill sought to control foreign policy so too did Roosevelt. The President would discuss issues at great length and in detail without informing his administration.[16] He was a poor administrator.[17] Nevertheless, Eden enjoyed his meetings with Roosevelt whom he found both dangerously 'charming' and 'perplexing'. Roosevelt 'seemed to see himself disposing of the fate of many lands, Allied no less than enemy. He did all this with so much grace that it was easy not to dissent. Yet it was like a conjuror, skilfully juggling with balls of dynamite, whose nature he failed to understand'. Eden was shrewd enough to see past the charm and Roosevelt ruthless enough to try to build upon it. Hopkins noted that Roosevelt suggested that Britain should release Hong Kong, but Eden wryly observed that he had not heard Roosevelt mention any similar offers by the United States.[18]

Back in Britain, Churchill's radio broadcast on 21 March from Chequers spoke of a post-war world in vague terms. This met with approval in the Foreign Office.[19] Eden's meeting with Welles in Washington proved to be more detailed and robust. Welles constructed an elaborate plan to return Indo-China to France, despite the unpopularity of the French regime, but said that 'we should claim world interest in the quality and direction of their administration' for the future. How this was to be achieved was not mentioned by Welles, who went on to enlarge upon trusteeship plans for Korea and the possibility of Britain handing Hong Kong back to China.[20]

The question of Indo-China was revisited in Eden's subsequent meeting with Welles and Roosevelt at the White House. Eden challenged that the President was being 'very hard on the French' who would no doubt strongly protest at such suggestions. Roosevelt had already foreseen such a charge and countered that 'France would no doubt require assistance for which consideration might be the placing of certain parts of her territory at the disposal of the UN'. The inference was clear to all present – the United States as the main creditor to France at the end of the war would be able to enforce such a policy. At this point Roosevelt's clear thinking was upset by both his and Murphy's previous pronouncements. Welles reminded the President that the United States had already agreed to the restoration of French territory, but Roosevelt countered that this only applied to North Africa. Welles was adamant that this was not the case. But Roosevelt would not be moved, the actual details could be arranged 'in the ironing out of things after the war'.[21]

Eden was experienced enough not to be belittled by the Americans and wise enough to avoid jumping into the Roosevelt–Welles divide. The President may have been at odds with Welles over issues concerning French territory, but Roosevelt generally preferred to work through Welles rather than Hull.[22] Eden knew how to play the American game. As part of his American excursion Eden endeared himself to his hosts with a speech to the Assembly of the State of Maryland. This called for the British Commonwealth to be a voluntary association and an instrument of development capable of moving members towards total independence.[23] Eden dutifully kept Churchill abreast of his discussions in Washington.[24] He wanted to co-ordinate British foreign policy and to create a better world.[25] Hull had already spoken to Eden about the need for some kind of Anglo-American accord to solve world problems.[26] But Churchill was not best pleased with the news that he received from America, especially regarding post-war ideals, and he telephoned Cadogan at the Foreign Office to vent his annoyance.[27]

Eden returned to Britain and reported the details of his discussions to the War Cabinet. He informed them that debates about French affairs were 'of a somewhat varied nature': Hull 'clearly hated' de Gaulle. Eden had received many complaints that the British 'had not done enough to support the American point of view'.[28] The United States was against the creation of a single French civil authority in exile to deal with French affairs and preferred to transact business with each rival French leader – Giraud and de Gaulle – separately. Roosevelt suspected that Britain only wished to resurrect France as a Great Power for selfish reasons whilst Leahy envisaged a malevolent British conspiracy to manipulate de Gaulle at American expense.[29] The British Embassy in Washington found it hard to decipher the fundamental principles behind American foreign policy towards France. It found only 'amateurishness and irre-sponsibility' mixed with 'uncertainty' and 'misleading information'.[30] Eden outlined his talks with Roosevelt to the Cabinet and referred to the conversation with Welles and the President about internationalising Indo-China. Eden believed that Welles' reaction concerning guarantees to the French empire meant that this would not be pursued any further. He also informed the Cabinet that he had met the Chinese Ambas-sador to the United States in Washington who had yielded the assurance that China possessed no territorial ambitions in Burma, Indo-China and Malaya.[31] The Foreign Office feared Chinese opportunism at Britain's weakness to extend into South and Southeast Asia – regions which had large indigenous Chinese populations.

Winant, the American Ambassador to Britain, met with Cranborne to discuss the Anglo-American drafts of the joint colonial declaration. The main difference between the drafts was the American emphasis on the word 'independence' for the colonies. Cranborne believed strongly that such a word could not be included in any declaration. Colonies removed from British protection could fall under the influence of less experienced nations in such affairs – the United States. Winant proposed substituting independence for 'social and economic development'. Cranborne was satisfied with the change in emphasis.[32]

Just as the Dominions Office continued to be suspicious of the sub-stance of the Anglo-American joint declaration, so too did the Foreign Office remain wary of the Wilsonian nature of American trusteeship and the Atlantic Charter.[33] Harvey also remained suspicious of Churchill and from his vantage point believed that the Prime Minister was 'botching' the peace.[34] Churchill was not content to let Eden direct Britain's for-eign policy towards America or to debate the shape of the post-war world. Churchill insisted that he had to be at the centre of Britain's relationship with the United States. He therefore set out for Washington to discuss – amongst other issues – his vision for the post-war world. Whatever Roosevelt's personal feelings of affection towards Churchill, his advisers had previously been wary of the effect that the Prime Min-ister had upon their leader. But this trip mellowed the misgivings of the Presidential entourage. Churchill could now be safely left alone with the President.[35]

In Washington Churchill found both Roosevelt and Hull vehemently anti-de Gaulle, but this was the least of his current worries. The special relationship and post-war issues had to be attended to first.[36] Churchill therefore set about grooming the Americans with gusto. On 22 May Churchill hosted a lunch at the British Embassy for a number of the senior members of Roosevelt's administration – Vice-President Henry Wallace, Secretary of the Interior Harold Ickes, Secretary of War Stimson, Chair of the Senate Foreign Relations Committee Thomas Connally and Welles. Churchill used the occasion to elaborate on his personal view of the post-war world. He envisaged the United States, the Soviet Union and the British Empire as the supreme powers responsible, to varying degrees, for three regional organisations. China would be pronounced a Great Power, but not to the same degree as the supreme three. France would assist in the policing of Europe. The world security organisation that Churchill pictured did not exclude an Anglo-American special relationship. Churchill would have been pleased with the reception that his ideas received. Welles and Connally were in complete agreement. Connally even ventured to express that 'the U.S. and England could run the world by themselves'. Churchill knew how to work his audience. He was in his element acting as the charming host, pontificating on great Anglo-American issues. Even Wallace found the proposals alluring: 'It was better bait than I anticipated'. But he did at least understand the difference between Churchill's showmanship and more firmly held beliefs, 'Churchill was not as definite as he sounded'. Nevertheless, upon leaving the embassy Wallace commented to Halifax that 'it was the most encouraging conversation . . . for the last two years'.[37]

The Americans believed that they were making progress with Churchill and vice-versa, although Brooke shrewdly noted that Churchill demonstrated a greater grasp of strategy than Roosevelt.[38] Churchill returned to the subject of the post-war world two days later during an intimate luncheon at the White House with Roosevelt, Wallace, Hopkins and Lord Cherwell. This time he met with more opposition from Wallace who believed that an Anglo-American alliance was a crude post-war mechanism. Churchill, fuelled by whisky, frankly asserted 'why be apologetic about Anglo-Saxon superiority . . . we are superior'.[39] Churchill's romantic vision of an Anglo-American alliance was built upon his unique position of being half American. He was the crucial link. He was the only one with the insight and the cultural heritage to navigate such waters. But neither the Americans nor the Foreign Office appeared convinced that this was anything but a dream. In London, Eden and Attlee were fed up with Churchill's 'lecturing' and 'hectoring' from Washington. Harvey noted that it was 'high time the old man came home. The American atmosphere, the dictatorial powers of the President and the adulation which surrounds him there, [sic] have gone to his head'.[40] The next day in Washington, Churchill confided in his doctor Lord Moran that Roosevelt appeared tired and his mind seemed 'closed' whereas for

Churchill the trip to Washington had reinvigorated him, allowing him to wallow in detail and do 'the work of three men'. The Americans were taken aback with his energy. Hopkins confessed to Moran: 'We have come to avoid controversy with Winston; we find he is too much for us'. Even Churchill's wife, Clementine, admitted: 'I don't argue with Winston, he shouts me down. So when I have anything important to say I write a note to him'. Churchill eventually arrived back in London content in the direction of his war.[41]

By this time Roosevelt had finally lost his patience with de Gaulle and was asking for his head on a platter.[42] He subsequently went further and declared that there was no such place or entity as France.[43] At the Allied Pacific War Council in Washington Roosevelt made strenuous remarks about Indo-China.[44] The Foreign Office continued to monitor the political situation in the United States and in particular American attitudes towards imperialism. The prospect of American elections in the forthcoming year explained for them some of Roosevelt's more lavish anti-imperial pronouncements. In Foreign Office analysis Roosevelt apparently feared that his opponent, Wendell Willkie, would mobilise the American electorates' anti-imperial sentiment against him.[45] However, the Foreign Office failed to comprehend that despite its often fanciful direction Roosevelt's abundant anti-imperialism was not merely an electoral whim. In June 1943 Roosevelt even suggested that Australia should purchase Timor from Portugal – a neutral nation.[46] It was left to Eden, in liaison with the American Ambassador in London, to co-ordinate the assurances to the Portuguese Government concerning the over-active imagination of an American President.[47] Likewise, if Roosevelt was merely a prisoner of the American electorate why did he not pursue a Japan first war policy rather than concentrating upon Germany? A nuance overlooked in London.[48]

The Foreign Office also had to contend with a lack of unity within Britain's National Government. Churchill was in step with Roosevelt and against the immediate recognition of an Allied France.[49] The Labour Party, however, was developing its own approach towards the issue of colonial development. The resultant policy statement advocated 'responsible self-government' for the colonies.[50] On 13 July the Conservative minister Stanley gave the fullest expression to date of British colonial policy. In a speech to the House of Commons he said that 'we are pledged to guide colonial people along the road to self-government within the framework of the British Empire'.[51] The subsequent paper *International Aspects of Colonial Policy* was sent to the Dominion Governments. It considered the establishment of a regional commission for

Southeast Asia.[52] If the British were to retain their colonies in the Far East the French would be unlikely to accept anything less.[53] Britain was weak. It could not stand alone and it was vulnerable to the demands of others. Any definitive policy would therefore need to be an imperial one agreed with the Dominions. The priority would be to protect the Commonwealth and the Empire in the Pacific. By its very nature this policy would have to involve the United States – a potential source of conflict. If American anti-imperialism in the Far East resulted in a weakening of France in Europe, then this would compromise stability much closer to home.[54]

Churchill returned to the United States and dined at Roosevelt's family home at Hyde Park on 14 August. In the privacy of Roosevelt's home and in a relaxed and informal atmosphere Churchill articulated the need for a flexible post-war Anglo-American relationship rather than Roosevelt's formal United Nations Organisation.[55] Roosevelt had initially intended to tackle Churchill at Hyde Park about the post-war world.[56] He still suspected that Britain was only acting out of self-interest.[57] But he chose instead to respond to Churchill six days later when he outlined his proposal for a post-war security organisation to the Prime Minister.[58] The Foreign Office feared that Roosevelt intended to use the Atlantic Charter as the blueprint for governing the post-war world. Even more worryingly it held that this blueprint was not 'static' and that Roosevelt intended that it was solely 'for him to interpret and secure the realisation of this as and when appropriate'. This could involve the United States acquiring the port of Cam Ranh Bay in Vietnam as an American naval base as part of any trusteeship settlement.[59] Churchill had agreed to the Atlantic Charter in order to gain American support, but he had deliberately avoided framing a clear-cut British policy based around it. At the Quebec Conference in pursuance of his post-war agenda Roosevelt challenged Cadogan about the Charter: 'Cadogan, I want to ask you a riddle – Where is the original Atlantic Charter?' Cadogan did not hesitate to expose Roosevelt to the ruthless reality of British foreign policy: 'That's an easy one, Mr President; it doesn't exist'.[60]

The Quebec Conference was also charged with the formation of the Southeast Asia Command (SEAC).[61] The British COS had believed that both French Indo-China and Siam should be included within the SEAC area of operations. However, in conference discussions between Churchill, Roosevelt and the Combined Chiefs of Staff (CCS), Admiral William Leahy – Chief of Staff to the President – revealed that the CCS had actually placed both Siam and Indo-China in the China

Theatre. Although Indo-China could have been placed within SEAC boundaries, the possibility of SEAC actually being able to conduct operations there remained in the distant future.[62] Leahy was content to leave Indo-China in the China Theatre but did raise the possibility of moving Siam into the SEAC sphere of operation.[63] The Quebec Conference also confirmed the operational management of SEAC. Mountbatten was appointed Supreme Allied Commander of SEAC and the American Lt.-General Joseph Stilwell his deputy. Brooke was not impressed with the choices. In his opinion Mountbatten 'lacked balance' and Stilwell was a 'small man with no conception of strategy'.[64] SEAC was organised along the same lines as the North African Command. Mountbatten was officially responsible for the co-ordination of all three Allied services – army, air force and navy. The only potential area of confusion was that Stilwell was also solely responsible for all American Southeast Asian forces and Chinese troops operating in Burma – forces outside of Mountbatten's remit.[65]

Following the Quebec Conference Roosevelt returned to Washington where he held lengthy talks with William Averell Harriman, his personal diplomatic representative, whom he was about to dispatch to Moscow to negotiate with Stalin. They touched on the substance of a post-war settlement and the future of France in greater detail.[66] Despite Roosevelt and many in his inner circle expressing vehement disdain concerning France and imperialism in general, they were not unsympathetic to Britain's vulnerabilities over colonial issues. Hull delivered a speech on 12 September in which he purposefully avoided the use of the word 'independence' but the subtext alluded to what might be achieved in the way of liberty.[67] Similarly, Churchill used a speech at Harvard University to further opine on the issue of greater post-war Anglo-American unity.[68] Churchill believed that he had developed a strong personal relationship with Roosevelt that had risen above the petty jealousies of both nations. Their friendship would build the romantic Anglo-American future: 'You know how I treasure the friendship with which you have honoured me and how profoundly I feel that we might together do something really fine and lasting for our two countries, and through them for the future of all'.[69] Churchill's daughter, Sarah Oliver, observed the Quebec courtship and felt that mutual affection, administration and understanding had been achieved. Yet at Quebec, the special relationship had not been equal. Churchill had permitted the United States to become the stronger partner. He had even allowed the American President to decide British policy in post-war atomic research.[70] Harvey remained sceptical of the consequences of Churchill's relationship with Roosevelt: 'the President's influence on him [Churchill] in political matters is disastrous. The PM's American half comes up more and more...the PM has no understanding of peace issues, and is a very old man with outdated ideas'.[71] Brooke was also concerned with Churchill's attitude at Quebec which he regarded as at best 'temperamental'. Brooke was 'slowly becoming convinced that in his old age Winston [was] becoming less and less well balanced'.[72] But Eden was less belligerent. He was anxious for Britain to maintain good, but not 'subservient', relations with the United States.[73] And even Brooke admitted that although the Cabinet without Churchill might be efficient it would also be 'headless'.[74]

Mountbatten departed for SEAC in October to assume his new duties. The Foreign Office also dispatched Maberley Esler Dening to SEAC to advise Mountbatten on political issues and foreign affairs. This would involve co-ordinating policy amongst the Allies; giving specific advice concerning Siam, Indo-China and political warfare; and representing the Foreign Office to the New Delhi Commission.[75] Upon arrival Mountbatten immediately discovered that 'Anglo-American relations in this theatre were far and away the worst I have ever come across'. Stilwell, Mountbatten's deputy, proved to be 'entirely anti-British'.[76] His Anglophobia was only equalled by his contempt for China whom he was also expected to serve. American personnel attached to SEAC quipped that it was an acronym for 'Save England's Asian Colonies'. Mountbatten set about trying to resolve the personality conflicts within his new command and between SEAC and the China Theatre. He was boosted in this by Churchill who indicated that Stilwell's position had become weak.[77] Mountbatten met Chiang Kai-Shek, the President of China, in Chungking and brokered a Gentleman's Agreement regarding Indo-China. This agreement permitted SEAC to attack Siam and Indo-China and if successful transfer them from the China Theatre. In the meantime Mountbatten would be able to execute intelligence gathering and other pre-occupational activities in Siam and Indo-China.[78] The Gentleman's Agreement built upon the existing ambiguities already established at the Quebec Conference – as to the boundaries of the two theatres within Southeast Asia – rather than resolving them. Mountbatten however believed that his solution had settled any future difficulties: 'I am never at a loss for advice to give others...he [Chiang Kai-Shek] accepted all my suggestions and a special certain difficulty appears now to have been resolved as a result of this conversation'.[79]

Mountbatten sent a personal note to Roosevelt informing him of the outcome of his meeting with Chiang Kai-Shek. The outcome was confirmed to Roosevelt by American Lt.-General Brehon Somervell who had also been present. Somervell had even helped to broker the Gentleman's Agreement.[80] Mountbatten's personal correspondence to Roosevelt, however, merely informed him of an amiable meeting with Chiang Kai-Shek to remove distrust and barriers between the commands, but it did not specifically mention the Gentleman's Agreement.[81] Similarly, Mountbatten's letters to Churchill and Brooke, Chief of the Imperial General Staff, concerning the meeting also failed to mention the Gentleman's Agreement.[82] Roosevelt seemed pleased with both SEAC and its Supreme Allied Commander and expressed confidence in the resolution between the commands, a success that he personally accredited to Mountbatten; but had he, Churchill and Brooke been misled?[83] If Mountbatten had made a more specific reference to the agreement and if Somervell had also mentioned it to Roosevelt, then could the Agreement – a growing source of disquiet – have been clarified at this stage and the later conflict between Britain and the United States concerning SEAC operations in Indo-China been avoided?

Mountbatten informed the British COS of his proposals to Chiang Kai-Shek regarding both Indo-China and Siam. These proposals were in essence the substance of the Gentleman's Agreement. But Chiang continued to express the impracticality of Indo-China and Siam being transferred to SEAC and jealously defended that political orchestration should be solely managed by China Theatre. This political dynamic was something that Mountbatten found detrimental to SEAC as he wanted to undertake pre-occupational duties independently of Chiang.[84] Yet had he already actually committed himself to such a compromise? Field Marshall Sir John Dill, responsible for the British Joint Service Mission in Washington, was under the impression that both Mountbatten and Roosevelt had agreed to political issues surrounding Indo-China and Siam being settled by a commission located at China Theatre Headquarters.[85] The SEAC-China Theatre difficulties did not pass unnoticed by their Japanese adversaries. The Japanese had not been idle and used the inter-theatre complications for wartime propaganda, citing that Britain's imperialist intention was to retain Indo-China and Siam after the war.[86] Differences between Chiang Kai-Shek and Mountbatten over theatre boundaries, the ambiguities of the Gentleman's Agreement and French participation in the war in the Far East would continue to reverberate in parallel to the trusteeship debate. These differences eventually culminated in an Allied crisis in the spring of 1945.[87] In the meantime

Mountbatten was convinced that Chiang Kai-Shek held a grievance against him – for not agreeing to his proposals.[88] Nevertheless, an informal discussion continued between Mountbatten and Chiang Kai-Shek and the essence of the Gentleman's Agreement was confirmed in a further verbal agreement in September 1944.[89]

In the meantime, if Churchill believed that he could direct the debate concerning the nature of Anglo-American post-war relations and the new world order, de Gaulle seemed determined to prove otherwise. He thrust the issue of Indo-China back into the foreground by establishing a committee to ponder the question of its status for the Allies. The Committee was also charged with considering the participation of French forces in the liberation of Indo-China.[90] France may not have existed but de Gaulle was not going to abandon its most important colony. In order to facilitate such plans even further de Gaulle's French National Liberation Committee asked for representation on the Allied Pacific War Council. This was the very body to whom Roosevelt had vented his desire not to restore the French Empire in January. The State Department naturally believed that Roosevelt would be against any proposal to include French representation on the council.[91] He had only recently reiterated to Hull the importance of placing Indo-China under international trusteeship.[92] But before the State Department took the matter further and liaised with the President it sought the opinion of the British Government.[93] Churchill ruled against the Foreign Office participating in any Anglo-American correspondence on this issue: 'better leave quiet for a bit. No need to reply for some days'.[94] But the matter was raised again two days later in a meeting at the Foreign Office with Stanley Hornbeck, a political relations adviser at the State Department. Hornbeck argued that although the French representation on the Pacific War Council did have some advantages, including being able to refuse French military missions, it did not automatically qualify France the right to return to Indo-China. The United States was not fighting the war to return colonies to colonial powers but to defeat mutual enemies.[95] Cadogan pursued Churchill on the inclusion of French representatives at Pacific War Council meetings.[96] But Churchill was unmoved: 'No need for action yet'.[97]

Meanwhile the Commonwealth Prime Ministers assembled for a conference in London. The South African Prime Minister Field Marshall Jan Smuts deplored American foreign policy which he regarded as being more focussed on financial issues than actually winning the war. Smuts also addressed the Empire Parliamentary Association. In a powerful speech titled 'Thoughts on a New World', he envisaged a revitalised

British Empire and Commonwealth that would act together with the United States and the Soviet Union to oversee the peace and the stability of the post-war world.[98] In Washington however, Roosevelt persisted in developing his theme of trusteeship with Hull and Leahy. This would be not only for French Indo-China but also Hong Kong.[99] Hull was subsequently dispatched to the Moscow Conference where he presented Roosevelt's trusteeship ideas to the Russians.[100] Roosevelt continued to believe that selfish British political motives were hampering his grand strategy. He was frustrated with the British attitude and vented his displeasure to the American Joint Chiefs of Staff on 15 November.[101]

Meanwhile Cadogan persisted in his efforts to establish French representation on the Pacific War Council. He wrote to Churchill: 'A refusal would confirm the French in their present suspicions that neither we nor the Americans (particularly the latter) wish to see them resume sovereignty over Indo-China. This would add to their sense of frustration and wounded pride'. Continued American hostility towards the imperial powers and the restoration of their colonies led Cadogan to conclude that 'there is much to be said for the colonial powers sticking together in the Far East'. Churchill had hoped to delay any decision, let alone action on the French participation in the war in the Far East, but de Gaulle was not prepared to stand on ceremony for the benefit of a British Prime Minister. With no response to their requests for representation forthcoming the French now asked for permission to send a military mission to SEAC. Cadogan used the opportunity to push Churchill into raising imperial interests above his relationship with Roosevelt.[102] Britain was already putting into place a mechanism to facilitate the free exchange of information between British and American organisations working in India and Southeast Asia with the establishment of a liaison committee in New Delhi.[103] Churchill did not rise to Cadogan's challenge and again preferred to delay having to make a decision noting 'this can certainly wait'.[104] Three days later Churchill's Private Secretary John Martin asked if the Prime Minister wished to mention the new French request to Mountbatten. Churchill's patience was wearing out: 'No nothing doing while de Gaulle is master'. Martin duly informed the Foreign Office.[105] The Foreign Office, the Colonial Office and the Dominions Office were all united in the belief that British policy towards French possessions should involve consultation with the Dominions lest a position develop where the Dominion Governments sided with the Americans against Britain.[106] When the issue of French representation was inevitably raised again a month later Churchill instructed Eden that Britain 'should adopt a negative and dilatory attitude'.[107] But this time he had reason to be cautious. Churchill had in the meantime attended the Cairo and Tehran conferences where Roosevelt and Stalin had fundamentally changed the dynamics of the post-war Indo-Chinese debate.

Cairo and Tehran

Churchill arrived in Cairo on 21 November for discussions with Roosevelt and Chiang Kai-Shek. Lord Killearn, the British Ambassador to Egypt, found Churchill in a 'very mellow and friendly mood'. Chiang Kai-Shek was housed in a neighbouring villa to Churchill and duly called upon him that evening.[108] Churchill was a tireless host but any expectation that he was to have his intimate discussions with Roosevelt had been upset by the early arrival of Chiang Kai-Shek. Reflecting on this incident in 1950 Brooke added a note to his diary entry for 21 November 1943 that the cart had been put before the horse and the opportunity of presenting a united Anglo-American front to Stalin had been lost.[109] Churchill's own memoirs noted that the conference was 'sadly distracted' by the Chinese delegation.[110] Chiang Kai-Shek had brought a large retinue of advisors and officials with him to Cairo, including Dr Wang Chung Hui – Head of the Chinese Government. The Chinese delegation hoped to use the conference, amongst other matters, to draw up an Anglo-Chinese agreement on post-war reconstruction in the Far East.[111]

Churchill was consumed with running the war and liaising with Roosevelt. But Churchill liked talking and he was an 'indifferent' listener. Moran feared this side of the Prime Minister's character. It displayed his lack of interest in people and his poor judgement of character.[112] The CCS met on 22 November followed by a larger meeting with Roosevelt, Churchill, Mountbatten, Stilwell, Major-General Claire Chennault – Head of the American Air Force attached to China Theatre – and Hopkins to discuss Mountbatten's plans for Southeast Asia. The Chinese delegation was invited to join the discussion the next day but the meeting quickly descended into a lethargic farce with first a Chinese general and then Madame Chiang Kai-Shek translating everything in tandem for Chiang. The subsequent meetings between the Chinese Chiefs of Staff and the CCS proved little better.[113] The Chiang Kai-Sheks and Dr Wang Chung Hui dined with Roosevelt and Hopkins that evening. Roosevelt once again held court on the future of French Indo-China. Both men were in agreement that China and the United States should help Indo-China achieve post-war independence.[114]

On 24 November Churchill hosted a dinner party for Chiang Kai-Shek and his wife. It was an informal affair predominantly made up of those with an interest in the Far East – Mountbatten, Moran, Adrian Carton de Wiart (Churchill's personal representative to China), Richard and Ethel Casey (Richard Casey was Minister Resident in the Middle East), Sarah Oliver and Lord and Lady Killearn.[115] Madame Chiang Kai-Shek acted as interpreter.[116] After dinner Churchill gave the Chiang Kai-Sheks a guided tour of his room.[117] The next day Churchill, Eden and Mountbatten resumed their discussions with Chiang Kai-Shek, but these were restricted by the usual conference photographs which occupied a portion of the official business for the day.[118] An 'off-the record' CCS meeting helped to restore the pace of the conference, but Chinese issues continued to look bleak.[119] Time was slipping away.

To make matters worse the Americans appeared to be obsessed with Chiang Kai-Shek.[120] Cadogan regarded the significance that the Americans attributed to the Chinese leader as 'ludicrous'.[121] Churchill's attitude towards both India and China remained 'Victorian'.[122] He wished to preserve the pre-war status quo, reinforced by a post-war Anglo-American alliance. At Cadogan's request Lord Killearn met with Dr Wang Chung Hui on the morning of 26 November. The Foreign Office was determined to ascertain Chinese post-war intentions. After lunch Eden and Cadogan entered the fray. Eden and Cadogan talked with Dr Wang Chung Hui at length about the possibility of an Anglo-Chinese agreement. The Chinese hosted a large tea party that evening at their villa. No agreement with the Chinese appeared to be forthcoming. Later in the evening Killearn, Churchill, Eden and Mountbatten met for an intense discussion about the present difficulties with the Chinese.[123]

Churchill was not aided by Roosevelt who had returned to the themes of his anti-colonial agenda from Casablanca. Macmillan witnessed the President 'browbeat' the Prime Minister yet again over France and Indo-China.[124] Yet Roosevelt was also thrown off course by Chiang and the demands of his wife. The President's assurance of Chinese membership of the Big Four along with vague references to trusteeship for Korea and Indo-China boosted Chiang's morale. The first draft of the Cairo Declaration approved the restoration of Chinese territories but omitted reference to the restoration of the European colonies. Subsequent negotiations produced little fruit for the British. However, the revised final communiqué did state that all Japanese conquests should be relinquished – the post-war status of the Asian colonies was not mentioned.[125]

At least Mountbatten was pleased with the direction that the conference had taken. Any criticisms of his dealings with the Chinese appeared unjustified given their poor performances in front of Churchill and Roosevelt: 'I am delighted that the Prime Minister and President and Combined Chiefs of Staff are at least being given first hand experience of how impossible the Chinese are to deal with. They have been driven absolutely mad'.[126] Mountbatten's inadequacies had been camouflaged. His own Foreign Office Political Officer, Dening, had only been present in Cairo because Carton de Wiart – located in the neighbouring China Theatre – had invited him. Dening would later complain to the post-war Labour Government about his lack of opportunity to brief Mountbatten before such meetings.[127]

In the meantime Churchill had relocated to Tehran. The Tehran Conference was the last meeting of Roosevelt, Stalin and Churchill as equals and it was Roosevelt's first meeting with Stalin. In many respects Churchill's position within the Big Three was in decline from the first day of the conference, as Stalin replaced Churchill with Roosevelt as his most important ally. Brooke remarked to Moran, 'This conference is over when it has only just begun. Stalin has got the President in his pocket'.[128] The discussions of the shape of the post-war world and the nature of the four policemen had profound implications for British policy towards French Indo-China and Churchill's relationship with the United States.[129]

No sooner had the conference begun than Roosevelt and Stalin met for bilateral discussions without Churchill in the President's quarters. The two leaders appeared to be getting on well together. Roosevelt in particular would have been pleased by Stalin's willingness to engage in a discussion on his pet subjects – anti-imperialism and French Indo-China. Stalin talked at length on the problems of the French ruling classes and their collaboration with Nazi Germany. Roosevelt responded that although Churchill believed that France should be rehabilitated as a strong nation, he did not share this view. Roosevelt was hanging Churchill out to dry. Churchill the old imperialist was not even being consulted. Roosevelt and Stalin were setting an unpleasant agenda for the post-war world. Stalin naturally agreed with Roosevelt and went on to explain that French Indo-China should not be returned to France. If Stalin had intended this as a trap to open Roosevelt up to discussing global post-war issues, when the Soviet Union was only committed to fighting a European war and had not as yet declared war on Japan, then the bait was taken by the President. Roosevelt responded that

> he was 100% in agreement with Marshal Stalin and remarked that after 100 years of French rule in Indo-China, the inhabitants were worse off than they had been before. He said that Chiang Kai-Shek

had told him China had no designs on Indo-China but the people of Indo-China were not yet ready for independence, to which he had replied that when the United States acquired the Philippines, the inhabitants were not yet ready for independence which would be granted without qualification upon the end of the war against Japan. He added that he had discussed with Chiang Kai-Shek the possibility of a system of trusteeship for Indo-China which would have the task of preparing the people for independence within a definite period of time, perhaps 20 to 30 years.

Stalin could not have been happier with Roosevelt's proposal and was in complete agreement.[130] He had been particularly shrewd as it was he who had raised the subject of Indo-China, thus playing effectively on Roosevelt's 'fears of post-war French stability and resentment against General de Gaulle', and entwining these fears with 'Roosevelt's Wilsonian beliefs in national self-determination'.[131] Roosevelt had opened the door for Stalin to deliberate on the future of imperial colonies and the general mechanisms for administering trusteeship. The prospect of Soviet officials participating in such a scheme would not have been lost on Stalin. Buoyed by the mutual feelings towards Indo-China the talks moved away from this subject and onto the future of India. Churchill would have been outraged had he been present, and both leaders agreed not to raise the future of India with Churchill in the official conference. Roosevelt felt that the best solution for India was to reform it from the bottom up along Soviet lines. Stalin starkly replied that this would mean a revolution. Harriman, who was present, was particularly impressed with Stalin's 'sophistication' on Indian issues.[132]

Churchill discovered in Tehran that his romantic visions of an Anglo-American alliance were not shared by Roosevelt. He found that he could not rely on the President's support in the Big Three deliberations, something of which the Soviets were quickly able to take advantage. He was 'appalled by his own impotence' and Britain's decline as a Great Power. He remarked to his entourage, 'There I sat with the great Russian bear on one side of me, with paws outstretched, and on the other side the great American buffalo, and between the two sat the poor little English donkey who was the only one...who knew the way home'. [133] If Churchill was unaware of Roosevelt's intimate talk with Stalin concerning Indo-China, London was not. With the conference still in session Attlee wrote to Churchill in Tehran predicting trouble over the future of Indo-China and seeking further clarification regarding Churchill's position.[134] Churchill responded that 'Britain does not pre-judge the question of the status of Indo-China any more than that of the...British possessions'. But Roosevelt and Stalin were prepared to pre-judge the status of both Indo-China and India. Churchill was unaware of the substance of their earlier tête-à-tête and believed that although Roosevelt contemplated some changes for Indo-China he had not as yet arrived at any definitive mechanism.[135]

The British delegation left Tehran on 1 December. Churchill, who had celebrated his 69th birthday the day before, appeared in better spirits than could have perhaps been expected.[136] Roosevelt joined Macmillan and Churchill in North Africa for an informal chat where once again the President launched into a discourse about French Indo-China.[137] The strain of managing the war however was beginning to tell on the Prime Minister. As soon as he reached Tunis, Churchill was struck down with a severe bout of pneumonia followed by two heart attacks.[138] It was left to Eden to brief the War Cabinet on the results of the Cairo and Tehran conferences. The Cairo Conference had revealed Roosevelt's continuing predilection to place Indo-China under some kind of international control. But Eden noted that at Tehran, Stalin had been particularly critical of France declaring that 'the French had not really tried hard in the war'. Stalin regarded France as 'rotten' and, revealing the nature of some of his discussions with Roosevelt, asserted Soviet-American agreement that not all of France's colonies should be returned at the end of the war.[139]

Churchill may have been gravely ill but both the colonial and Indo-Chinese debates were gathering momentum and continuing to afflict him. In Washington Hull proposed a joint Anglo-American declaration regarding colonial policy. The British Colonial Office was not enamoured with Hull's initial draft which perceived deeper meaning into the murky substance of the Atlantic Charter. Particular concern was given to the proposed pledge that 'peoples who aspire to independence shall be given an opportunity to acquire independent status'.[140] Meanwhile the French National Committee of Liberation released a declaration in the name of de Gaulle publicising the political and economic development of Indo-China in a 'free and intimate association' with France.[141] Roosevelt too was enlarging upon his ideas for the development of Indo-China. He met with Chinese, Turkish, Egyptian, Russian, Persian and British diplomats in Washington and despite the open audience asked them not to repeat what he was about to say. Roosevelt was certainly being mischievous in his tactics. Eden was subject to a similar experience of American politics during his March trip to Washington. In his memoirs he recalled that 'Diplomacy is never off the record. The only advantage of pretending that it can be is to pursue diplomatic ends by undiplomatic means'.[142] On this occasion Roosevelt revealed that:

> He had been working very hard to prevent Indo-China being restored to France who during the last hundred years had done nothing for the Indo-Chinese people under their care. Latter were still as poor and as uneducated as they had ever been and this state of affairs could not be allowed to continue. He thought that Indo-Chinese who were not yet ready for elective institutions of their own should be placed under some United Nations trusteeship, which would take them toward the stage when they could govern themselves.

The British representative duly telegraphed Eden who informed a convalescing Churchill of Roosevelt's latest musings.[143] Despite warnings to the contrary Churchill was dismissive of the brewing crisis. He had frequently heard Roosevelt's deliberations on this issue but he had 'never given any assent to them'. This was a matter for the end of the war. Churchill believed that the United States would not forcibly remove territory from France without making an agreement with a French government that had been freely elected by the French people, again a matter for the termination of the war or at the very least the liberation of France and the holding of free elections. Churchill was confident in his stance. Roosevelt had already made numerous declarations on 'the integrity of the French Empire', and the Prime Minister asked to see these.[144]

Eden, however, was not convinced that Roosevelt's current attitude and endeavours should be so readily dismissed. He advised Churchill that a 'note of caution' should be sounded in Washington. He requested that Halifax meet with Hull to establish whether Roosevelt's Indo-Chinese statements actually represented 'a concerted White House-State Department policy'. Eden considered that it was very important for Britain to have a 'definite policy on this matter'. The issue was becoming ever more complicated. It would be irresponsible to let it drift. The French remained eager to establish a military mission attached to SEAC and had already set one up in Chungking. The possibility of French troops and warships being used in the Far East was accelerating.[145] Churchill agreed with Eden that Halifax should contact Hull, but he remained adamant in his belief that 'questions of territorial transfer should be reserved until the end of the war'. In the meantime a memorandum was drawn up that provisionally set out Foreign Office policy as supporting the return of French possessions.[146] This would be subject to any international and collective security arrangements accepted by the colonial nations in concert with the Dominions. The paper had already been forwarded to Attlee's post-war committee for consideration. But the Foreign Office felt that if the Americans were determined to remove the French from Indo-China then Britain may not have any choice but to go along with them.[147] Britain required full United States participation in post-war collective security. Britain also needed to avoid the instability of the Dominions siding with the United States.[148] Halifax consulted with Hull on 3 January 1944 and discovered that the Secretary of State 'knew no more about it that I did'. Halifax concluded that Roosevelt's remarks clearly 'did not represent any settled policy in which [the] State Department has occurred'. Halifax regarded the whole affair as 'woolly' whilst Hull 'supposed' that it would be an issue for future consultation between Roosevelt and Churchill.[149]

Although Churchill was content to dismiss speculation over the future of French Indo-China, the Foreign Office was not. Cavendish Bentinck was one of a number of officials who were both highly suspicious and critical of Roosevelt's trusteeship policy. Roosevelt was deluded as to the actual extent of his power and motivated not by benevolence but by ruthless dollar imperialism.

> President Roosevelt is suffering from the same kind of megalomania which characterised the late President Wilson and Mr Lloyd George (the latter to a lesser extent) at the end of the last war and proved the former's undoing. ...
>
> I trust that we shall not allow ourselves to quarrel with the French, without being on very strong grounds, for the benefit of a United States President, who in a year's time, may be merely a historical figure.
>
> If Indo-China is not restored to France on the ground that 'the poor Indo-Chinese' have had no education and no welfare (I have never heard that the Indo-Chinese were any more unhappy than the share croppers of the Southern United States), the Dutch and ourselves may later on be told that the oil resources of the Netherlands East Indies and Borneo have never been properly developed, nor the rubber resources of Malaya, that the natives are insufficiently educated according to Washington standards and that these territories must be placed under United Nations trusteeship (perhaps with United States oil and rubber controllers).

The President's double standards were all too evident to those in Whitehall. America, a segregated nation, was lecturing the colonial powers about welfare and development. The forthcoming American elections did at least provide the possibility of Roosevelt's removal from office and the easing of Anglo-French relations – relations that were necessary for the long-term security of Europe.[150]

Eden was troubled by the escalating Indo-Chinese crisis. Roosevelt's policy seemed at best hazy.[151] But in Churchill's continued absence these 'very big issues' could not be considered by the War Cabinet. The only course of action for the moment was further discussion between the Foreign Secretary and his senior civil servants with a view to developing a uniform imperial policy with Australia, Canada and New Zealand. In the meantime if the French published Roosevelt's previous pledges on the restoration of the French Empire the results would be 'devastating'.[152] The Foreign Office also remained suspicious of Chinese intentions towards French Indo-China, and it firmly believed that it was both irresponsible and impossible to prevent France from taking part in the war in the Far East. The French had an intimate knowledge of Indo-China, which both Britain and the United States did not, and a substantial number of troops and ships available in North Africa for any such campaign. A British response of 'No thank you; we prefer to have more of our own soldiers killed' in the Far East would require some kind of explanation to the British public.[153] The Defence Committee had already decided that the French mission to SEAC should be dispatched as soon as possible. Its presence would help to limit 'incidents' with French troops on the Sino-Indo-Chinese border and also to provide valuable support to Mountbatten.[154]

Roosevelt heralded the dawning of the New Year with yet another outburst to Churchill about de Gaulle. He was particularly vexed at the inclusion of French representation on the Allied Commission for Italy. Roosevelt was angered by de Gaulle's policy of 'infiltration'. He complained to Churchill that de Gaulle's 'presence there will, as we know from experience, cause controversy and more trouble with the French Committee'. But Roosevelt did at least recognise the difficult restraints placed upon Churchill by what Roosevelt regarded as the interfering and pro-French nature of the British Foreign Office. He sympathised 'I know the problems you have with your own Foreign Office' and lamented 'I [only] wish you and I could run this Italian business. We would not need any help'.[155] The implication being that great men of destiny should not be limited by those of lesser stature – especially maverick French generals or the British Foreign Office. Macmillan, no doubt too pro-French and of lesser stature, reflected on his working relationship with the Prime Minister and the Churchill of destiny: 'He is a really remarkable man. Although he can be so tiresome and pig-headed, there is no one like him. His devotion to work and duty is quite extraordinary'.[156]

3
Churchill's Isolation

Brooke was promoted to Field Marshal on 1 January 1944. A new year may have dawned with the Chief of the Imperial General Staff attaining the 'top rung of the ladder', but such promotions were insignificant compared to the Allied policy battles still taking place.[1] Britain's official responses to the questions raised by Roosevelt's policy of trusteeship, anti-imperialism and the possibility of French participation in the war in the Far East continued to vex officials in Whitehall. At the Foreign Office, Cadogan was aghast at the unprofessional fashion in which the President conducted intra-Allied business.[2] A British rejoinder to Roosevelt's Indo-Chinese questions was not aided by the deterioration in the relationship between Mountbatten and Stilwell within SEAC.[3] The two commanders were never suited to get along at the best of times. Mountbatten was related to a number of European royal families – Edward VIII was the best man at his wedding. Stilwell was a hard-talking American anti-imperialist known as 'vinegar Joe'. Their mutual distrust and animosity became symbolic of the Anglo-American war effort. Was America fighting for the return of European imperialism or was this a ruse to attain access to new markets and business opportunities? Trusteeship was certainly not without its financial benefits. The Foreign Office was against finding a local Southeast Asian solution to the Mountbatten–Stilwell dispute. It held that the source of all intra-Allied Indo-Chinese problems lay in Washington. Until this was addressed localised negotiations were unlikely to yield any positive results.[4]

In the meantime, the Foreign Office reassessed the record of the French administration in Indo-China in order to counter Roosevelt's claims about colonial under-development.[5] The submission of France in Europe to Germany and in the Far East to Japan did not endear either France or European colonialism to the American President.[6] Britain was wary about potential criticism of its own colonial record. The British reputation in Southeast Asia was hardly outstanding. It too had been damaged by its failure to withstand the Japanese advance into the region.[7] Britain therefore began to initiate its own colonial development policy towards the region. Post-war constitutional change was explored for Malaya and Borneo.[8] Political evolution was matched with planning for the post-war economic reorganisation and reconstruction of Malaya, Borneo, Hong Kong and the Pacific dependencies. All of these had fallen ingloriously into Japanese hands.[9] Stanley, the Colonial Secretary, later argued – in November 1944 – that colonial development would keep the Commonwealth and the Empire in close contact with the metropole. This would enable Britain to continue to play a major role in world affairs, but it would do so under the guise of a very different imperial framework to the pre-war model.[10]

London

Eden was forced to approach Churchill again on 11 January 1944 concerning the future of French Indo-China. The Foreign Office had received a statement from the British Embassy in Chungking. This report strongly deplored Roosevelt's stance concerning the future of French Indo-China. The severity of the assessment left Eden with little option but to forward the statement to the Prime Minister. The embassy account not only warned about the immediate danger of a precedent for British decolonisation being established, but it also emphasised the danger to both Anglo-French relations and 'post-war collaboration in Western Europe' if Roosevelt succeeded with his trusteeship plan. Western disunity could also mobilise indigenous Asian peoples against Western influence at this critical wartime juncture. The report specifically highlighted the danger of the Chinese agreeing with Roosevelt, therefore supporting America against France's wish to return to French Indo-China after the war. The statement did not doubt that the Chinese hoped to put forward their own economic and political agenda for Indo-China under a Chinese-mandated trusteeship system rather than a United Nations administration.[11]

The account appeared to galvanise Churchill into action. Contrary to his previous tactic of dismissing Indo-Chinese questions out of hand, Churchill now decided that the Foreign Office should undertake 'very strong' consultations with the State Department. Yet this was not a signal for the Foreign Office to assume direct management of Anglo-American Indo-Chinese issues – in liaison with the State Department – as

Churchill instructed that any direct communications between himself and Roosevelt on this issue must be left until a 'later' and as yet unspecified date.[12] Churchill intended to avoid Indo-China as an issue, thus preventing a rift between himself and Roosevelt, by encouraging the appeal to the State Department. Churchill was not being shrewd in appealing to the State Department for affirmation of British policy. Indeed American anti-imperialism could produce a negative reaction. Churchill no doubt held that the involvement of another government bureaucracy would result in further analysis, confusion and delay. It later transpired that the State Department was unprepared to develop a policy towards Indo-China at this point in time. This was rectified later in the spring when Washington began to evolve a coherent policy in parallel to Roosevelt's grand strategy.[13]

In the meantime Roosevelt, unhindered by State Department restraints, continued to pursue his utopian vision for Indo-China. On 18 January, Roosevelt held wide-ranging talks in Washington with Halifax over lunch. When the topic of conversation turned to the issue of Indo-China, Roosevelt was not at all embarrassed by his previous pronouncements. Halifax had already conferred with Hull, who had admitted to being kept in the dark by the President on this matter; he therefore considered that Roosevelt's thoughts did not represent a 'settled' State Department policy. The President, however, jovially informed the British Ambassador that his expressions on this subject represented his 'considered view'. Halifax cautioned Roosevelt that his lectures would be reported back to the French. But the President, who was enjoying sparring with Halifax, responded 'I hope they will'. Roosevelt turned to the heart of his Indo-Chinese thoughts – the need to remove Indo-China from French control. Britain feared Chinese intentions towards Indo-China, but Roosevelt was not so concerned. He was 'satisfied' with Chiang Kai-Shek's motivations. Roosevelt added to his main argument by revealing that Stalin liked the idea of placing Indo-China under some kind of 'international trusteeship'. His thesis was that Chiang Kai-Shek could be trusted: Stalin was in full support but Roosevelt feared that the real problem was Churchill. The President emphasised that he had mentioned it '25 times' to Churchill; however 'the Prime Minister has never said anything'. Roosevelt appeared to have turned the tables on the British. His was the predominant view between the four Great Powers. Britain was isolated and the Prime Minister was incommunicado on this subject. Was this an example of dextrous verbal sparring between Roosevelt and Halifax? If so, Roosevelt had just revealed Britain's vulnerability as a Great Power to American dominance. Or did Roosevelt really understand Churchill's predicament? The Prime Minister wished for Britain to remain a world power. The Anglo-American special relationship was crucial to his vision but at the same time Churchill remained uninterested in post-hostilities planning – he was the man of the moment, not of the future. If Roosevelt truly understood Churchill's foreign policy motives then Churchill's silences should have been of no surprise. Churchill was guarding his special relationship against an Indo-China provoked crisis.

Roosevelt was keen to demonstrate to Halifax the clarity of his 'considered' thinking. He denied that his previous 'pledges' about the veracity and the standing of the French Empire were either contrary or relevant to his current plans. The confusion had arisen because Murphy, the President's diplomatic envoy to North Africa, had exceeded his brief. Halifax was not impressed with the President's about-face. He contended that Welles had also made strong public statements on this issue. Halifax was losing patience with his host and his annoyance clearly showed. Halifax informed Roosevelt that he did not care for the President's plan and that, when indeed he did discuss it with the Prime Minister, Halifax hoped that this would not take the form of a 'monologue'.

Halifax also cautioned against a precedent for decolonisation being established. The President might include the 'bright idea' that the Dutch East-Indies or Malaya could also be placed under trusteeship. Roosevelt interrupted Halifax's conjecture to dismiss any such suggestion. The British and the Dutch colonial records were beyond doubt, however 'the French were hopeless'. Halifax countered that the Allies needed to restore France as a Great Power rather than create division and resentment in any future world order. Could not the President at least consider the proposals of the British Colonial Secretary, Stanley, of regional councils to administer trusteeship issues? But Roosevelt was in too playful a mood to take the idea seriously. He did agree about the 'general future of France' but on the specific topic of trusteeship he was prepared to be ruthless: 'tell Winston I gained or got three votes to his one as we stand today' – China, the Soviet Union and the United States versus Britain.

Halifax warily informed the Foreign Office, 'I am left feeling that he has got this idea in his mind a bit more than is likely to be quite wholesome'.[14] Cadogan shared Halifax's assessment: 'this is one of the President's most half baked and unfortunate obita dicta'. He warned that Britain had 'better look out', lest the same argument be used against the British Empire.[15] Eden was in complete agreement with this analysis of Roosevelt's trusteeship scheme.[16] The Foreign Office however did not officially rise to Roosevelt's provocation. It hoped to soften slowly the

American attitude towards French territories whilst at the same time maintaining that the French must be included in all deliberations about the future of Indo-China. Likewise, the Foreign Office believed that it was safer not to consult with the Chinese for the moment, and that any wider move to involve the Chinese in discussions and not the French should be resisted 'strongly'.[17]

Roosevelt may have succeeded in provoking Halifax, but the Foreign Office remained more considered in its reaction, and Churchill was not about to be sidetracked from his main objective of maintaining a Europe-first wartime strategy.[18] The Foreign Office was also against 'taking the initiative' in debating Indo-China with the Americans within the SEAC and China Theatres – despite the growing tensions between these theatres concerning clandestine operations. The root of all of their problems lay in Washington and not the Far East.[19] This frustrated the senior leadership within SEAC. Dening, the Chief Political Adviser to Mountbatten, questioned the essence of Britain's role in Southeast Asia to the Foreign Office. Allied Far Eastern strategy was an American effort; Britain was essentially subservient to its wartime partner. Therefore 'for the Southeast Asia Command there appears to be no role at all, except to cover General Stilwell's supply route and to employ British forces at the maximum disadvantage to themselves with minimum effect upon the enemy'.[20] Churchill did attempt to relieve SEAC's Indo-Chinese problems. He proposed, half-heartedly, to Mountbatten and Roosevelt, that any emergencies should be resolved in Washington.[21] This move could only have been perceived by Mountbatten as unhelpful and would no doubt have been warmly received by the President.

Meanwhile, Roosevelt wrote to Hull to reaffirm his trusteeship policy: 'France has had the country – thirty million inhabitants for nearly one hundred years, and the people are worse off than they were at the beginning'. The President saw 'no reason to play with the British Foreign Office in this matter'. He was absolutely resolute, 'France has milked it for one hundred years. The people of Indo-China are entitled to something better than that'.[22] Halifax's concern about Roosevelt's trusteeship intentions appeared justified. At a press conference in Washington, several days after the President's reassurances towards the British Ambassador concerning British decolonisation, Roosevelt turned his anti-colonial wrath upon the nature of the British Empire. Britain was charged with the same crime of under-development in the Gambia as the French had been in Indo-China. Britain had exploited the indigenous people for economic gain. A United Nations committee should be sent to investigate.[23] In the meantime, de Gaulle had held the Brazzaville

Conference which had rejected post-war self-government for the French colonies.[24] The stage was set for conflict. Allied unity was subservient to Roosevelt's war aims, and Roosevelt's justification for trusteeship of French Indo-China set a dangerous precedent for Britain.

The Australian and New Zealand Governments held a joint conference in Australia to debate common regional concerns.[25] Peter Fraser, the New Zealand Prime Minister, announced that he wished to see the Atlantic Charter 'implemented to the fullest' extent.[26] This certainly alarmed Whitehall. Australia and New Zealand appeared to be advocating support for trusteeship – independent of consultation from Britain. To counter the threat, Whitehall responded with the bait of an international regional council. Australia and New Zealand accepted the idea of a regional council and for the moment division with Britain subsided.[27] In the meantime, Australia and New Zealand agreed to the establishment of an advisory regional organisation. This would include Australia, Britain, France, New Zealand and the United States. Its brief was to develop a common policy towards the economic, political and social development of indigenous colonial peoples. Australia volunteered to host a South and Southwest Pacific conference for the regional organisation members – plus Dutch and Portuguese representatives – to discuss regional security, post-war development and welfare policies.[28] Britain was eager to maintain the support of Dominions. Halifax visited Canada and in Toronto he gave a speech to the British Empire Club. The speech affirmed commonwealth unity to preserve Britain's post-war position as the fourth Great Power. William Mackenzie King, the Canadian Prime Minister, was not pleased with Halifax's oration. He interpreted the speech as promoting a London-centric post-war imperial policy.[29] Neither was Eden satisfied. The Foreign Secretary attempted to restrict further outbursts by requesting that all such engagements be cleared by the Foreign Office.[30] However Lord Cranborne, the Dominions Secretary, revealed wider Whitehall divisions by agreeing with the speech. After all, a strong British Empire was vital to the post-war peace.[31] Even Churchill expressed some sympathy towards Halifax.[32]

Although Churchill was happy to play the role of the deferential political partner within the special relationship, he was wary about how this translated into military practice – especially in the Far East. Churchill held that British forces should not act in a supplementary capacity to the Americans in the Pacific. If such a situation were to arise, this would create immeasurable political problems concerning the sovereignty of Borneo and Malaya. A Japanese retreat, in the face of an overwhelming American-led offensive, would enable the United States to implement international trusteeship to the 'former' colonies and Britain would be unable to do much about it.[33] Likewise, Churchill's deference to Roosevelt did not blind him to the international implications of the turbulent waters of American political life. The Prime Minister informed the House of Commons that the forthcoming presidential election in the United States could revive the public prospects of American anti-imperial sentiment. He was not personally concerned by the shallow consequences of election dramas. But Churchill cautioned, 'a lot of rough things will have to be said about Great Britain and popularity is to be gained in that large community in demonstrating Americanism in its highest forms'.[34]

The War Cabinet Post-Hostilities Planning Sub-Committee concluded that British possessions in the Far East – Australia, India, New Zealand and territories in the South Pacific – were susceptible to the actions of a hostile power using Indo-China. The recent actions of the Japanese exemplified this hazard and justified this thesis. However, the paucity of Britain's status as a Great Power was revealed in the analysis. The Committee highlighted that without American assistance Britain would be unable to address any future threat. Roosevelt's deliberations over the future of French Indo-China were therefore paramount to the maintenance of Britain's position within the region. Although Britain would welcome American involvement in the defence of Indo-China, if the United States removed Indo-China from French control the hostility and the resentment of the French would 'seriously endanger' any post-war collaboration. This would result in an 'unfriendly' relationship with France that could affect British security in other parts of the world. The Committee therefore recommended that American participation in the defence of Indo-China must be sought. However, rather than deprive France of its territory, American interest should be recognised by the institution of United Nations bases.[35] Eden presented the Committee's conclusions to the War Cabinet as part of a wider paper on Indo-China and French possessions in the Pacific. Eden pressed the Cabinet that this was not a future problem but one with grave immediate consequences concerning Britain's relationship with the French Committee of National Liberation and Britain's current political warfare activities in Southeast Asia. He concluded that if the Cabinet favoured continued French sovereignty – something which it would be impossible to deny – then the subject should be pursued with the Americans to prevent any future differences of opinion.[36] The War Cabinet approved of Eden's paper on 24 February 1944. British policy would be to pursue the maintenance of French sovereignty over Indo-China subject to the establishment of international bases which would help to protect British interests in the region. Britain would also liaise with the Dominions Governments concerning the establishment of a co-ordinated policy vis-à-vis the Americans.[37]

Churchill, however, was not going to be bullied into taking any necessary action by the War Cabinet – led by the Foreign Secretary or the Dominions Secretary. His prime concern was to protect his special relationship with the President. A special relationship that was vulnerable to American sensitivities concerning European imperialism and war aims. Churchill feared raising Indo-Chinese matters with his American partner during a presidential election year lest Roosevelt seize upon them and use them to play to anti-imperial sections in the American press and electorate. Churchill therefore held the trusteeship debate to be of minor significance compared to the continuation of the Anglo-American special relationship for Allied wartime and post-war co-operation. Churchill was prepared to hide from the earnestness and seriousness of Roosevelt's intent. He was also willing to forestall Whitehall from setting any 'ponderous machinery in motion'. Churchill informed Eden and Cranborne that the President's pronouncements were 'particular to himself'. They were merely 'chance remarks' of little significance, 'made in [passing] conversation'. Despite growing evidence to the contrary, Churchill denied that any decisions, let alone actions, were needed on this issue for the foreseeable future. He concluded that any consideration of this topic could be logically postponed until the Dominions' Prime Ministers arrived in London for wider discussions – a delay of two months.[38] Cranborne was not prepared to dismiss the subject so readily. He argued for an immediate consultation with the Dominions in order to produce a more meaningful discussion later in London.[39] Churchill seemingly agreed to Cranborne's request, but only with the pre-condition that he would first have to approve of any telegram before it was sent.[40] Churchill would therefore be able to censor any approach to the Dominions and also control the timing of the telegram by using his customary delaying techniques, thus preventing Cranborne's immediate consultation.

Churchill's only tactic appeared to be delay. He felt disinclined to heed the caution of others or even to allow others to chart a way forward. Foreign Office correspondence to the Prime Minister received similar treatment.[41] A separate correspondence by Cranborne to the War Cabinet highlighted that the Dominions Office supported the creation of regional commissions as part of the 'parent/trustee status of the Atlantic Charter', but it also held that this concept was impractical for

Southeast Asia.[42] Nevertheless for the moment, Churchill's simple strategy of delay prevailed. Eden noted five months later – September 1944 – that the Dominions had still not been conferred with about British policy towards French Indo-China. Churchill's intransigence could not, however, prevent the Dominion Governments from developing their own policies. Australia informed Hull that it was entirely in favour of a French return to Indo-China.[43] Churchill may have been reluctant to defend French imperialism in the Far East vis-à-vis his special relationship with America, but when Roosevelt's chance remarks were directed towards the future of the British Empire Churchill was not as disinclined to offer a strong defence: 'my irrevocable principle is that no Government of which I am the Head will yield one square inch of British territory or British rights in any quarter of the globe except for greater advantages or moral scruples'.[44]

The Colonial Secretary, Stanley, noted with disquiet the American hypocrisy concerning the creation of a benevolent trusteeship and its undoubted economic benefit to the advancement of the American market empire.[45] The Foreign Office was aware of the growing global mercantile rivalry between Britain and the United States, and the paradox that Britain's continued Great Power status was dependent upon Anglo-American co-operation. The United States was 'a land looking for opportunity', and overseas oil, rubber, tin, communications and civil aviation industries were suitable economic targets for acquisition.[46] The Indo-Chinese rubber industry would, no doubt, be of commercial interest to American manufacturers. By challenging Roosevelt's plans for Indo-Chinese trusteeship, the Colonial Office and the Foreign Office were defending the European colonial empires against the onslaught of dollar imperialism. The economic nature of trusteeship was hidden beneath eloquent American language that advocated 'a responsibility... to dependent peoples who aspire to liberty'. The United States was relatively untarnished in this respect – America led the way with its promise of independence to the Philippines following the war.[47] In contrast Churchill's predictions about the presidential election had come true: Britain was viewed by the American public as exploitative towards its colonies and preventative of self-government.[48] Nonetheless, Foreign Office intransigence proved that, despite Churchill, Britain still had an independent foreign policy and that it was still a world power. Churchill had to tread carefully to protect his special relationship with Roosevelt against American public opinion and the British Whitehall establishment. Churchill may have been the weaker partner, but as far as he was concerned he was the fulcrum of the Anglo-American partnership.

Churchill spent two days before the start of the Dominions Prime Ministers' Conference with Field Marshal Smuts at Chequers. On the afternoon of 29 April they discussed the nature of the future world order. Fraser joined them for tea. On 1 May the conference opened in London.[49] Churchill had done his groundwork and grooming well. Brooke observed that the old imperial relationships appeared 'strong'.[50] The Dominions Prime Ministers were particularly complementary about Churchill's wartime leadership and the general direction of British foreign policy.[51] Britain could depend on the continued support of its empire vis-à-vis the other Great Powers.

The French Committee of National Liberation unsurprisingly remained resolute to regain French Indo-China. Mountbatten observed, at first-hand, French intent to establish a small military mission either at SEAC or China Theatre headquarters in order to facilitate this eventuality. He stressed to the British COS the importance of SEAC hosting the mission lest the French decided to concentrate all of their efforts upon the China Theatre and thereby diminish British influence in the region.[52] French General Zinovi Pechkoff, de Gaulle's representative to Chiang Kai-Shek, had already observed that as France possessed a fleet in the region it was by now engaged in the war against Japan. Major-General Leslie Hollis, the War Cabinet Secretary at the Ministry of Defence, brought the matter before the Prime Minister for his consideration.[53] Churchill – unperturbed by War Cabinet conclusions and Colonial, Dominion and Foreign Office concerns – was unmoved by Mountbatten and the COS's desire for greater direction. Churchill continued to do nothing. He instructed the Foreign Office, 'It will be better to delay. One can always concede'.[54] General Hastings Ismay, Chief of Staff to Churchill in his capacity as the Minister of Defence, reluctantly informed the Foreign Office, 'For the time, therefore, there is nothing we can do'.[55] Cadogan mused upon Churchill's unrelenting obduracy and the consequent idleness of British policy that, 'I can only infer that the P.M., knowing as I do President Roosevelt – and Admiral Leahy's – sinister intentions regarding Indo-China, is careful not to do anything that might imply our recognition of French input there'.[56]

Lord Selborne, Head of the Special Operations Executive (SOE) which was responsible for the political warfare and pre-occupational duties in Indo-China on behalf of SEAC, was less philosophical. Selborne harried both Churchill and Eden concerning the necessity to accept a French mission at SEAC. He argued that any delay would impair SOE operations and, in view of Roosevelt's 'calculated indiscretions', add to French paranoia in relation to the direction of British intentions in the region.[57]

Eden agreed with Selborne. Although Eden did recognise that the Prime Minister did not appear to want to discuss the future of Indo-China with Roosevelt, Indo-Chinese problems were now disrupting military operations rather than political deliberations.[58] Action was needed. Yet Churchill remained indifferent towards the petition. His anger at again being dragged into Indo-Chinese deliberations was evident. He ridiculed Eden:

> It is hard enough to get along in SEAC when we virtually have only the Americans to deal with. The more the French can get their finger into the pie, the more trouble they will make in order to show they are not humiliated in any way by the events through which they have passed. You will have de Gaullist intrigues there just as you now have in Syria and the Lebanon.
>
> Before we could bring the French officially into the Indo-China area, we should have to settle with President Roosevelt. He has been more outspoken to me on that subject than any other colonial matter, and I imagine it is one of his principal war aims to liberate Indo-China from France. Whenever he has raised it, I have repeatedly reminded him of his pledges about the integrity of the French Empire and have reserved our position. Do you really want to go and stir all this up at such a time as this?
>
> I do not like the idea of Mountbatten's command becoming a kind of minor court with many powers having a delegation there. The fact that the Dutch have a section is because we are studying those countries which they own with a view to attack and we certainly have no plans in prospect for liberating Indo-China.
>
> On the other hand, I recognise that the arrival of the 'Richlieu' (for 3 months) in Indian waters gives the French certain valid grounds...
>
> It is erroneous to suppose that one must always be doing something. The greatest service SOE can render us is to select with great discrimination their areas and occasions of intervention.

Churchill could not have been less ambiguous concerning his fear. He had elevated trusteeship from a 'chance remark' to one of Roosevelt's 'principal war aims'. The most important aspect of Churchill's wartime policy was his special relationship with America and this in itself was difficult enough to manage without the complications of French or Indo-Chinese issues. Added to this Churchill was aware of the problems within Mountbatten's command – the strained Anglo-American relations, personality clashes, the ambiguous presence of a French battleship and so on. Delay appeared to offer the simplest immediate solution – the war in the Far East was unlikely to end in the foreseeable future.[59]

Churchill's delaying tactic was not well received by the Foreign Office. Harvey dryly observed that the 'President has become more and more obstructive in all French matters and the Prime Minister runs away from them'.[60] Cadogan was less sympathetic: 'It's a girls' school. Roosevelt, P.M. and – it must be said de Gaulle – all behave like girls approaching the age of puberty'. Nevertheless, beneath the tantrums the Foreign Office strove to concoct a consistent British foreign policy – even if this was, at times, in direct opposition to Churchill. At the May meeting of the Dominion Prime Ministers, the Foreign Office and the Prime Ministers had formed a united front against Churchill concerning his views on regional councils for the post-war world.[61] Churchill would not let them do the same over French Indo-China. It was his foreign policy to command – he was His Majesty's First Minister.

In the meantime, a sub-committee of the War Cabinet Post-Hostilities Committee considered the extension of post-war base facilities to the United States in greater detail. A report issued on 23 April highlighted that the closeness of French territory to the British Empire necessitated continued friendship and the possible use of French bases. Provided the British extension of base facilities to the United States was clearly justified, as solely a 'step towards setting up a world security system', the Committee foresaw that no previous Anglo-American understanding could distort a similar prospect of sharing resources with France.[62] The unwritten implication in the report was that any future Anglo-American relationship must not be seen as a threat to France or other lesser nations.

Mountbatten appeared perturbed with the lack of direction from London. He again raised the prospect of a French military mission being attached to SEAC with the COS on 1 June. Mountbatten believed that it was of the utmost military importance to obtain the full co-operation of the French for pre-occupational work in Indo-China.[63] This could only be established through a military mission. Churchill requested that the COS report to him about this subject before taking any action.[64] Therefore the COS repeated their request for clarification to Churchill – the fundamental query being whether the mission was still to be conceded.[65] Eden suspended a further Foreign Office appeal to the Prime Minister.[66] Churchill was consistent in his response. He asked Hollis: 'Is there any reason why we should not wait and see how we finish up with de Gaulle?'[67] Allied theatre policy was again subservient to Churchill's big political picture. The COS was unwilling to harass the

Prime Minister further. Mountbatten's requirements were to be ignored. The COS was in agreement with Churchill. There was no need for them to pursue the topic at this juncture. They absolved themselves of all responsibility by charging Mountbatten: 'On the instructions of the Prime Minister a decision is to be deferred for the time being'.[68]

The COS may have decided that it was convenient to defer to Churchill's direction on Indo-Chinese matters, but other branches of the British Government were less than happy with Roosevelt's pro-nouncements or Churchill's inactivity. Brendon Bracken, the Minister of Information, was particularly scathing about Roosevelt: 'Now that Roosevelt is talking to God he may be even more unreasonable. We have got to tell the gentleman that Europe cannot be wrecked by his Dutch obstinacy'.[69] Even Churchill was capable of making mirth at Roosevelt's expense: 'I think it would be a good thing to let the President know the kind of way de Gaulle interprets friendliness. I have now had four years' experience of him, and it is always the same'.[70] Roosevelt would have agreed: 'Prima Donnas do not change their spots'.[71] American reluctance to agree to the return of French overseas possessions had already led to disagreements between the President and de Gaulle.[72] Churchill also had his difficulties with de Gaulle; however, with D-day on the horizon Bracken believed that Churchill was becoming more level-headed about French affairs. Nevertheless, Churchill could be as difficult as his French nemesis and continued to harangue both British and French representa-tives with Churchillian eruptions when particularly vexed. The British Ambassador to France, Duff Cooper, was an extreme Francophile and his pro-de Gaulle stance provoked Churchill to quip that Cooper was 'a cat purring at the feet of de Gaulle' but that Churchill had never actually met a 'decent' Frenchman.[73] Bracken was also targeted for mockery by the Prime Minister. He was a Foreign Office 'lackey' and a 'hack' who had displayed thus far 'more ignorance than its normal inhabitants'.[74]

On 7 July Churchill chaired a meeting of the War Cabinet. When the conversation turned to the future structure of the world organi-sation, Churchill suddenly announced that he had a prior luncheon engagement and left the Cabinet to its task. Cadogan was not impressed with the Prime Minister's attitude. He feared that Churchill's lack of interest in the future world organisation would hinder the British del-egation to the Washington post-war conference at Dumbarton Oaks (August–October 1944).[75] Churchill saved his frustrations concerning post-hostilities planning for Eden. He scoffed to his Foreign Secre-tary: 'Nobody cares a damn about the United Nations'.[76] But Eden was tiring of Churchillian outbursts. Britain's interests would be better served by developing an independent foreign policy instead of having to defer to America for approval. Churchill's special relationship allowed both the United States and the Prime Minister to block Foreign Office initiatives.[77] The 'honeymoon stage' of the special relationship was over. But in French affairs Roosevelt's behaviour could at best be described as 'ornery', and Churchill favoured siding with Roosevelt rather than France. Eden was wary of damaging Anglo-French relations during a crucial period in France's national rebirth. Yet, he was caught in an impossible situation. Churchill, Macmillan, Hull, Roosevelt, the American Joint Chiefs of Staff and the British COS all sought to direct British foreign policy in competition with the Foreign Secretary.

Churchill did not enjoy post-war planning.[78] The Prime Minister was old and fatigued. He did not understand post-war business. The Americans adhered to a vision of the post-war world organisation that used territorial trusteeship to achieve its ends. When Churchill was informed of this by the Foreign Office he responded in a 'cynically jocular' fashion and settled the future world order in a 25-minute Cabinet session.[79] Churchill liked to swamp himself with the details of wartime management. Nevertheless, even with military strategy the Prime Minister was exhausted and as a result he failed to see such problems within a wider context. Brooke felt that Churchill's leadership was 'wandering and meandering'.[80] Lord Moran, the Prime Minister's doctor, observed how isolated within government Churchill had become. This isolation was exasperated by his dislike of perceived trouble makers.[81] In contrast, Roosevelt appeared to be energetically setting the agenda for post-war decolonisation. In a speech, the President announced that the future of the people in the Pacific would be intertwined with America for years to come.[82]

De Gaulle, in Washington, announced that France would not give up its empire.[83] Meanwhile, by coincidence, the French delegation in Washington had acquired correspondence between Welles and Vichy. This urged that French Indo-China make every assistance available towards the Japanese in Indo-China. [84] Cadogan believed that such revelations, despite their age, could prove to be of acute embarrassment to Roosevelt. But Eden was less convinced even though the revelations included an offer of unqualified support to return Indo-China to France.[85] However, the changed geo-political situation following D-day and the annihilation of the Axis-orientated Vichy France permitted the British COS to reconsider the matter of affixing a French military mission to SEAC.[86] Metropolitan France temporarily ceased to exist. The French National Committee of Liberation under de Gaulle began to assume control of mainland France behind the advancing Allied armies. Indo-China, which had previously rallied to Vichy rather than de Gaulle, continued to serve in collaboration with its Japanese occupiers as part of the Axis movement. Tensions mounted between the French colonials and the Japanese. The SOE estimated that French forces in Indo-China totalled 54,000. It became apparent that Indo-China was the only part of the Vichy regime to survive. As the resurrection and rehabilitation of France as a Great Power became increasingly likely, Churchill reacted to this changing situation by agreeing to a French military mission and also the *Corps Leger* being attached to SEAC.[87] The COS therefore considered that it was an appropriate time to recommend to the American Joint Chiefs of Staff plans for the French participation in the war in the Far East.[88] The Foreign Office fully agreed.[89] Both the Foreign Office and the War Office were embarrassed by the absence of an immediate American reply. The War Office recommended that if nothing was decided by the end of the month then French General Roger Blaizot should undertake a personal visit to Mountbatten.[90] The Foreign Office admitted to being ignorant of the content of Roosevelt and de Gaulle's recent discussions in Washington.[91] Yet it also acknowledged its impotency until Churchill and Roosevelt had discussed the issues at stake.[92]

The War Office distrust of the American Joint Chiefs of Staff proved unfounded. The American Joint Chiefs of Staff duly re-evaluated the appeal and agreed with the French request to partake in the war against Japan; their only caveat being that French political warfare operations should be restricted to the area of SEAC.[93] The military planners in London and Washington appeared to be acting in unison. Roosevelt, however, did not approve of the new Anglo-American military consensus either to involve France in the war in the Far East or to establish a French military mission at SEAC. Such ideas challenged his command of French imperial policy and specifically his plans for Indo-China. The President turned to a familiar Churchillian tactic – delay. Roosevelt declared that presidential approval of the American Joint Chiefs of Staff plans could not be countenanced until he had the chance to converse about them with Churchill at Quebec. This discussion could not be held via their regular exchange of telegram correspondence, or over the telephone, but only at their next wartime conference meeting.[94] The President was in a mischievous mood before the Quebec Conference. He quipped to Henry Morgenthau, Secretary of the Treasury, that he had genuinely not known that Britain was bankrupt. The only solution that he could offer was to go to London and seize the empire.[95]

The British Foreign Office remained appalled with the American attitude towards SOE operations and Far Eastern obduracy. Such issues
were 'molehill[s]' and not 'mountain[s]'. It was dryly observed that
even 'if we were a nation of angels we would still be suspected by
some Americans of having sinister motives for anything we did'.[96]
Mountbatten attempted to bring further pressure to bear upon Eden by
notifying him of rumours, concerning an American *volte-face* towards
Indo-Chinese problems, circulating in Southeast Asia.[97]

The continued rehabilitation of France and of Anglo-French relations provoked greater contact between the Foreign Office and René
Massigli – the French Ambassador in London. The War Cabinet met
on 14 August, without Churchill, to discuss again the future of French
Indo-China and other mutual issues likely to arise in upcoming dialogue
between Massigli and Eden. Unsurprisingly, the War Cabinet re-affirmed
its conclusions of 24 February – the maintenance of French power – and
approved of Eden's suggestion that the initiation and direction of debate
on this topic should be left to Massigli.[98] In contrast to the position
adopted by Roosevelt, Britain could not be seen either to pre-judge or to
direct the Indo-Chinese question. Roosevelt was the aggressor. The Foreign Office depicted empathy towards France. Its real allegiance lay in
re-establishing both a strong France in Europe and American assistance
in post-war global management.

Massigli's subsequent meeting with Eden at the Foreign Office produced, as expected, negotiations about Indo-Chinese matters. Massigli
observed that the United States had not as yet clarified its position
towards Indo-China. Even de Gaulle's recent talks with Roosevelt had
been of the most 'vague' nature on this topic. Aware of French sensitivities concerning Indo-China and also of Roosevelt's bold plans for a
change of sovereignty, Eden chose instead to address Massigli's remarks
from a purely British perspective. In order to protect future international
security Britain was prepared to donate base facilities to the employment of the international community if other nations were prepared to
do likewise. Britain would not withdraw from its global responsibilities.
It was a non-negotiable case of 'what we have we hold'. Eden enquired
of Massigli that if Britain was prepared to undertake membership of an
international security process – which involved a period of consultation and a joint use of bases – then would France also be willing to
participate in such a scheme. Massigli responded from a personal perspective that he did not believe that France would object towards these
proposals as long as questions about French sovereignty over such areas
were no longer at stake.[99] Massigli proposed that in the absence of any

direction from Washington, concerning the attachment of a French military mission to SEAC, Blaizot should be permitted to make a 'temporary personal visit' to Mountbatten. Eden agreed to 'favourably consider' the proposal even if an American response was not forthcoming. Dening was subsequently consulted to ascertain Mountbatten's views.[100]

Quebec and Cairo

Churchill travelled to Quebec on the *Queen Mary* to partake in further consultations with Roosevelt. Churchill appeared old and tired. Brooke, although an admirer of the Prime Minister's achievements, was frustrated with Churchill: 'He [Churchill] knows no details, has only got half the picture in his mind, [and] talks absurdities'. Brooke thought that the Prime Minister was unwell. He kept holding his head in his hands.[101] The voyage revived Churchill, but, in contrast Churchill found Roosevelt at the Quebec Conference 'very frail'.[102]

John Colville, Churchill's Private Secretary, telegrammed to the Prime Minister at Quebec to remind him to discuss Indo-Chinese issues with the President.[103] The stalemate concerning the French participation in the war in the Far East and the establishment of a French military mission and the *Corps Leger* at SEAC needed to be broken. Curiously, despite Churchill's newly found enthusiasm for the French mission and his general support for a French contribution towards the war in the Far East, Churchill could not find the opportunity to raise these matters with the President in Quebec, although international trusteeship for Germany (the Morgenthau Plan) was discussed at dinner on 13 September. Nor could Churchill seem to find another convenient moment, following a further reminder, whilst he visited Roosevelt at his home at Hyde Park in upstate New York.

The Quebec Conference had focussed on numerous post-war policy issues including the government of France and American financial guarantees to Britain.[104] The absence of a disagreement about French Indo-China ensured the conference's success. Colville enquired of the Foreign Office as to whether the Foreign Secretary should pursue the Indo-China issue by asking Churchill to telegraph to Roosevelt. Eden decided that, for the moment, it would be advisable to wait. He copied his response to Hollis.[105] Both Allied leaders chose to bury their Indo-Chinese concerns at the Second Quebec Conference: Churchill – because he feared upsetting Roosevelt so close to an American presidential election; Roosevelt – since a delay kept him as the fulcrum of the international trusteeship debate. At the parallel Dumbarton Oaks Conference (August–October) a similar degree of progress was made. Independence for the European colonies was not explicitly discussed. A new idea concerning 'voluntary' trusteeship was proposed. But it was ruled that this could not be discussed by the conference – further analysis was pending.[106] John Curtin, the Australian Prime Minister, warned Churchill of the potential public relations disaster if America won the war in the Far East and recovered captured territories 'relatively' unaided by the other Allies. This would irrevocably damage Britain's presence in the Pacific.[107] The Foreign Office proposed making another appeal for the Prime Minister to consult with the Dominions.[108] Eden cautioned that the Foreign Office needed to discover what had actually taken place at Quebec before proceeding.[109]

Mountbatten, however, was exasperated by the lack of direction from the Allied leadership. His pre-occupational activities for Indo-China could not begin until its status had been resolved at the highest level. French involvement in the war in the Far East, SOE operations, the attachment of a French military mission and *Corps Leger* to SEAC, the ongoing disagreements between SEAC and China Theatre concerning intra-theatre boundaries all required urgent attention. He also wanted Churchill, Roosevelt and the CCS to endorse formally his Gentleman's Agreement with Chiang Kai-Shek.[110] Churchill, though, would not be drawn into taking his previous ruling further by negotiating a joint solution with Roosevelt or formally endorsing the Gentleman's Agreement. He informed both Eden and Ismay that Mountbatten's questions should be dealt with by the COS; thereby relegating Mountbatten's problems to military concerns and deflecting the need for him to take decisive political action. The COS naturally decided that for the moment these matters could be postponed – they were not of an urgent military nature.[111] The vague Gentleman's Agreement permitted flexibility towards some of the difficulties and avoided the problem of having to achieve a formal settlement.[112] Mountbatten was not however prepared to wait. Action was needed, and his position had already been compromised as Britain had by now accepted the contribution of a French battleship for employment in the Far East against the Japanese. Clarification was justified as French sailors were about to engage in Far Eastern operations. Additionally, if delays pertaining to the deployment of a French military mission persisted or if the mission was located in China Theatre, Mountbatten believed that this would fundamentally disrupt both China Theatre operations and British policy in the Far East. In the meantime Mountbatten agreed to receive Blaizot's informal visit.[113] Eden weighed SEAC concerns but conceded Foreign Office impotency on this issue vis-à-vis Churchill and Roosevelt: 'This is all very well but <u>PM</u> may take same view as President'.[114]

SEAC and the Foreign Office were in agreement upon British objectives in Southeast Asia and the requirement to include consultation and co-ordination with the French. Mountbatten was relieved by Eden's support and remained in personal correspondence with him concerning such issues.[115] British Foreign Office policy necessitated some kind of action to satisfy French demands and restore intra-Allied associations, but the Anglo-American stalemate over Indo-Chinese issues prevented any such action. It was a source of embarrassment to Eden and the Foreign Office.[116] The Foreign Office continued to agree with Mountbatten that the direct result of the current impasse could be the establishment of a French military mission in China Theatre, to the detriment of British influence in the region. John Sterndale Bennett, Head of the Far Eastern Department at the Foreign Office, petitioned to Churchill that he should contact Roosevelt and resolve the situation.[117] He also informed him that Allied policy within SEAC could be enhanced by informal Anglo-French liaisons. A provisional private visit had been arranged for Blaizot to meet Mountbatten at SEAC headquarters. Eden was in agreement with the assessment and supported the appeal to the Prime Minister.[118] Ultimately, American permission was required because SEAC was a combined Allied theatre.[119]

The French still anticipated formal Allied permission to deploy their forces in the war against Japan. In contrast to the agreement attained in August, the American Joint Chiefs of Staff now reflected the attitude of their Commander in Chief and appeared indifferent towards the appeals of the British COS to decide the matter. The only solution appeared to be for Churchill and Roosevelt to come to some kind of workable solution for all of the parties concerned. On the other hand, it was in neither of their interests to agree to a conference, the deadlock served to shield their respective agendas. Nevertheless, Churchill at last appeared willing to consult with both Eden and Mountbatten at Cairo, at the end of October, concerning a possible settlement. Yet aware of the strength of Roosevelt's convictions and jealous about guarding his special relationship, Churchill continued to hesitate about pursuing the subject directly with the President. He was caught in two minds about how to proceed. Churchill instructed Eden to 'draft a telegram to the President' but advised that this should be undertaken at the Foreign Secretary's 'leisure'. The draft would have to be agreed by the Prime Minister and he was in the short term unprepared to do so. Safety appeared to necessitate delay. Churchill counselled Eden that the President would not be fond of the French being permitted to partake in Indo-Chinese affairs. It seemed logical to the Prime Minister that 'we had better keep this particular item till other more urgent matters have been settled'. After all, the war in Southeast Asia was unlikely to progress before 1946. Churchill timidly contested: 'I am trying to improve on this'.[120]

Pressure was building in Whitehall against the Prime Minister. At the Foreign Office Sterndale Bennett informed Pierson Dixon, Eden's Principal Private Secretary, that there was a real danger of all Indo-Chinese operations being entirely managed by the United States unless urgent action was taken.[121] Hollis, on behalf of the COS, wrote to Churchill and advocated that it was now time for the Prime Minister to contact Roosevelt and reach an agreement for the establishment of a formal French military mission at SEAC and general French participation in the wider war against the Japanese. He included a draft telegram for the Prime Minister's consideration.[122] Eden was in agreement with the COS recommendation.[123] The informal liaison between SEAC and the French could not be allowed to continue indefinitely. French Indo-Chinese issues stalked Churchill. Offering no respite, they accompanied him to Moscow where the COS appealed to the Prime Minister to agree to Foreign Office proposals.[124]

The debate moved to Cairo where Mountbatten joined Churchill and Eden for discussions. He too pressed Churchill for a verdict and offered the Prime Minister the benefit of his expertise.[125] Whilst Churchill was in Cairo the American Government's decision to recognise the Provisional Government of France was announced. Mountbatten's enthusiasm that this necessitated full recognition of the Blaizot mission was for the moment both premature and erroneous. Churchill and Roosevelt had not reached a mutual agreement.[126] However, Churchill appeared to bow to the CCS and Foreign Office pressure, although he did query whether the proposed draft telegram to the President was in fact contradictory.[127] This proved to be a non-contradiction as it transpired that Churchill had confused the parameters of 'planning for political warfare' with 'operational planning'.[128] Nevertheless, the Prime Minister told Eden that he should 'proceed' as the COS suggested for the preservation of the French military mission at SEAC, and Dening was instructed that the Prime Minister had approved the Blaizot mission. Despite evidence to the contrary this was not a definitive statement by the Prime Minister to resolve the status of the mission. Churchill instructed Eden: 'There is no need for me to telegraph to the President'.[129] He then referred the issue back to Eden, who would be unable to pursue it further until he returned to London.[130] Churchill had played a feint. There was no longer an informal French military mission attached to SEAC but neither was there clarity. Churchill had weighed his options and decided to act unilaterally to protect both SEAC and his special relationship with the President. Ambiguity served him well.

In the meantime, the French resolved to take matters into their own hands and settle the issue of their Far Eastern involvement for themselves. In September, Vice-Admiral Fenard approached the Commander in Chief of the American Fleet and enquired whether the French Navy could be supplied with an aircraft carrier to conduct operations off the Indo-Chinese coast. The request was forwarded to the CCS for their consideration.[131] When the matter eventually reached Churchill three months later, the Prime Minister was reluctant to act. Churchill may have been willing to support the ambiguous attachment of a French military mission to SEAC, but he was unprepared to permit France to develop the capacity to conduct its own operations in the South China Sea. Churchill blamed the strain of 'heavy work' for his inability to consider the request with the due care and diligence that it deserved. He therefore asked for the subject to be returned to on a later and more appropriate occasion.[132]

The United States was just as unwilling to support the deployment of French forces in the Far East. It appeared to the British Joint Service Mission in Washington that familiar political as well as naval deliberations were influencing an American response. In London, the First Sea Lord held that the Americans were 'studiously avoiding any definite commitment'. If the French wished to pursue the prospect of their naval forces operating off the Indo-Chinese coast as part of Allied Far Eastern operations, then the British Admiralty held that it might just be able to aid its French counterparts with the renovation and refurbishment of French naval vessels. The Admiralty could offer less indistinct assistance towards the French only if Churchill and Roosevelt resolved their differences and provided clear direction and leadership. However, the President and the Prime Minister were spared from having to address the problem. The Allies were neither able to find any naval vessels to provide the French with nor, as it transpired, were they able to carry out the necessary repairs. Therefore an executive decision did not have to be made at this juncture.[133] Churchill, unsurprisingly, seized the opportunity for further procrastination. He observed that the French would be indignant at the rebuff, but that in reality they had little choice but to accept the wait. If the French protested at their treatment the issue would have to be resolved by a dialogue 'between the Heads of

Government'.[134] This would not be in the best interests of France as any future conference would be dominated by Roosevelt. The American fleet, however, was not forbidden from carrying out operations against Indo-China. On 11–12 January 1945, American aircraft carrier strikes sunk 30 ships and damaged 9 others.[135]

At the same time as Churchill's deliberations concerning the French fleet, stories circulated in Washington concerning Mountbatten's future as the Supreme Allied Commander of SEAC. His intended demise was due to his tempestuous dealings with an unspecified American general.[136] Mountbatten had already had a turbulent association with Stilwell, his deputy. Stilwell had been recalled to Washington in October and his position was taken by Al Wedemeyer – another American general but one who had previously maintained amicable relations with Mountbatten as his Deputy Chief of Staff. Wedemeyer, however, now considered it his duty as Chief of Staff to Chaing Kai-Shek to protect China Theatre affairs at the expense of SEAC.[137] M. Francfort, of the French Embassy in London, protested to Sterndale Bennett about Wedemeyer's pronouncement that French Indo-China was located within the China Theatre.[138] Mountbatten considered that the SEAC–China Theatre boundaries remained unresolved considering French Indo-China, an issue that he had not discussed at Cairo with Eden or Churchill. The first Quebec Conference had placed Indo-China within the China Theatre and Siam within SEAC. These boundaries were at odds with Mountbatten's later Gentleman's Agreement with Chiang Kai-Shek. Mountbatten now audaciously asked for clarification to the problem that he had helped to create.[139] The American Joint Chiefs of Staff had already re-clarified that Indo-China lay within China Theatre boundaries, any change would be taken after a successful invasion.[140] The haphazard nature of Mountbatten's command did not pass unnoticed in London. Brooke and even Churchill remained wary of Mountbatten's capacity to manage SEAC responsibly. Mountbatten was 'quite irresponsible, and tries to be loved by all, which won't at all work!... I [Brooke] am afraid however that Mountbatten will be a constant source of trouble to us and will never really fit the bill as Supreme Commander'.[141] Brooke's personal thoughts, penned in his diary, proved prophetic when in 1945 Mountbatten was at the centre of another Anglo-American crisis concerning French Indo-China.

The Foreign Office was still committed to solving the unsettled Indo-Chinese problems that existed between Britain and the United States concerning SOE pre-occupational activities, the employment of French forces in the war against Japan and the ambiguous status of the French military mission attached to SEAC. These issues were not assisted by the tempestuous nature of the relationships between Mountbatten and his American deputies. Churchill, though, still could not settle such matters with Roosevelt. He proposed that the Foreign Office should purse these topics with the State Department. The Foreign Office was initially wary of the suggestion, and it was hesitant of actually achieving a positive solution because the ultimate resolution rested with Roosevelt.[142] Eden, however, thought that the Foreign Office should at least attempt to resolve the crises via the British Ambassador in Washington before proceeding to lobby Churchill for a more direct approach to be made to the President.[143] Eden was tiring in his struggles with the Prime Minister, who seemed more energetic in foreign affairs as the military situation simplified.[144] Halifax was therefore directed to approach the State Department and persuade them to decide upon a solution to the Indo-Chinese problems in liaison with the President. He was reminded of the recent failure to resolve the issue at the second Quebec Conference, when Churchill and Roosevelt had not found an opportunity to discuss the matter.[145] Based upon the history of the Indo-Chinese debate Eden would have expected very little from the new initiative, but there was little harm in attempting to circumnavigate Churchill and Roosevelt's obduracy and reassess the prevalent mood in Washington. To reinforce the enterprise the Foreign Office notified Winant, the American Ambassador in London:

> It would be difficult to deny French participation in the liberation of Indo-China in light of the increasing strength of the French Government in world affairs, and that, unless a policy to be followed toward Indo-China is mutually agreed between our two governments, circumstances may arise at any moment which will place our two governments in a very awkward situation.[146]

The warning proved far-sighted when in March 1945 the Japanese disposed of the Vichy regime in Indo-China and precipitated another crisis in the Anglo-American relationship concerning Indo-China.

In Washington the State Department challenged Roosevelt to ascertain both clarity and direction regarding his Indo-Chinese policy. Roosevelt was forced to defend his trusteeship predilection.[147] The President received timely support from Major-General Bill Donovan, Head of the Office for Strategic Services (the forerunner of the Central Intelligence Agency). Donovan's analysis of Southeast Asia indicated that Britain, France and the Netherlands all intended to re-colonise the region as soon as possible.[148] This interpretation was supported by separate assessments from Wedemeyer at SEAC and Patrick Hurley, the American Ambassador to China.[149] Roosevelt explained to Stanley Hornbeck, now his Ambassador to the Netherlands, that he did not as yet have a specific French Indo-China policy but that some kind of provision would be made for independence.[150] American foreign policy was Roosevelt's personal fiefdom. Pragmatic and magnanimous, he 'was an ambiguous combination of political manipulator and visionary. He governed more often by instinct than by analysis'.[151] He did not have to make a final political decision about Indo-China until the cold light of day following the end of hostilities. As the main creditor nation America would call the shots in the post-war world. The British Foreign Office was certainly worried by Roosevelt's fluidity and lack of plans. In contrast, Roosevelt expected to be consulted by Britain on all matters relating to Indo-China.[152]

In the meantime, Oliver Stanley advised the War Cabinet Armistice and Post-War Committee that Southeast Asia was an ideal candidate for a regional commission.[153] Churchill was vexed with the Committee and his response was draconian. He temporarily 'banned' the Committee from meeting.[154] Brooke visited Churchill on the morning of the 12 December 1944. He observed that the Prime Minister 'was quite incapable of concentrating on anything but his breakfast and the Greek situation'. A meeting later the same day provoked further consternation from Brooke: 'Quite impossible to get the P.M. to even begin to understand the importance of the principles involved. ... He *cannot* understand a large strategical concept'. Brooke was depressed at his leader's inability to focus on the important issues at hand. The Chief of the Imperial General Staff even considered his resignation.[155] Attlee, the Deputy Prime Minister, in conjunction with Stanley prepared another paper for the War Cabinet to discuss on trusteeship. The paper was an attempt to prevent the United States from dictating both the agenda and the course of international trusteeship.[156] The Cabinet met on 20 December to discuss the world organisation and territorial trusteeships. Cadogan was appalled with both Churchill's conduct and his management of the meeting: 'A complete madhouse – P.M. knows *nothing* about it'. It was all 'utterly futile'. Cadogan believed that the ageing Prime Minister was 'failing'. Colville noted how the strain of maintaining the special relationship with America was placing an enormous amount of pressure upon Churchill. The Prime Minister's paperwork was in a 'frightful state'. He was tired and neglected complex issues of state.[157] Indo-China was no exception.

Nevertheless, the trusteeship dispute would not dissipate. Churchill, although an ardent advocate for the protection of the British Empire, continued to neglect the direction of the international trusteeship debate. The Prime Minister enquired of Eden on New Year's Eve, 'How does this matter stand? There must be no question of our being hustled or seduced into declarations affecting British sovereignty in any of the Dominions or colonies. Pray remember my declaration against liquidating the British Empire'. Churchill observed with irony that the United States expected to retain a number of Japanese islands for its own post-war security requirements. He 'blessed' such imperialist intentions and whatever 'form of words' that the Americans used to justify their actions. But Churchill warned: ' "Hands off the British Empire" is our maxim and it must not be weakened or smirched to please sob-stuff merchants at home or foreigners of any hue'.[158] Eden was equally emphatic in his response to Churchill: 'we are anxious to persuade the Americans not to go in for half baked international [trusteeship] regimes'. The American hypocrisy was evident to both the Prime Minister and the Foreign Secretary. On the one hand the United States promoted trusteeship for French Indo-China based upon anti-imperialism, but on the other it expected to create its own colonial territories on similar security grounds to the British Empire.[159] Churchill asked John Martin, his Private Secretary, to research the trusteeship issue for him and ascertain: 'if we are really being jockeyed out or edged near the abyss' by the Americans.[160] Martin's reply insisted that there was no apparent danger to the British Empire.[161] Eden and Stanley concurred.[162] Dening warned that the logic of history dictated that the former colonial governments were the best 'qualified' to liberate Southeast Asia. To deny this qualification to French Indo-China would create 'disorder' and threaten regional stability.[163]

As part of Churchill's new initiative, for dialogue between the Foreign Office and the State Department, Halifax 'repeatedly' approached the State Department in order to state the Foreign Office's Indo-Chinese concerns. The State Department, however, appeared unwilling to reappraise French Indo-Chinese policy in consultation with the Foreign Office. On 26 December Edward Stettinius, the new Secretary of State, informed Halifax that a solution lay solely in the hands of the President.[164] Early in the New Year Halifax again raised the Foreign Office anxieties with the Secretary of State. This time Stettinius revealed that the President considered any political or military activity concerning Indo-China to be untimely. In the meantime Roosevelt had already proposed that he should review all of the relevant questions with the Prime Minister. This implied further delay. Halifax therefore remonstrated with

Stettinius about the importance of attaining a rapid solution. He high-lighted that Mountbatten desperately needed some kind of an answer in order to clarify SEAC military planning. Stettinius was unmoved and refused to take the matter further.[165] The Foreign Office was exasperated by the American intransigence: 'This throws us back to where we were before the [second] Quebec Conference. The President refuses to discuss Indo-China with anyone save the P.M. and when he meets the P.M. he does not mention it'.[166] The Foreign Office was equally frustrated with American suspicions concerning the recovery of the British Empire and the American preoccupation with self-determination. From an American perspective 'recovery' could only be interpreted as an enslavement of 'native peoples'.[167]

Several days later Halifax had the opportunity to question Roosevelt directly about pre-occupational activities in French Indo-China. He vented his disappointment with the President's communiqué for further talks with Churchill, which was relayed via Stettinius. The President opened his response with a characteristic 'tirade' about the status of French Indo-China. Halifax pressed Roosevelt for a ruling that would alleviate Mountbatten's strategic concerns and end the current deadlock. The President chose to respond with both clarity and ambiguity:

> if we felt it important we had better tell Mountbatten to do it and ask no questions. He did not want in any way to appear to be committed to anything that would seem to prejudge [a] political decision about Indo-China [that was] in a sense favourable to [the] restoration [of the] French status quo ante which he did not wish to see restored.[168]

Mountbatten had been given permission to commence pre-occupational duties, as long as he did not prejudice Roosevelt's political agenda, and only if future questions and confirmation were not requested of the President. Dening clearly understood the nature of the offer that was being presented to SEAC by Roosevelt. Blaizot and the French mili-tary mission were already informally established at SEAC. Mountbatten could immediately begin pre-occupation duties. The co-ordination and administration of these activities would fall under the jurisdiction of the vague Gentleman's Agreement already established between Chiang Kai-Shek and Mountbatten. Washington did not need to be involved in any future consultations. Although this meant that the CCS would also be isolated from the operations – a potential source of future conflict. Nev-ertheless, the further involvement of Roosevelt could only harm SEAC operations rather than enhance them.[169] Roosevelt's cryptic statement to Halifax was the most favourable pronouncement by the President towards the Foreign Office on these issues. Halifax, Mountbatten, the COS and the Foreign Office all saw the need to accept the bait and unanimously decided that 'we should let this particular sleeping dog lie'. Eden seized the opportunity to draw a line under the affair and return foreign policy to the diplomats and away from both SEAC and the Joint Service Mission in Washington. He ruled that any future discussions were to be solely managed by the Foreign Office.[170] Halifax, wary that Roosevelt could potentially deny or change the terms of their discussion, suggested that he should liaise with General Marshall to protect Britain's impromptu agreement.[171] This measure met with approval from Dening and SEAC.[172] Halifax was therefore instructed to discuss the President's remarks with Marshall.[173]

Roosevelt had not softened his stance towards French Indo-China, although he still regarded the details of how trusteeship would be both implemented and operated as purely a post-war concern.[174] Stanley, visiting Washington for Anglo-American negotiations concerning dependent territories, had an audience with the President. Roosevelt confirmed his intention to place French Indo-China under trusteeship and urged Britain to commit itself to a clear programme for decolonisation.[175] The President playfully asked the Colonial Secretary whether Britain had 'purchased' Hong Kong in 1841. This was a blatant attack on European imperialism. Stanley was equally ruthless in his response. He cited that the episode in question occurred at a similar time to the Mexican War.[176] America could be accused also of the evils of imperialism.

4
Churchill's Realignment

Eden continued to try and produce a coherent direction for British foreign policy that would protect Britain's national interests. Part of this policy was to restore France to a position of strength within Europe and therefore, by association, re-establish the French Empire. Paris had been liberated in 1944 and the de Gaulle administration had been recognised by the Allies as the legitimate Provisional Government of France in October 1944. It was intended for France to be rejuvenated as a Great Power. France was already a member of the Allied European Advisory Commission. The Allies had by now agreed that France would also administer one of the post-war occupation zones within Germany. Similarly, France would have to hold one permanent seat on the United Nations Security Council. Therefore it appeared logical to Eden that de Gaulle should attend the forthcoming Allied conference at Yalta in February 1945. Yet Churchill remained sceptical about post-war planning issues. He believed that too much effort could be expended in this direction. Churchill considered it appropriate to delay planning until the cold light of day of the post-war world had finally dawned.[1]

Malta and Yalta

On 16 January 1945, Eden wrote to Churchill and repeated to the Prime Minister the familiar Foreign Office argument that Britain and France shared a number of common global interests. Eden pressed Churchill about the Prime Minister's least favourite topic – post-hostilities planning. Britain needed to plan for the future and this necessitated co-operation with the French.[2] Churchill was also warned by the British Joint Planning Staff of a new American twist to the trusteeship debate. It appeared that Roosevelt was planning for France to retain post-war

administrative control of New Caledonia – an innocuous decision on its
own. But the President was also contemplating that France would not
be responsible for New Caledonia's post-war defence. The Joint Planning
Staff believed that Britain was being tested by Roosevelt. The President
was considering what he could get away with regarding decolonisation.
New Caledonia was a relatively unimportant colony but it could provide
a useful precedent for establishing an Allied trusteeship policy towards
French Indo-China.[3]

Churchill was unconvinced with Eden's arguments regarding France
and post-hostilities planning. The Prime Minister believed that France,
no doubt, would be useful in the future. Eventually it would be rehabilitated as a Great Power but not yet; for the moment the Prime Minister
was unconvinced that de Gaulle should be called to attend a meeting
of the Big Three. Roosevelt's views about de Gaulle were widely known,
and Churchill feared that the presence of de Gaulle would quickly shake
Allied unity and dissolve the conference proceedings into a farce: 'we
shall have the greatest trouble with de Gaulle, who will be forever
intriguing and playing two off against a third'.

Churchill was clear. France had not yet completed its prescribed
restorative treatment: 'France has enough to do this winter and spring
in trying to keep body and soul together'. It could not 'masquerade' as
a Great Power merely to remove its war guilt and balance out its earlier
capitulations to Germany and Japan. Churchill regarded the prospect
of having to deal with de Gaulle in such circumstances as wearisome.
France was ripe for restoration but de Gaulle was not. The Prime Minister
protested to Eden that his was a personal quarrel with de Gaulle rather
than a general slur against France because the French general posed a
significant danger to Allied unity. Churchill enjoyed his personal tirade
against de Gaulle:

> I cannot think of anything more unpleasant and impossible than
> having this menacing and hostile man in our midst, always trying
> to make himself a reputation in France by claiming a position far
> above what France occupies, and making faces at the allies who are
> doing the work.[4]

Eden begged the Prime Minister to reconsider his stance. He remonstrated that the Prime Minister's attitude could turn France towards
Russia for assistance. After all, De Gaulle was not beyond such behaviour
if he believed that he had been personally snubbed. The prospect of a
Franco-Russian alliance concerning post-war co-operation posed serious

problems for British security in Europe and elsewhere. Churchill was not persuaded by Eden's conjectures.[5] It was hard enough for the Prime Minister to maintain Great Power unity without de Gaulle being part of the equation. Besides, the threat of a potential post-war crisis did not constitute an effective counterweight to actual wartime politics. Churchill would not back down.

The Foreign Office wanted de Gaulle to attend the Yalta Conference. It was scornful of Churchill's dissemination of British foreign policy and blamed the debacle on Roosevelt, 'Are we going to acquiesce in the President's veto again?' Stalin also favoured de Gaulle attending the conference. Eden met with Massigli to soothe ruffled French feathers and to reassure him that Britain favoured French participation. The French were also content to blame Roosevelt for their omission.[6] The British Ambassador to France, Duff Cooper, noted from Paris that in general the French administration appeared to be accepting their exclusion from Yalta better than Cooper had expected, but he was unable to vouch for the reaction of de Gaulle: 'with him [de Gaulle] grievances are an accumulative poison of which he never seems to rid his system'.[7]

In Southeast Asia, following the problems with establishing the Blaizot mission, Dening was disheartened with the general direction of Allied policy towards French Indo-China.[8] Dening believed that the United States was only blocking the deployment of the French *Corps Leger* for political reasons.[9] All was not well within SEAC. The Foreign Office was forced to implement a security clampdown after one of Dening's restricted and confidential telegrams appeared in American hands in Washington. Sterndale Bennett, Head of the Far East Section of the Foreign Office, curtly reminded the War Office that SEAC was a joint Allied command rather than solely a British affair. American staff attached to SEAC would continue to have access to War Office correspondence, but Foreign Office material needed to be restricted solely to British personnel.[10]

The Prime Minister left London for Malta. This Anglo-American meeting prior to the main conference at Yalta was to permit Churchill the opportunity of personal discussions with Roosevelt and to renew his special relationship before they met with Stalin. Churchill hoped that talks at Malta would enable the Prime Minister and Roosevelt to establish a unified Anglo-American position about the creation of the United Nations.[11] The Malta Conference, however, proved to be an anti-climax. Both Churchill and Roosevelt suffered bouts of illness at the conference. Allied business therefore was severely limited.[12]

Churchill and Roosevelt travelled on from Malta to Yalta to meet with Stalin. It was the first time that all three had been together since the Tehran Conference of November 1943. The journey to the Crimea town of Yalta, located north of the Black Sea in the Ukraine, was a long and tiring one for both Churchill and Roosevelt – and it clearly took its toll on the President's health. Eden believed that despite the President's obvious frailty this did not effect Roosevelt's judgement. But Cadogan disagreed: 'most of the time he [Roosevelt] hardly knew what it [the conference] was about'.[13] Roosevelt was not above admitting his physical frailty. On one occasion he quipped: 'Yes, I'm tired – and so would you be if you'd spent five years pushing Winston uphill in a wheelbarrow'.[14]

As the conference met, Russian armies were sweeping into Germany from the east and Anglo-American forces were advancing from the west. The conference agenda was therefore to put down the foundation stone for the shape of the post-war world. Roosevelt's dislike of colonialism was evident at Yalta. Eden sardonically noted that Roosevelt's 'principled' agenda permitted former colonies to become politically and economically subservient to the United States.[15] Within this context Roosevelt's suggestion for United Nations trusteeships was examined by the Big Three, but Churchill vetoed the President's proposals.[16] Eden described Churchill's defence as 'eloquent' but Moran, Churchill's physician, witnessed a great deal of 'histrionics' and shouting by the Prime Minister.[17] Nevertheless Churchill was adamant. He was opposed to 'such a departure which might well be pressed upon nations like Britain, France, Holland and Belgium who have had great colonial possessions by the United States, Russia and China who have none'.[18] Churchill's bold threat was evident to all present. The Prime Minister would not permit trusteeship to establish a precedent for decolonisation. Churchill feared that Roosevelt's proposal was a Trojan horse designed to acquire property, by false pretences, by nations which currently did not posses access to such territories. The Prime Minister had, in a simple veto, aligned himself with the British Foreign Office, the Dominions and the other imperial nations against Roosevelt and Stalin. It was an important watershed in Anglo-American relations. Churchill had acted unilaterally and decisively against Roosevelt to protect not just the British Empire but all European colonies. Churchill had placed British foreign policy above his special relationship with Roosevelt, a path that previously he had feared to tread.

Churchill and Eden fought also at Yalta for the full restoration of France but Roosevelt was not interested in Europe or achieving a balance of power. The President favoured the creation of a new world order with peace and security guaranteed by Britain, China, Russia, the United States and the United Nations organisation.[19] In the discussion that followed the veto, Churchill, Roosevelt and Stalin agreed to the proposition of voluntary trusteeship being established. The concept of voluntary trusteeship had initially been proposed by the Dumbarton Oaks Conference (August–October 1944). Now it received the attention of the leaders of the Big Three before being debated further at the San Francisco Conference (April–June 1945). For Roosevelt, voluntary trusteeship was not a victory for Churchill but a stalling of the inevitable.[20] Voluntary trusteeship was just another elastic foreign policy concept.[21] American minutes of these Yalta discussions confirmed the President's approach. The five governments that would eventually have permanent seats on the United Nations Security Council could consult with each other about the 'machinery' for dealing with territorial trusteeships. Yet it 'would be a matter of subsequent agreement as to which territories . . . would actually be placed under trusteeship' and this debate was not contemplated either before or during the San Francisco Conference – in the meantime only 'machinery and principles' could be discussed.[22]

Despite Churchill's decisive action, of vetoing one of Roosevelt's principal personal war aims, his new found enthusiasm for an independent British foreign policy did not extend any further. Churchill did not confront Roosevelt at Yalta about French participation in the war in the Far East. The Prime Minister reasoned that as the President had not taken any military advisors to Yalta it would be inappropriate therefore to contest the matter with Roosevelt because realistically he could not be expected to consider any proposals in detail.[23] Eden discussed the Prime Minister's stance with senior British officials and concurred with Churchill's conclusions.[24] Yet Roosevelt took great interest in the military situation within Indo-China. The President regularly received 'Magic' decryptions of Japanese signals intelligence – his interest heightened by dreams of trusteeship.[25] Nevertheless, considering Churchill's flash of boldness in resisting Roosevelt's plans for trusteeship, his reluctance to face up to the President about French participation in the war against Japan was unsurprising. Anglo-American relations between SEAC and China Theatre were strained and contentious. To have raised such issues would have only irritated Roosevelt further and provoked a strong backlash. Churchill had just torpedoed Roosevelt's trusteeship proposal in front of Stalin. The Prime Minister had also unified all of the European colonial powers against the United States and placed their common cause above the value of his special relationship. Churchill could only push Roosevelt so far without provoking a hostile response. The Prime Minister therefore feared pressing for further gains. Churchill also was probably concerned that the exhausted Roosevelt could not have been expected to pursue the matter without further military briefings. Would Roosevelt – who used any conversation as an extension of his political intrigues – have been as generous as not to have pressed his advantage merely because the health of the Prime Minister is doubtful? Roosevelt was adroit at adapting his policies to take advantage of any situation.[26]

Indeed, Roosevelt had already met with Stalin in private prior to Churchill's act of veto and discussed trusteeship in greater detail. Roosevelt told Stalin that he was not prepared to let Britain participate in the trusteeship scheme for Korea. Stalin recognised the danger to Allied unity of Churchill's exclusion. Stalin replied that Churchill would certainly 'kill us' and he therefore advocated that the Prime Minister should be invited to participate in such a plan.[27] The President went on to highlight to Stalin the danger for Britain of a precedent for decolonisation being established via his trusteeship proposals. Stalin was prepared to participate in Roosevelt's decolonisation deliberations. He was not convinced that Britain was, in fact, the correct nation to oversee Burma. Roosevelt placed the plight of the Burmese, the Indo-Chinese and the Javanese together. They were all in need of assistance. Roosevelt revealed that de Gaulle had already requested that America supply a number of ships to France in order to facilitate a return to Indo-China. Stalin enquired as to how the President had left this appeal by de Gaulle. Roosevelt answered: 'de Gaulle said he was going to find the troops when the President could find the ships'. But Roosevelt playfully added that he had not been able to locate any vessels.[28] Stalin was still not yet committed to the war in the Far East. Both Britain and France relied upon American patronage to maintain the operational status of their armed forces. Roosevelt could easily refuse logistical aid to de Gaulle, and thereby prevent a French return to Indo-China and maintain the direction of his Indo-Chinese policies.

Perhaps Churchill was aware of Roosevelt's personal discussions with Stalin about trusteeship and Indo-China prior to his showdown on this matter at Yalta; nevertheless Churchill did not press the President about further French participation in the war against Japan. Roosevelt, on the other hand, was far more ruthless towards Churchill. At a press conference aboard the *USS Quincy* following the Yalta Conference, Roosevelt had a 'personal talk' with members of the media concerning trusteeship. The President informed them that for the past two years he had been deeply troubled about Indo-China. Chiang Kai-Shek had revealed to Roosevelt that France had underdeveloped Indo-China and economically drained the region for its own benefit. The President explained to the assembled journalists how an international trusteeship committee – comprising of one French, one or two Indo-Chinese, one Chinese, one Russian and possibly one American and one Filipino representative – should be established to 'educate' Indo-China for self-government in the same way as the United States had prepared the Philippines for independence. But it had transpired in discussions that the difficulty in implementing such a solution lay with Britain: 'Stalin liked the idea. China liked the idea. The British don't like it. It might bust up their empire, because if the Indo-Chinese were to work together and eventually get their independence, the Burmese might do the same thing to England'.

Roosevelt understood that his utopian vision set a precedent for decolonisation and provided a focal point for Asian nationalism vis-à-vis European colonialism. Twice the President reiterated to his journalistic audience that trusteeship would make the British 'mad'. Roosevelt concluded that it was 'better to keep quiet just now'. One journalist fell into the President's snare. Roosevelt was asked if Churchill expected that all areas of the world would be returned to the pre-war status quo. The implication in the question was that the United States was only fighting the war in order to restore European colonialism. Roosevelt responded with a perfect media sound byte: 'Yes, he [Churchill] is mid-Victorian on all things like that'. Churchill was a product of the Victorian age but the President had just labelled him in American eyes as an imperialist of the worst kind.[29]

Dening wrestled also with the general French attitude towards the return of Indo-China. He was convinced that France intended for Britain to restore French Indo-China at any cost. He enquired curiously of Sterndale Bennett, 'Do they expect us to bear their cross for them?' The French attached to SEAC appeared to display the same negative traits that Churchill feared that de Gaulle would have brought to the Yalta Conference – if he had been invited. Dening concluded: 'I am gradually gaining the impression that the French we have [here] are either *mal élèves* or just stupid, or trying to pull a fast one'.[30] The stage was set for further high policy conflict.

At the same time as Churchill's Malta and Yalta discussions, relationships between SEAC and China Theatre deteriorated even further. On 29 January 1945, Wedemeyer wrote to Mountbatten to reassert China Theatre's sole claims to administer Allied operations both in and towards Indo-China. Wedemeyer informed Mountbatten of his detailed plans to co-ordinate and integrate all Anglo-French-American clandestine operations under his command.[31] Wedemeyer was supported in his stance by Admiral William Leahy – Roosevelt's Chief of Staff.[32] The British COS sought to protect Mountbatten from Wedemeyer and his powerful patron in Washington. The COS requested that Lord Halifax, the British Ambassador, contact General George Marshall, Head of the American Army, and share with him Roosevelt's ambiguous approval of Mountbatten's clandestine operations in Indo-China and by implication China Theatre. The COS hoped that by informing Marshall of Roosevelt's tacit backing of Mountbatten future conflict between Mountbatten and Wedemeyer could be avoided.[33]

Lt.-General Adrian Carton de Wiart, Churchill's personal representative to Chiang Kai-Shek, was not known for his ability to agree with Mountbatten.[34] Carton de Wiart was aware of the vague but long-standing Gentleman's Agreement between Mountbatten and Chiang Kai-Shek. From his vantage point within China Theatre, he thought that the only way to resolve the Mountbatten–Wedemeyer disagreement would be for the CCS to produce a definitive ruling on the areas of dispute. Carton de Wiart believed that Wedemeyer was so entrenched in the righteousness of his cause that only a ruling by the CCS would be able to alter his stance.[35]

The relationship between Mountbatten and Wedemeyer was also clouded by their relationships with Chiang Kai-Shek. Despite previous guarantees to Britain that China possessed no imperial aspirations towards Indo-China – and in particular the northern Vietnamese province of Tonkin – Chiang Kai-Shek was not adverse to enlarging his area of influence or expanding Chinese territory. Chiang Kai-Shek, therefore, added to the Mountbatten–Wedemeyer and Anglo-American misunderstandings in order to promote his own interests. He often told both Mountbatten and Wedemeyer completely contradictory stories in order to confuse and divide the Allied commanders.[36] These actions did not aid Anglo-American co-operation. Both Mountbatten and Wedemeyer believed that they possessed a legitimate *modus operandi* to conduct operations within French Indo-China. Mountbatten could base his assumption upon his Gentleman's Agreement with Chiang Kai-Shek and Halifax's agreement with Roosevelt. Wedemeyer could point to the terms of reference agreed at the first Quebec Conference (August 1943), which established the boundaries of SEAC and China Theatre. These terms clearly placed French Indo-China within the sphere of China Theatre. As both Allied commanders continued to sanction independent clandestine operations within French Indo-China the relationship between the two theatres continued to disintegrate. Suspicion, mistrust and paranoia set in.

The escalating disagreement was made even more problematic when two British aircraft were shot down by American night fighters over Tonkin. SEAC had failed to alert China Theatre of their operations that night over northern Indo-China. The Allied deaths, caused by a lack of communication, were highly embarrassing to both SEAC and China Theatre, even though the British were ultimately more culpable than their American counterparts.[37] British Air Vice-Marshal John Whitworth-Jones, on behalf of SEAC, acknowledged responsibility for the tragedy. He counselled that the investigation be stepped down and that a communications blanket be imposed to ensure that 'sealed lips' prevented any further news about the affair from leaking out.[38]

Despite strained Anglo-American relations and tragic incidents in the field, Wedemeyer still hoped for a resolution to his differences of opinion with Mountbatten. On 10 February, he again contacted Mountbatten about their problems. In a warm and friendly letter Wedemeyer acknowledged that he and Mountbatten were poles apart regarding Allied policy towards French Indo-China. Wedemeyer informed Mountbatten that the only way to determine the matter would be to seek arbitration at a senior level. He no doubt hoped that an appeal to the CCS would result in a second ratification of the boundary terms of the first Quebec Conference. Wedemeyer therefore proposed to prepare the necessary paperwork and inform his higher authorities in order to clarify the Indo-Chinese issue once and for all.[39] Wedemeyer's sincerity appeared genuine but already he had let slip, within the China Theatre command, his anti-imperialist feelings. He was 'quite unable to understand why the British Commonwealth holds together, still less why it should do in the future'.[40] Wedemeyer's contempt for European imperialism was apparent to all. Later the French General Jean Boucher de Crevecoeur (who as a Lt.-Colonel had been seconded to SOE at SEAC in November 1943) was equally judgemental about Wedemeyer. Crevecoeur equated the cause of Wedemeyer's unhelpful attitude to the combination of his German ancestry and his exchange student internship at the Berlin Military Academy.[41]

Carton de Wiart reiterated to Churchill the crux of the Mountbatten–Wedemeyer quarrel. Wedemeyer bitterly resented SEAC involvement within French Indo-China. He believed that SEAC could not undertake any Indo-Chinese operations without his prior permission. Carton de Wiart was troubled by the dispute. He accurately prophesied that if the situation regarding French Indo-China was not rectified in the near future it would result in significant trouble for all concerned.[42] Churchill was against discussing military matters with Roosevelt at the Yalta Conference, but at least he had asked the Foreign Office for its advice.[43] In the meantime, British intelligence discovered that the internal situation was about to change within Indo-China. The Japanese forces that had previously coexisted alongside their Vichy collaborators appeared to have finished their preparations for the formal annexation of Indo-China and the removal of the last remaining Vichy territory. Churchill noted the activity with interest.[44]

Churchill may not have wished to push the President regarding French Indo-Chinese military matters at the Yalta Conference, but these matters were rapidly gathering a momentum of their own. The British War Cabinet COS Committee reassessed, in post-hostilities planning, the strategic significance of French Indo-China to British defence within Southeast Asia. It concluded that Indo-China was the single most important area within the region. Indo-China would become the vital 'anchor' for a chain of bases that would form a protective arch and cover Burma, Malaya and northern Borneo in order to shield wider British interests in Australia and India from future threats. The security of this chain of bases necessitated strong, stable and amiable governments in Indo-China and Siam, as well as unwavering support in Malaya. It also necessitated closer ties with France and Holland. If the Soviet Union did decide to establish a presence in the region – in particular within southern China – then Indo-China would become even more significant to protecting the British Empire. This would call for full Anglo-French-American-Commonwealth co-operation in maintaining Indo-China's defence.[45]

The British Foreign Office was unprepared to allow the COS solely to manage the growing tensions between SEAC and China Theatre. Wider Anglo-American relations and British post-hostilities planning were threatened by the Mountbatten–Wedemeyer dispute. This was rapidly escalating into a wider crisis than a mere military disagreement. Patrick Hurley, the American Ambassador to Chiang Kai-Shek, visited Washington for policy discussions with the Roosevelt administration concerning Chinese affairs. Halifax warned Eden that Hurley was 'the arch gossip of the world' but he cautioned the Foreign Secretary that Hurley also had 'a good deal of influence at the White House'. Halifax's vigilance was well placed. Hurley was a 'flamboyant nationalist and unrelenting Anglophobe'. One prominent historian has even ventured to describe him as a 'buffoon among ambassadors'.[46]

Wedemeyer was present in Washington at the same time as Hurley. Despite another bout of illness Roosevelt saw both Hurley and Wedemeyer separately. The President told them that he remained committed to independence for French Indo-China and instructed them not to supply French forces in the region. Therefore Roosevelt continued his campaign against French control of Indo-China. The British Colonial Secretary Stanley correctly gauged that trusteeship remained Roosevelt's ultimate goal; his fears were confirmed by Halifax. Roosevelt envisaged that United Nations trusteeships would be set up at the San Francisco Conference. He needed the agreement of Britain and France for such schemes, but he was not yet ready to challenge them openly. The post-war world had not yet emerged and the Allied debt to the United States still had to be calculated. By June 1945 the British war debt would total 3355 million pounds, approximately a quarter of its national wealth. Britain needed the United States to be generous. Nevertheless, Churchill instructed Holland and France to lead the European fight and object to trusteeships at San Francisco.[47]

Eden seized the opportunity presented by Hurley's impending return to China to invite the Ambassador to London on the journey back to Chungking. The British COS advised Eden that the invitation could also be extended to Wedemeyer. This would permit both the Foreign Office and the COS to debate Indo-Chinese issues with the two senior American officials in the region and form their own assessment of the Mountbatten–Wedemeyer clash.[48] But Wedemeyer subsequently declined his invitation.[49] Churchill believed it likely that the American Joint Chiefs of Staff had prevented Wedemeyer from visiting London to protect him from being subjected to British 'persuasiveness' regarding Indo-Chinese issues.[50] From SEAC, Dening ominously warned the Foreign Office that Wedemeyer did not intend to leave Indo-Chinese issues in a permanent state of flux.[51] He expected further action by Wedemeyer.

Just as Churchill had neglected the direction of the trusteeship debate late in 1944 so too he had ignored the finer details of the Mountbatten–Wedemeyer dispute. The Prime Minister appeared devoid of ideas or direction and appealed to both his Foreign Secretary and the COS to ascertain British policy. On 1 March Churchill wrote to Eden and Ismay and asked: 'What action do we take?'[52] Stettinius had informed Halifax during their January exchanges that Roosevelt would raise Indo-Chinese political and military issues with the Prime Minister. But the President had so far failed to do so. Unless, of course, Roosevelt regarded the Yalta dialogue as part of this process, in which case military matters had still received no such attention. The Foreign Office concluded that – because of Wedemeyer's renewed hostilities towards SEAC, his appeal to higher authorities and his anti-imperial beliefs – Indo-Chinese issues could not be delayed any longer.[53] The time for action had arrived.

Three days after Churchill's enquiry, Eden responded. The Foreign Secretary knew how to manipulate Churchill's fears; it could be guaranteed that the Prime Minister would strive to protect his perceived special relationship with Roosevelt above everything else. Eden therefore argued that the Mountbatten–Wedemeyer disagreement would have a negative impact upon Anglo-American relations. It would produce 'a constant source of friction'. The only recourse that Eden could envisage, to resolve the situation to a satisfactory degree, was for Churchill to make a direct appeal to Roosevelt. This was the very path that the Prime Minister feared to tread, but it was the route that he was now being asked to take. Eden believed that the solution to all of their problems in this dispute lay with Roosevelt. The President needed to formally endorse the Gentleman's Agreement between Mountbatten and Chiang Kai-Shek as both the appropriate apparatus to administer the boundary between SEAC and China Theatre and as the justification for SEAC French Indo-Chinese operations. Under this arrangement, the local management of clandestine activities would be individually left to the respective Allied commander – Mountbatten or Wedemeyer. But the two commanders would be expected to exchange 'intentions, plans and intelligence' in all areas of joint concern.

Eden was not prepared to act single-handedly concerning military policy. The Foreign Office had already been instructed to ask the COS for their views on the proposal. In the meantime, Churchill appeared to fall for Eden's bait. The Prime Minister hesitantly agreed to 'consider an approach' to the President. Nevertheless Churchill demonstrated consistency with his tactics of the past two years, to delay and only to proceed on his own terms. The Prime Minister ruled that the approach to the President could only be made when the relevant Foreign Office papers and COS briefings had been collated into a unified coherent statement.[54]

Churchill was trapped. He needed to protect his special relationship with Roosevelt as this was the cornerstone of his wartime policies. This relationship had to be protected at all costs. The Mountbatten–Wedemeyer dispute threatened this relationship. The previous tactic of delay, however, had now unravelled because of two events: firstly, Wedemeyer's appeal for assistance to higher authorities and patrons – Hurley and Leahy – and therefore by implication Roosevelt; secondly, the Foreign Office had linked the dispute to negative and damaging

Anglo-American confrontations. Churchill could not escape the Indo-Chinese issue. Yet, by asking for the amalgamation of the Foreign Office and COS briefings he had once again advocated a policy of delay. But this strategy had been played once too often. This time Eden had anticipated the manoeuvre and Foreign Office had prepared an adequate response. The Foreign Office proposal and the COS response were already in preparation. The draft had begun in the 48 hours in between Churchill's initial enquiry to Eden and Ismay and the subsequent reply made by Eden to Churchill on 4 March.[55] The Foreign Office approach was verified by the COS the next day.[56]

Vietnam

Churchill was desperately trying to balance his special relationship with Roosevelt against intra-Allied theatre conflicts and one of the President's principal war aims – the removal of France from Indo-China. On 9 March another element was added into the Prime Minister's complex equation. The Japanese launched their long suspected *coup d'etat* against the Vichy regime in Indo-China. The French authorities, who had previously been in charge of the government of the colony but under close Japanese supervision, were overwhelmed quickly and most French opposition crumbled. Nonetheless, a number of French troops under the leadership of General Marcel Alessandri refused to surrender and endeavoured to regroup at Son La in western Tonkin. The shackles of white colonialism were broken. The Vietnamese Emperor Bao Dai and the Cambodian King Norodom Sihanouk were permitted by the Japanese to proclaim their independence from French rule but remained within Japanese-governed 'Greater East Asia'.[57]

Eden again wrote to Churchill on 11 March concerning the Mountbatten–Wedemeyer dispute. Alessandri's forces had been fighting the Japanese for 48 hours. This time Eden presented Churchill with the finalised Foreign Office and COS briefing papers. Eden informed the Prime Minister that, as a precaution, Mountbatten's operations within French Indo-China were to be for the moment limited. The British COS had not yet received a reply to suggestions made to their American counterparts concerning French participation in the war against Japan. This was because of the 'inaction' of the President. Eden was suspicious that the Americans never would respond to the proposals, although he acknowledged that the whole affair was mired in ambiguity because of Roosevelt's 'off the record' remarks. These comments, made by Roosevelt to Halifax, indicated that the President was prepared 'to turn a blind eye' towards operations that Mountbatten considered of vital importance to SEAC.

Wedemeyer however adhered to a more fixed delineation between SEAC and China Theatre. With a distinct lack of guidance and instruction from the American Joint Chiefs of Staff, Wedemeyer appeared to adhere to a course of action based upon his own initiative. He declared that he would not permit any SEAC operations within French Indo-China that had not obtained his previous assent. After all Indo-China was located within the China Theatre war zone. Eden observed that although Wedemeyer's position was 'technically' accurate, Wedemeyer had not taken into account the terms of the oral Gentleman's Agreement between Mountbatten and Chiang Kai-Shek, the conditions of which Churchill was aware and which Wedemeyer had ignored. The British COS supported the Foreign Office's wish for a joint Anglo-American declaration endorsing the Gentleman's Agreement – with a framework for Mountbatten–Wedemeyer liaison established as part of the statement. Similarly, the COS agreed with Eden's assessment of the dispute. The conflict was by now so embittered and entangled that Britain was 'not likely to obtain a satisfactory solution except through your [Churchill's] personal intervention with the President'.[58]

The following day, with French troops still engaged against Japanese forces deep within Japanese Greater Asia, French General de Saint Didier approached the British Joint Service Mission in Washington and urgently requested information on Japanese operations as well as immediate British assistance.[59] At the same time, Churchill resolved to act. The grave situation within Indo-China and the unhelpful Mountbatten–Wedemeyer dispute necessitated decisive action. French troops could not be left unaided to suffer a forgotten defeat far behind enemy lines. Nevertheless, Churchill responded to the challenge ponderously. He contacted Ismay and requested that a brief be drawn up giving the history of proceedings within French Indo-China since the beginning of the Second World War. Churchill appeared vague and hesitant. The Prime Minister was unsure of the status of Indo-China. He was uncertain as to whether it was still a Vichy territory or a part of de Gaulle's resurrected French Empire. Likewise Churchill was puzzled as to whether or not there actually were any French troops garrisoned there. Room for confusion certainly existed. Indo-China was the only French territory not to unite behind the banner of de Gaulle's provisional government after the emancipation of Paris. But the circumstances were hardly conducive for it to do so. Large numbers of Japanese troops were stationed within French Indo-China which was a vital logistical base for Japanese operations within Southeast Asia. Japanese forces had

previously co-existed in an uneasy affiliation with their French counterparts. This relationship was strained when Indo-China became the
lone Vichy province. Churchill finished his request to Ismay with the
telling remark: 'I have not followed the affairs in the country for some
time'.[60]

The French Government naturally was anxious about the crisis in
Indo-China. French troops were engaged in fighting Japanese forces
far from Allied support deep within Japanese Greater Asia. They were
outnumbered and outgunned. At the same time as Churchill's ponderous deliberations Massigli contacted Eden about the crisis. The French
Ambassador sought to solicit a direct guarantee of British assistance from
the Foreign Secretary. He requested that Britain provide the necessary
transportation for the 600 men, of the French *Corps Leger* to the Far East,
to be transferred to reinforce the French resistance against the Japanese.
Eden took note of the appeal and reported the matter to Churchill for
his consideration.[61] The Prime Minister referred the request to the COS
to obtain their considered opinion – resulting in a further delay.[62]

Churchill finally appeared to be galvanised into action on 17 March –
five days later. Nonetheless his attention was not directed upon the
immediate crisis within Indo-China and the need to assist French troops
resisting the Japanese. The Prime Minister had instead decided at last to
adopt a personal approach to Roosevelt concerning the Mountbatten–
Wedemeyer dispute. Wedemeyer was at that moment in Washington
for a number of policy briefings with the Roosevelt administration.
The timing of Churchill's approach appeared advantageous. The Prime
Minister humbly reminded the President of Mountbatten's claim and,
using his personal friendship with Roosevelt as leverage, appealed to
the President's excellent nature to assist in rectifying the situation:

> as you [Roosevelt] know he [Mountbatten] has an oral understanding
> with Chiang Kai-Shek that both he and the Generalissimo shall be
> free to attack Siam and Indo-China and that the boundaries of the
> two theatres shall be decided when the time comes in accordance
> with the progress made by their respective forces. The Generalissimo
> agreed after Sextant [the Cairo Conference] that this understanding
> extended to pre-occupational activities.
>
> I am told that Wedemeyer feels difficulty in recognizing this oral
> understanding in the absence of instructions to that effect from his
> superior authorities.
>
> This is a situation from which much harmful friction may spring.
> Could not you and I clear it up by jointly endorsing the oral
> understanding which seems a sensible and workable agreement?

Churchill had accepted the Foreign Office recommendations. The Prime Minister requested of Roosevelt an agreement that both he and the President formally recognise the Gentleman's Agreement. Likewise, Churchill also suggested that some kind of infrastructure needed to be developed to permit for the 'full and frank exchange of intentions, plans and intelligence'.[63] It had taken Churchill five days to reflect upon the Foreign Office and COS proposals and then implement them. But the outcome marked a significant step. Churchill had moved even further towards alignment with the Foreign Office over Indo-China and away from his long-standing position of isolation between Britain and the United States on this issue.

In the meantime, the battles between the Japanese forces and the limited French resistance to the *coup* continued. The British War Cabinet Joint Intelligence Committee Sub-Committee considered the plight of the resisting forces and an appropriate British response. Addressing the urgency of the crisis, the Committee recommended that SEAC augment provisions to the French troops fighting the Japanese in Indo-China.[64] Consideration was given to the dropping by parachute of machine guns and ammunition to besieged French troops.[65] In Washington, General Marshall summoned Field Marshal Sir Henry (Jumbo) Wilson, Head of the British Joint Service Mission in America, to discuss the Mountbatten–Wedemeyer conflict. Wilson understood that the CCS had been unable to agree, at the Cairo Conference November 1943, in which Allied theatre to locate French Indo-China.[66] Considering Churchill's reference to the Cairo Conference in his appeal to Roosevelt, Wilson was no doubt correct in his assessment of the Cairo Conference minutes, but he had failed to comprehend that regardless of deliberations at Cairo a workable solution had been agreed three months previously at the first Quebec Conference.[67] It was this agreement that Wedemeyer based the justification for his stance upon. Both Churchill and the British COS adopted selective amnesia and consented to the direction that Wilson proposed to adopt in his negotiations with the Americans – a strategy purely based upon the failures of Cairo.[68]

In Southeast Asia, Mountbatten was delighted with the formal appointment of the French military mission to SEAC.[69] Similarly, a message from Mountbatten to American Lt.-General Somervell mentioned that on a recent trip to Chungking Mountbatten was 'delighted' that the Gentleman's Agreement was being 'honoured'.[70] Such remarks can only be described as curious given the context of the Mountbatten–Wedemeyer dispute. Mountbatten appeared undaunted by the political debate that raged around him.

Ten days after the launch of the Japanese *coup* against the French in Indo-China Churchill turned his attention towards assisting the French resistance. Nevertheless, yet again, the problem of over-burdening his special relationship with Roosevelt prevented a direct approach to the President. Instead, Churchill told Wilson to inform Marshall that:

> The Prime Minister feels that it would look very bad in history if we were to let the French force in Indo-China be cut to pieces by the Japanese through shortage of ammunition, if there is anything we can to do save them. He hopes therefore that we shall be agreed in not standing on punctilio in this emergency.[71]

This was Churchill's most robust and direct intervention yet on behalf of the French troops. The appeal to avoid an injustice necessitated an emergency response that rendered current disagreements irrelevant. Eden agreed with the Prime Minister's approach to Marshall and urged for it to be dispatched immediately.[72] At the same time the COS instructed Wilson to ask Marshall if it would be possible for Wedemeyer to send supplies to the French troops.[73] The following day Churchill went even further. The Prime Minister charged Ismay that Mountbatten was to take 'emergency action' to aid the French troops.[74] Churchill was not going to wait for a decision from Washington. His time for action had arrived; delay was not now an option.

In Washington, Marshall met with Wilson for further talks. He revealed that Major-General Claire Chennault, the Head of the American Air Force in China Theatre, had been instructed to fly ordnance supplies to the besieged French troops.[75] At the same time as the frantic high policy debate being waged between London and Washington, regional Allied commanders sought on their own initiative to assist the beleaguered French troops. With Wedemeyer in Washington, American Major-General Robert McClure had already ensured that the American Army Air Force assisted the French during the first week of the *coup*. 28 American sorties were flown as a direct response to French requests for assistance. This was purely an emergency action as by 16 March the American Air Force had recommenced its regular bombing activities and would not assist in logistically aiding French troops without receiving authorisation from Washington. Likewise independent from the American aid efforts, SOE's Far Eastern Branch, Force 136, which consisted of 36 French military staff, assisted the French troops fighting the Japanese. Both of these examples of micro-assistance occurred before Churchill and Marshall's macro-interventions.[76]

Small numbers of French troops continued to resist the might of the Japanese armed forces which had assumed control of most of Indo-China. On 22 March these diminutive French forces made another appeal for more equipment and the recommencement of logistical support by the American Air Force. The resistance within Indo-China was led by the French General Marcel Alessandri. He had organised an orderly retreat by French forces to Son La – located in the mountains of north-western Tonkin this was approximately half way between Hanoi (the provincial capital) and the Chinese border. Alessandri was not hopeful of his situation. He believed that Son La would fall to the Japanese within two days.[77] However, Alessandri managed to rally his fatigued troops and successfully reinforced them with additional units who were fleeing towards the Chinese border. Five days after Alessandri's initial assessment Son La was still held by the French. 4500 French troops occupied Son La and a further 2000 held the city of Luang Prabang in Laos. This prompted further French requests for finance and medical supplies to assist the beleaguered troops.[78] In Washington, the British Joint Service Mission decided that it was both 'embarrassing' and 'unfortunate' that the CCS refused to offer Allied French troops the necessary assistance.[79] Britain therefore made plans to forward the finances and medical supplies requested by the French troops on its own.[80]

In contrast to the stark silence emanating from the CCS in Washington, Mountbatten was informed by Admiral James Somerville of the Royal Navy delegation in Washington that the American Joint Chiefs of Staff was not altogether in favour of Roosevelt's policy of trusteeship for Indo-China.[81] From China Theatre Chennault complained to Marshall at the lack of Allied co-ordination concerning the flurry of activity taking place within Indo-China.[82] Chennault was in danger of raising the Mountbatten–Wedemeyer dispute above the immediate crisis. Marshall met with Wilson to discuss Chennault's complaints. He acknowledged that although certain issues remained unresolved regarding the Mountbatten–Wedemeyer disagreement, it appeared essential that SEAC should liaise with China Theatre lest it create even more trouble between the Allied commands. Marshall insisted that: 'Whatever the differences which remained unsettled regarding priority rights in Indo-China operations, it seems to me that Mountbatten's Headquarters should at least notify Chungking of what they are doing or we are riding for a fall out there'.[83]

Roosevelt responded to Churchill's appeal concerning the ongoing difficulties between Mountbatten and Wedemeyer. The President agreed that a mechanism needed to be established to empower total and truthful talks between the Allied commanders. However, his telegram to the Prime Minister requested that Churchill concur to 'all Anglo-American-Chinese military operations in Indo-China, regardless of their nature be[ing] co-ordinated by General Wedemeyer'.[84] Roosevelt had boldly proposed that Wedemeyer was to be the final arbitrator over Mountbatten's clandestine operations. Marshall agreed with Roosevelt's position, but he was unconvinced that Wedemeyer could actually direct Mountbatten's deployments.[85] The British Foreign Office regarded Wedemeyer's position as nothing more than a 'nominal co-ordinator' with no power of actual veto over Mountbatten's operations. It also insisted that the French should be involved in all future discussions.[86]

Hurley, in Washington, informed Wilson that American policy towards French Indo-China still remained rather 'nebulous'. Despite Churchill's triumph at Yalta, the spectres of trusteeship and anti-imperialism had not been exorcised from the Roosevelt administration. Hurley advised Wilson that Britain should expect further difficulties with both the President and the State Department concerning Hong Kong. Likewise, the administration was disconcerted that lend-lease equipment was being used for the recovery of colonies over and above the desire to propagate the war against Japan further.[87] In American eyes Pandora's Box was still open and the future of the European colonies still far from certain.

Hurley had been invited and had accepted the invitation to visit London on his return journey to Chungking.[88] Churchill hoped that it would be possible for Hurley to call upon the Prime Minister.[89] The visit was an ideal opportunity for the Foreign Office to assess Allied interests in the region from both American and Chinese perspectives. The Foreign Office placed a high degree of value on Hurley's stopover and accordingly prepared a briefing paper. The briefing outlined Hurley's personal views and opinions and detailed the best direction to be taken during his visit. The individual assessment of Hurley was not encouraging; it concluded that, although his 'bark is probably worse than his bite', he held the most 'crude ideas' about the nature of British imperialism. Hurley's suspicions about European imperialism were well known within China Theatre. He had told the Dutch Ambassador to China bluntly that the United States was not about to rectify the wartime 'mess' for the return of British and Dutch imperialism in the Far East. Hurley was apprehensive of an Anglo-Dutch-French conspiracy that was designed to rejuvenate their imperial spheres of interest whilst at the same time keeping the Americans in the 'dark'.[90] But, the brief did give some scope for optimism. The Foreign Office had discovered that Hurley was not at all pleased with Roosevelt's approach towards Indo-China. It therefore leapt to the conclusion that Hurley would be 'receptive' to the British standpoint regarding Indo-Chinese matters. Considering that the Foreign Office's own analysis portrayed Hurley as an anti-imperialist, an assessment that assumed that an alignment was possible with Hurley against Roosevelt was at best naïve. No consideration was given to the possibility of Hurley being more radical in his anti-imperialism than the President.[91]

Churchill read the brief on Hurley with interest. He notified Colville that he had been advised to speak 'bluntly' because Hurley appreciated forthrightness; but Hurley's resultant visit to London turned out to be something of a let-down for the Foreign Office. The meeting that was arranged between Churchill and Hurley did not amuse the Prime Minister. Hurley did not wish to engage Churchill in his favourite past-time of wide-ranging conversations and kept his statements limited to 'civil banalities'. Churchill boldly informed Hurley that Britain would not give up territory that was under its 'flag'. The British COS fared little better in their meeting with the American Ambassador to China. When pressed upon Indo-Chinese matters Hurley restricted his dialogue to underlying trends in Indo-China and could not be enticed on the status of its political future.[92]

In the meantime, Churchill had returned to his usual strategy of avoiding confrontation with Roosevelt – delay. By 31 March Churchill had not yet replied to the President's telegram of 22 March outlining a strong American-led solution to the Mountbatten–Wedemeyer difficulties. Churchill confessed that he felt 'a little shy of overburdening' his American colleague. Churchill could not bring himself to believe that Roosevelt could have meant to have been so cold and forthright in response to a personal appeal by the Prime Minister. Churchill romanticised that the President's reply was 'obviously not his own'. The Prime Minister was clearly hurt by the tone of Roosevelt's telegram. After all they possessed a special relationship. The manner of the ruthless dismissal of a personal appeal by the Prime Minister laid bare the true nature of the special relationship – American dominance. When the chips were down America could dictate the road to be taken and Britain could only blanch at the prospect. Churchill's response to his subornment was to ignore the cause of his discomfort. The Prime Minister therefore decided not to provoke Roosevelt any further regarding the Mountbatten–Wedemeyer dispute.

Despite both Foreign Office and COS belief that the current difficulties could only be solved through mediation between Churchill and

Roosevelt, the Prime Minister ruled that they would have to be resolved by the COS. Churchill's logic was that the President was clearly 'very hard pressed' and the Prime Minister wanted 'to keep him as much as possible for the biggest things'.[93] The Anglo-American intra-theatre dispute was thereby relegated by Churchill to a position of lesser status. However, three days later Churchill appeared to have had second thoughts. In what could only be interpreted within Whitehall as an acute about-turn, the Prime Minister reversed his original instructions and informed Hollis that he was now willing to discuss the issue with Roosevelt in 'a day or two'.[94] Even now Churchill was unprepared to rush. He had relented and overturned his previous ruling but the result was an open-ended commitment to pursue the matter with the President with no definitive timetable for action. The Prime Minister could not understand why the Foreign Office 'always had to be active' and also why it 'never could see when it was wise to do nothing'.[95]

Mountbatten and Wedemeyer at last met to discuss their disagreement. The conference produced a full and frank exchange between the Allied commanders. Mountbatten repeated to Wedemeyer the legitimacy of SEAC operations within French Indo-China. This was based upon the endorsement of both the American Joint Chiefs of Staff and the President of the terms of the Gentleman's Agreement. Mountbatten was not prepared to disavow his Indo-Chinese *modus operandi*. He submitted to Wedemeyer two documents for consideration during their talks. The papers proved Mountbatten's assertion that he possessed American support at the highest levels for the terms of the Gentleman's Agreement. The mediation appeared to have the desired affect. Mountbatten and Wedemeyer agreed that in future Wedemeyer could only reject SEAC activities that clashed with China Theatre operations.[96] But Wedemeyer's subsequent paper to Washington, about the conference, added a further caveat. Wedemeyer claimed that British activities could not be performed until approval had also been given by Chiang Kai-Shek.[97] The stage was therefore set for, yet again, further accusations and recriminations.

Churchill finally wrote to Roosevelt on 11 April regarding the resolution of the Mountbatten–Wedemeyer dispute. However, delay had served the Prime Minister well. Mountbatten and Wedemeyer had appeared to reach an accord concerning SEAC and China Theatre operations within French Indo-China. Nonetheless Churchill was at last prepared to take a stand against the President. He began by reinforcing Mountbatten's understanding of the new agreement with Wedemeyer and using this as the basis for an Anglo-American settlement. Churchill stated that Mountbatten would make certain that Wedemeyer was 'continually informed' of all SEAC activities. This was because China Theatre forces would be operating within the same vicinity. Likewise, the Prime Minister adhered to a safety valve against further misunderstandings being established – all future disagreements were to be arbitrated by the CCS.

Churchill next embarked upon a firmer stand against his great American ally. The Prime Minister strongly warned Roosevelt that he could not permit any of Mountbatten's operations within Indo-China to be subjected to Wedemeyer's consent. He reiterated bluntly to the President his previous warning to Marshall: 'it would look very bad in history if we failed to support isolated French forces…or if we excluded the French from participation in our councils as regards Indo-China'.[98] Words that Churchill had not dared to communicate directly to Roosevelt during the previous month were now boldly sent to the White House.

For the last two years Churchill had been trapped between the President and the British Foreign Office in an attempt to protect his highly romanticised special relationship. The Prime Minister had seen himself as the fulcrum attempting to balance the aspirations of two different and conflicting worldviews. But after months of delay and tactical manoeuvrings Churchill had returned to the fold. His telegram to Roosevelt clearly brought into line British military policy concerning Indo-China with his post-Yalta political stance on colonialism. Churchill had defended all of the colonial territories of all the European nations against the lustful intentions of the Americans, the Chinese and the Russians. From now on this applied in the military sphere just as much as the political. Alas Roosevelt did not have the chance to reply to Churchill's watershed communication – he died the following day.

San Francisco and Potsdam

Roosevelt's death was a significant turning point for American foreign policy. This had been the President's sole preserve. American foreign policy had been robbed of its chief architect just as the European war drew to a close and the birth pains of a new word order commenced. This was even more the case for Indo-China than elsewhere. Roosevelt had made it one of his principal war aims to implement trusteeship and begin the process of decolonisation. Fate removed Roosevelt from the stage at precisely the moment at which he was needed most and for which he had planned for so long. Now Roosevelt's Vice-President Harry S. Truman was propelled into the limelight, but Truman was no Roosevelt. Truman's first actions upon ascending to the office of the presidency were designed to stabilise the ship of state at this crucial wartime juncture. The new President needed to avoid any unnecessary administrative fallout caused by a change in the Commander in Chief. Truman therefore initially implemented few changes to either Roosevelt's team or the policies of the late President. Wedemeyer certainly benefited from Truman's policy of continuation.

Churchill was heartbroken at the news of Roosevelt's death. The relationship on which he had staked so much had been destroyed.[99] Yet Churchill's grief was for more than just his vision of Anglo-American geopolitics. Churchill genuinely held both a warm and romantic regard for Roosevelt. They were comrades in arms and at times intense rivals, but they preserved a degree of mutual affection that was unique. It illustrated both the quality of their relationship and the similarity of their burdens on the lonely path that they trod.

Therefore it was left to Truman to respond to Churchill's telegram of 11 April which had boldly laid out British policy and SEAC terms of reference within French Indo-China. Truman confirmed to Churchill that Wedemeyer had conveyed that an agreement had been reached whereby Mountbatten would now inform Wedemeyer of SEAC operations. But Wedemeyer's account to Washington appeared to introduce new and additional terms to the agreement as understood by Mountbatten. The report stated that all SEAC Indo-Chinese activities would now also have to be approved by Chiang Kai-Shek. In addition, if the proposed SEAC Indo-Chinese operations could not be incorporated with China Theatre strategy then Mountbatten would be obliged to withdraw his plans and cancel the operations. Truman attempted to follow in the footsteps of Roosevelt and approved of Wedemeyer's stance. The new President told Churchill that Wedemeyer's explanation offered the most 'satisfactory method of solving the problem'. If future disagreement arose, Truman agreed with Churchill's suggestion that it should be reported to the relevant Allied Chiefs of Staff for arbitration by the CCS.

Truman addressed directly Churchill's dark warning that history would judge the Allies harshly for not supporting the French troops fighting the Japanese. He revealed to the Prime Minister that Wedemeyer had already been 'instructed to give the French resistance groups such assistance as is practicable without prejudice to his present or future operations'. It would, no doubt, be left for Wedemeyer to decide how he should best define words such as 'practicable' or 'prejudice', let alone 'present or future operations'.[100] Indecisiveness and ambiguity reigned.

Churchill decided that Truman's proposition appeared to offer a practical solution to their difficulties despite the limitations that Wedemeyer's additional terms placed upon Mountbatten's activities. Truman had agreed to relegate any future disagreements to the CCS and away from the political arena. Churchill was free now to groom the new President for another special relationship away from the potential political fallout resulting from a bitter Anglo-American intra-theatre dispute. Truman had also acted in the favour of the beleaguered French troops in Indo-China. Yet there was a familiar presidential silence concerning further French participation in the more general war in the Far East or Allied councils about Indo-China. Churchill was resigned to accept what he had been offered. He instructed Ismay for 'Action this day' on Truman's telegram.[101] Ismay duly referred the matter to the COS for their consideration. Four days later, Ismay was able to inform the Prime Minister that the COS had decided to trial the motion that Truman had suggested to Churchill.[102] The following day Churchill informed Truman that Britain was prepared to attempt to undertake the President's direction.[103] The two heads of state had agreed that Mountbatten had the right to operate within French Indo-China.[104]

In his reply to Truman, Churchill had not softened the terms of his complaint to Roosevelt from 11 April. Churchill had weighed the compromises inherent in Truman's resolution. The Prime Minister had not acted alone, he had sought the advice of the COS and his response to Truman was not a knee-jerk reaction but a considered stand developed over the course of six days. An ill-judged response could damage Anglo-American relations and set a disastrous tone for Churchill's new special relationship with Truman. Therefore during this six-day pause Churchill had re-evaluated Anglo-American relations. The Prime Minister came to the conclusion that he had detected a subtle shift in the American political landscape. Churchill believed that the time was now ripe to discuss greater French and Dutch participation in the war against Japan with the Truman administration. Churchill told Eden of his conviction. The Foreign Secretary was in Washington, on behalf of the British Government, to attend Roosevelt's funeral.[105] Churchill's hunch was justified although Eden still had plenty of work to do. Ten days later the British COS informed Mountbatten that the CCS had agreed that the French *Corps Leger* would be moved to Ceylon as soon as possible for deployment in the Far East.[106] Churchill had triumphed, but the real victory belonged to the Foreign Office. The Prime Minister had returned to the fold and was advocating a direction that the Foreign Office had long ascribed to.

At the same time Churchill reviewed the hard-won victory that he had achieved at Yalta concerning voluntary trusteeship. The Prime Minister continued to hold that he was opposed to the European colonial powers relinquishing territory into the hands of those that had no previous experience of such matters – China, Russia and the United States.[107] The Foreign Office observed with contempt the American duplicity in accepting aid from colonial areas whilst at the same time championing the cause of trusteeship based upon accusations of European underdevelopment: 'the Americans have not disdained the use of our territories particularly India and Burma and the considerable resources which those territories have made available for them'.[108] It was acerbically noted that:

> The 'fundamental principle on which the very existence of the United States rested' was...in abeyance when the US wrested what is now Southern California, Arizona, New Mexico and Texas from the Mexicans, and when the North forced the Confederate southern states to stay within the Union.[109]

In the meantime the French Government issued the Brazzaville Declaration. This aimed to entwine the political aspirations of the French metropole and Indo-China as one component within a new French Union. The Declaration was progressive and signified a more benevolent post-war direction for Franco-Indo-Chinese relations. The French Union was to form the main mechanism for the post-war administration of the French Empire. True self-government would not be possible; nevertheless 'liberty' would be allowed but only within the boundaries of the Union.[110] The French remained suspicious of the motives of others.[111] De Gaulle attacked the American stance towards France and called for American supplies for French troops operating against the Japanese.[112] Massigli met Cadogan at the Foreign Office to ascertain French 'arrangements' for the future Allied 'command' of Indo-China.[113] The COS wanted the Foreign Office to defer any response until the intra-Allied boundary review had been completed. In the meantime, the COS advised the Foreign Office to instruct the French Ambassador that, due to occupational activities within Europe and Cadogan's presence at the San Francisco Conference, a response was not possible. The Foreign Office was not 'convinced' by the COS assessment.[114]

Britain organised a meeting of the Dominions Prime Ministers to co-ordinate a unified response to United Nations policies prior to the San Francisco Conference. Trusteeship was included in their discussions.[115] Australia and New Zealand were critical of Britain for adopting the Yalta changes on trusteeship without first consulting with them. But at San Francisco they supported the British line.[116] Similarly, the five Security Council nations were set to discuss trusteeship before San Francisco. No debate of definite territorial transfers was thought likely at the forthcoming United Nations Conference.[117] Roosevelt had been a strong advocate of trusteeship but, even before his death, other nations appeared to be steering his vision for decolonisation into a different sunset.

The Foreign Office chose now to reply to Dening's qualms, voiced from SEAC in February, concerning French objectives in the region. Dening believed the French to be '*mal élèves*' who intended for Britain to be responsible for 'bearing their cross for them' regarding Indo-China. Dening was instructed from London that official British policy was 'to help her [France] to recover her former strength and influ-ence and to cultivate the closest possible relations with her. We regard a strong and friendly France as an essential factor for our post-war security'.[118] The Foreign Office and the Prime Minister were operating in step with one another. It was imperative for Britain to continue to protect the welfare of all of the European colonial powers concerning trusteeship – voluntary or otherwise – lest a model for decolonisation be accepted that could annihilate the European colonial system. The main-tenance of the extra-European colonial system was not the only issue at stake. The internal peace and security of post-war Western Europe relied upon political stability and economic rejuvenation in order to face the expected future threat from Russia. Leadership of a grouping of European colonial powers would preserve Britain's position as a Great Power. The British Empire and Dominions acting alongside the other European Empires would act as a counter weight to the growing power of Russia. This would be threatened by trusteeship.[119]

Eden was dispatched to San Francisco by Churchill for United Nations negotiations. In Eden's absence, the Prime Minister assumed direct responsibility for the management of the Foreign Office. This proved to be something of a disaster. Churchill failed to deal with the vol-ume of Foreign Office work in addition to his normal responsibilities. He became a 'bottleneck' to policy. Churchill was tired and exhausted. Colville observed the impact upon the Prime Minister's leadership, 'He

[Churchill] does little work and talks for far too long' and he 'weed[s]' 60 percent of the Foreign Office telegrams.[120]

Despite the adoption of a new set of guidelines regarding SEAC and China Theatre activities within French Indo-China, the Mountbatten–Wedemeyer conflict continued unabated. With the lack of American assistance, Mountbatten considered it his duty to continue to supply and assist French troops and resistance groups fighting the Japanese.[121] In Washington, Wilson discovered that the American Joint Chiefs of Staff had reassessed their position on Allied intra-theatre boundaries. The outcome of this review appeared favourable to Mountbatten. The American Joint Chiefs of Staff was now unlikely to object to Indo-China being added to an enlarged SEAC during the course of any theatre boundary re-examination. In spite of the recent turbulent Anglo-American history concerning French Indo-China, Marshall was unsure as to how the White House would receive such a proposal or where the existing policy of the executive branch of the American Government resided on such matters.[122]

Mountbatten was not pleased with either Wedemeyer's general attitude or his interpretation of their guidelines. He insisted that Wedemeyer had introduced 'new factors' and new 'interpretations' into the Gentleman's Agreement with Chiang Kai-Shek. Wedemeyer strongly protested to Mountbatten that Indo-China was of the utmost strategic importance to China Theatre. As Commander in Chief to Chiang Kai-Shek, Wedemeyer believed that he could not be held by the terms of the Gentleman's Agreement – especially Mountbatten's interpretation of the ambiguous accords. In addition this was also an agreement to which Wedemeyer had not been an original signatory. Wedemeyer noted that as a Supreme Allied Commander, Chiang Kai-Shek required prior notification of all external operations scheduled to take place within China Theatre. Yet this observation failed to acknowledge that Mountbatten was also a Supreme Allied Commander and therefore senior to Wedemeyer. Nevertheless Wedemeyer's onslaught continued. He assailed Mountbatten's comprehension of the Gentleman's Agreement as being contrary to 'standard military practice'.[123]

Mountbatten was hurt by the ferocity of the attack. His only response was to reel away from a further entanglement by insisting to Wedemeyer that the conflict would have to be resolved 'officially'.[124] Referral to the CCS was the mechanism for arbitration. From Washington, Wilson assured both the British COS and Mountbatten that Wedemeyer was only entitled to veto SEAC activities within French Indo-China that conflicted with China Theatre operations. The problem was that Wedemeyer believed that he possessed the right to veto all of Mountbatten's operations.[125] Wilson confirmed that Wedemeyer was not permitted to reinterpret the terms of the Gentleman's Agreement. Yet Wedemeyer was not operating alone, he was supported and encouraged in his disagreement with Mountbatten by Hurley. Marshall warned Wilson that both Hurley and Wedemeyer were sending powerfully written anti-British telegrams to Washington from Chungking.[126]

The hostility displayed in the attacks shocked Marshall. He told Wilson that: 'there must be an extraordinary importance to the clandestine operations being carried out...to justify the possible creation not only of ill will but of a feeling that there is a lack of good faith'. Mountbatten felt justified in his position as reports from Burma highlighted the importance of Indo-China as a Japanese supply base for the Burma front. Marshall decided that the American Joint Chiefs of Staff would not bring the Mountbatten–Wedemeyer dispute before the CCS for arbitration. He considered that already there had been ample correspondence at the highest levels on this matter. Truman and Churchill as well as Marshall and Wilson had all been engaged in this process. Marshall believed that nothing new would be achieved by involving the CCS.[127] Wilson was taken aback. Marshall had prevented Wedemeyer from using the American Joint Chiefs of Staff to raise his conflict with Mountbatten before the CCS – the dedicated forum for arbitration. Wilson was amazed at Marshall's conviction that nothing would be realised. He concluded that 'there is more in it than meets the eye'.[128] The British COS reply to Wilson lamented that 'if Wedemeyer acted in the spirit of his directive and if good liaison is established in Chungking, the difficulties would cease'. The COS therefore requested that Marshall should 'advise' Wedemeyer of this.[129] The COS had read between the lines of Marshall's statements and concluded that the tide had turned against Wedemeyer.

Differences still existed between SEAC and China Theatre concerning operations within French Indo-China. The view from the Foreign Office was that Wedemeyer had behaved 'very badly' and was attempting to restrict greater SEAC activity against Japan. French interests were temporarily aligned with Britain, but the Foreign Office warned that the French understood that it was with the United States that they would have to establish a rapport and therefore they might have to change direction.[130] In India, Britain arranged for the French to use amenities to educate and to equip French colonial administrators in order to successfully step into the breach and administer Indo-China upon liberation.

In China, the American Office of Strategic Services lent its support to an indigenous Vietnamese nationalist coalition that had established a resistance movement against the Japanese. Commonly known as the Vietminh, this group, led by the Communist Ho Chi Minh, supplied the United States with intelligence reports about the Japanese and rescued American pilots shot down over Vietnam in return for supplies and training.[131] SEAC and China Theatre thus continued to develop parallel policies to one another concerning French Indo-China.

When the war in Europe ceased on 8 May, Britain began to focus greater attention on the outstanding conflict against Japan. Brooke discussed with the British COS the possible reassignment of French Indo-China from China Theatre into SEAC. The COS conference concluded that SEAC boundaries should be expanded to embrace Indo-China.[132] The COS informed the Joint Service Mission in Washington of their decision.[133] Churchill approved of the proposed change on 19 July.[134] Wedemeyer naturally objected to the relocation but his influence was waning. Indo-China was a side issue for the American Joint Chiefs of Staff compared to operations within the Pacific Theatre.[135] The American Government was anxious to ascertain British and Chinese views for a rapid settlement of the boundary dispute.[136] Compromise was in the air. Even Chiang Kai-Shek indicated a willingness to place French Indo-China into SEAC operational planning for future action against Japan but not to formally change the theatre boundaries.[137]

Sir Neville Butler, Superintending Under-Secretary of State at the Foreign Office, lunched with John Hickerson, Sub-Head of the European Office of the State Department, at the San Francisco Conference. Hickerson revealed that the American stance at Yalta concerning voluntary trusteeship had been designed by the State Department to allow for a 'climb down' from the late President's hard-line approach. Hickerson believed that voluntary trusteeship would not now be forced upon the French but that they could activate it if they so desired. He revealed that the State Department considered Roosevelt's stand on trusteeship a step 'too far' and voluntary trusteeship a necessary 'face saver' for America.[138] Eden told Truman at San Francisco that he was 'satisfied' that all trusteeship questions would soon be settled, although the British delegation did have a lot of problems with the Russian negotiators concerning trusteeship. Russia supported full independence for all colonial areas. On the other hand the French representatives objected to the use of the word 'independence' in the draft of the United Nations Charter. Georges Bidault, the French Foreign Minister, also announced that France was not prepared to place Indo-China under any form of trusteeship. France was flexing its muscles. It had been accorded a permanent seat on the United Nations council. Once again it was a Great Power.

Eden was impressed with Stettinius' negotiating skills, especially considering the polarised French and Russian positions. The San Francisco Conference progressed in a direction amiable to Britain. Eden also liked Truman's confidence and decisiveness. The President informed Eden: 'I am here to make decisions, and whether they prove right or wrong I am going to take them'.[139] The United Nations Charter established at San Francisco included apparatus for the management of trusteeships – chapter 12. Self-government and self-development were important principles included within the text. But the voluntary system for trusteeship developed at Yalta was enshrined as article 77.[140] France would not lose Indo-China to an American trusteeship and a precedent for decolonisation was avoided.

The CCS and the leadership of the Big Three assembled at Potsdam, just outside Berlin, for the European victors' conference (18 July–2 August). In the triumph of the moment and the sobriety of the location, doubt and suspicion were forgotten. Truman congratulated Mountbatten with his success at SEAC. The President said that both he and the American Joint Chiefs of Staff were 'grateful' with the 'impartial way' that Mountbatten had managed SEAC and conducted its affairs. Truman flattered Mountbatten that: 'we in America regard you in exactly the same light as Eisenhower is regarded by the British; that is, we really do appreciate your integrity, and the admirable way which you have run your command'.[141] Had Wedemeyer been party to the conversation he would have probably choked at his Commander in Chief's sycophancy. But he would have expressed full agreement with Brooke's assessment of Mountbatten at a COS meeting a couple of weeks later: 'Seldom has a Supreme Commander been more deficient of the main attributes of a Supreme Commander than Dickie Mountbatten'.[142]

Churchill would not be at the helm to steer Britain into the postwar world. The British general election result was declared during the Potsdam Conference. Churchill was deposed from office by the electorate. It was a grievous blow to a prime minister who had struggled to preserve so much in the face of such adversity.[143] But Churchill's health at Potsdam was once again failing, and yet again he was having trouble mastering his brief.[144] The time had come for the old warhorse to take a rest.

The Potsdam Conference confirmed changes to the Allied theatre boundaries between SEAC and China Theatre. But as a concessionary gesture to Chiang Kai-Shek, Truman and the new British Prime Minister Clement Attlee separated Indo-China between SEAC and the China Theatre along the 16 parallel.[145] China would be responsible for northern Vietnam and northern Laos. SEAC was to assume responsibility for southern Vietnam, southern Laos and the whole of Cambodia for all further Allied Land Force operations. The Foreign Office feared a negative French reaction to such a measure. Cadogan, in particular, could not 'pretend to be happy' with the proposal. But the Foreign Office did not raise any formal objection as the CCS considered the division to be of military importance. In August following the dropping of the Atomic bombs on Hiroshima and Nagasaki, SEAC became responsible for the administration of the Japanese surrender within southern Indo-China.[146]

5
Trusteeship's Denouement

The San Francisco and Potsdam Conferences had appeared to reconcile Anglo-American differences concerning Indo-Chinese trusteeship. Within a matter of months, France had been rehabilitated as a Great Power. Its imperial grandeur was resurrected alongside its metropolitan rebirth. Only the Soviet Union, out of the Big Three, continued to support full independence for colonial peoples. But Russia was still not engaged in the war in the Far East and Stalin had been robbed of the opportunity to influence such events by the death of Roosevelt. Never again would Stalin be able to indulge in personal flights of fancy with an American president – to stand shoulder to shoulder as men of destiny and divide the world into spheres of influence according to their whims – as they had done at Tehran when Roosevelt had offered India to Stalin. The age of American foreign policy being based upon the impulses of an indecisive juggler king was over. Truman was taking United States diplomacy in a different direction.

Truman may have been inexperienced in foreign policy but he was at least decisive. He was also a team player who was eager to rely upon experts in the State Department, or the Joint Chiefs of Staff, to make up for his lack of knowledge. As Truman slowly asserted himself in his new role, he also quietly removed from office the sycophants from Roosevelt's circus and the more liberal elements of the Democratic Party – all of who saw themselves, rather than Truman, as the natural heirs and guardians of Roosevelt's foreign policy.[1] American foreign policy therefore became more critical of Russia and in doing so it required the United States to covet the support of the old world imperial powers upon whom Roosevelt had desired to enact trusteeship: Belgian, Britain, France, the Netherlands and Portugal.

Churchill was naturally devastated by the loss of his special friend – Roosevelt. Much has been made of their partnership. It was an alliance that 'saved' the world. But Churchill's romantic special relationship was, in reality, fraught with difficulties, one of the most dangerous of which was the question of trusteeship for French Indo-China. After Roosevelt's death, the Foreign Office was content to allow Churchill to realign himself with their policies. The change of an American president permitted the Foreign Office, at the San Francisco and Potsdam conferences, the luxury of not only diffusing Roosevelt's trusteeship policy but also combining American, British and European interests for the rebirth of European imperialism.

Within a matter of months, Roosevelt's grand strategy of international trusteeship for French Indo-China had unravelled. The speed of this American foreign policy *volte-face* was impressive. A grave threat to Anglo-American relations had been averted. Yet the resolution of the trusteeship debate and the preservation of Churchill's special relationship with the United States had more to do with a shift in the balance of power within Washington than merely the death of the trusteeship architect – as important as this proved to be.

Resolution

Just as the origin of Britain's conflict with the United States over Indo-Chinese trusteeship lay in Washington, so too did its resolution. Despite the political acumen of the British establishment – whether in the Dominions Office, COS, Foreign Office or the political elite – and the personal diplomacy of Churchill and his special relationship with the United States, resolution of the conflict came about through a number of changes outside of their control. The most important of these alterations were a transformation in Franco-American relations, a shift in power within the Washington establishment and the sudden change in president at a crucial wartime juncture.

Roosevelt has often been portrayed as having a foreign policy that was unique.[2] He certainly had many allies within the Washington establishment and elsewhere who were ready both to agree and to indulge in his anti-imperial and anti-French sentiments. Important advisers such as Hull, Hurley, Leahy, Stilwell, Wedemeyer and Donovan (the latter was the Head of the Office of Strategic Services, the forerunner of the Central Intelligence Agency) provided Roosevelt with an appreciative audience for his views and were all natural accomplices against the British and the French. But this does not mean that Roosevelt's distinctive approach to

American foreign policy was welcomed by all those that he led. Large elements of the State Department, the armed forces and even the inner sanctum of the administration within the White House, were not in agreement with the President or his incongruous group of flatterers.

As early as February 1943, Roosevelt was already receiving strong opposition from the State Department towards his anti-French feelings. The State Department Sub-Committee on Security Problems was advocating that it was in America's interest for France – and in so doing the French Empire – to be restored as a Great Power. France would therefore be able to become a strong component in American policy against Russia. The perceived wisdom was that any future threat to American security would come from communist rather than imperialist ideology. Because of the President's personal animosity towards the French, a year later, the State Department Country and Area Committee on the Far East went as far as to declare Indo-China a unique colonial question rather than part of mainstream policy. Roosevelt would have no doubt been pleased with such apparent anti-colonial feeling. Nonetheless, Indo-China's exclusive status outside of conventional colonial thinking indicated that all was not well within the State Department. Indeed, Indo-China's special designation hardly set a precedent for decolonisation. Similarly, the actual composition of the Committee reflected Washington divisions towards such issues. When the Committee voted on two possible solutions for post-war Indo-China, there was an even split between those that supported Roosevelt's trusteeship scheme and those that subscribed to the possibility of permitting a limited French return.[3]

In spite of strong protestations from the State Department about future threats to American security, Roosevelt was able initially to keep the State Department isolated from his high policy pontificating about trusteeship for French Indo-China. American foreign policy was his personal domain, but even he was ultra-cautious about its operation. He once informed Henry Morgenthau, Secretary of State for the Treasury: 'You know I'm a juggler and I never let my right hand know what my left hand does'.[4] Roosevelt was indecisive, inconsistent and contradictory in order to further his aims. He could infuriate his own advisers just as much as he did the British Foreign Office.

Yet by 1944 – when paradoxically Roosevelt appeared to Halifax to be at his most zealous in his quest to dispose of Indo-China – the State Department had begun to challenge Roosevelt's dominance of foreign policy. Initially, the State Department merely questioned China's commitment to the principles of the Atlantic Charter. But as the problems surrounding Roosevelt's fourth global policeman (China) grew, China's importance to American foreign policy diminished. In the process Roosevelt's policy of trusteeship for Indo-China was undermined.[5] In these circumstances officials at the White House and within the State Department sought to develop – separately for the moment – a more coherent American policy towards Southeast Asia and specifically Indo-China. Therefore, just as Roosevelt appeared to be at his most vociferous concerning Indo-Chinese issues, the Washington bureaucracy was laying the very foundations that would eventually restrict his free-wheeling policies.[6]

In the meantime, the second Quebec Conference (August–September 1943) appeared to offer Roosevelt good cheer. Churchill had sufficiently stroked his ego and Roosevelt had led Churchill to believe that their special relationship had risen above the animosities and petty jealousies of both nations. In the process, a clearly flattered Churchill signed up to American war aims – one of which was an end to old world imperialism as exemplified by the French in Indo-China – as the United States assumed the role of the senior partner in the relationship. This had left Churchill at the mercy of an American president whose wartime objectives included a very different vision of what the post-war world would look like. At this juncture, Brooke and Eden correctly discerned the threat posed by Roosevelt. Yet they both failed to readdress the balance as Churchill was committed to a romantic vision of Anglo-American unity. This notion made Roosevelt's war aims easier to achieve. But paradoxically, the Quebec Conference also undermined Roosevelt's most fanatical anti-imperial policy. The conference had further diminished the importance of China and Southeast Asia to American military and foreign policy objectives. The conference had decided to centre United States policy in the war in the Far East towards a stratagem of island hopping across the Pacific Ocean.[7] This had moved the focus of American wartime planning away from the Chinese and Southeast Asian theatres, and Britain naturally sought to step into the strategic vacuum.

Meanwhile, Roosevelt persisted in advocating a policy of trusteeship for French Indo-China. But events also continued to threaten his clarity on this issue. By October 1944 the majority of France had been liberated and de Gaulle's Provisional Government had established itself in Paris. Roosevelt's diplomatic recognition of the French Provisional Government signalled an important blow against Nazism in Europe. The United States, the champion of oppressed peoples, had resurrected France from tyranny. No doubt Roosevelt viewed trusteeship for the Indo-Chinese as a similar form of emancipation. Nevertheless, the diplomatic recognition of the Provisional Government further blunted Roosevelt's vision for Indo-China.[8] An independent French Government – established by the Allies – under the stewardship of de Gaulle was never going to permit an American president to dictate the rebirth of a once proud imperial nation, let alone allow Roosevelt to administer the decolonisation of one of its most important colonies. In order to remove the stains of the defeat of 1940 and the subsequent Vichy collaboration, French belligerence could be expected in all areas of national pride. Similarly, Britain and France would be thrown together as uneasy allies against Roosevelt-led anti-imperialism. The President's Indo-China policy had definitely become more complicated, however the juggler was not defeated and Indo-Chinese trusteeship remained an attainable goal. After all, the United States was a creditor nation. France was in debt and would need American finance to re-establish itself. Roosevelt could afford to be patient and bide his time. He held the purse strings of the French recovery.

France – now reconstituted as a European power – sought to assert its interests further and the State Department found itself temporarily aligned with French concerns. Both were keen to see Roosevelt's foreign policy fiefdom further restricted.[9] In the light of rapidly changing international circumstances, on 1 November 1944 the State Department took the initiative and lobbied the President for clarification about current American policy towards French Indo-China. In his response, Roosevelt revealed that as far as he was concerned nothing had changed. No American aid was to be given to the French with respect to Indo-China and all American officials were expected to refrain from political discussions about the future of French Indo-China. He alone would decide upon the timing and implementation of American Indo-Chinese policies. In addition, Roosevelt anticipated that he would naturally be consulted by the British and the other colonial powers about their future plans for Southeast Asia.[10] Trusteeship was still very much at the forefront of the President's mind. He was confident enough of his vision and purpose to impose draconian terms on both the Allies and his administration in order to implement it.

On 30 November Hull retired as Secretary of State because of ill health and was replaced by Edward Stettinius. With Stettinius' appointment by Roosevelt, a delicate change in the direction of American foreign policy had taken place. Stettinius' promotion from Under-Secretary was evidence that Roosevelt would continue to regard foreign policy as his personal fiefdom. Yet with Stettinius' advancement the European Office within the State Department had been brought to the forefront of American decision making.[11] The post-war world had not yet dawned, but planning for a new age intensified as subtle changes within the Washington old guard gradually took place. The war in Europe was rapidly drawing into its final stages; yet in the Far East the war was expected to continue well into 1946.

At the turn of the year Stettinius met with the Secretary of War, the Secretary of the Navy and Roosevelt's special adviser – Harry Hopkins. The purpose of the meeting was to re-evaluate Roosevelt's approach towards French Indo-China. All agreed that the President's indecision was a grave policy error which was damaging the newly re-established Franco-American relationship.[12] Failure to address the Indo-Chinese question could pose significant problems for American European policy. The British would have been pleased with Hopkins' involvement in such discussions. Cadogan considered that Hopkins was 'the only practical and more or less effective member of the [presidential] entourage'.[13] Oliver Harvey was equally as supportive: 'Harry Hopkins has something of the Baptist missionary about him, earnest, ignorant, worried, determined to help, woolly, but he is a good friend to us'.[14] On this occasion the British trust was not misplaced and Hopkins – Roosevelt's closest confidant – undermined his beloved chief. Hopkins advocated that the time had now come not just for a complete reappraisal of American foreign policy towards French Indo-China but also of the entire approach by the administration towards the Franco-American relationship. Hopkins demonstrated the depth of his convictions by embarking upon a personal visit to Paris. French rehabilitation and usefulness to American foreign policy gathered momentum within the State Department. When Georges Bidault, the French Foreign Minister, sought to return Hopkins' overtures with a visit to Washington later in the spring, State Department officials actively encouraged the blossoming Franco-American relationship. The importance of the trip was underscored by Bidault's reception by the Vice President – Harry S. Truman. Resentment and distrust on both sides appeared to be thawing. In such circumstances Indo-Chinese trusteeship looked out of place. It appeared to be a diminishing possibility. It seemed to be a foreign policy quirk: unique to Roosevelt and out of step with a growing State Department vision for the future of American foreign policy and the creation of the post-war world order.[15]

Nevertheless, despite the rejuvenation of France a significant stain remained upon the French wartime record that enabled Roosevelt to continue to press for Indo-Chinese trusteeship. France may have been liberated in Europe but in French Indo-China a Vichy-led French regime

still existed. As long as this persisted and Frenchmen seemed to be col-
laborating with the Japanese in their efforts against the Allies, Roosevelt
could continue to indulge in his pursuit of trusteeship with moral
vigour. Yet in the rapidly changing global circumstances, the ambiguity of the previous Vichy regime continuing to be the sole bastion of
French treachery proved short lived. The Japanese *coup* of 9 March in
Indo-China against the Vichy authorities clarified French international
standing. The last remaining and highly symbolic vestige of collaboration with Germany and Japan had been removed.[16] Indo-China had
become an enemy-occupied territory in Southeast Asia. French troops
were at last openly fighting the Japanese. The French Government thus
sought to liberate its Southeast Asian occupied territory and free its
population from tyranny in the same vein as the British (who were
attempting to orchestrate efforts towards Burma, Hong Kong, Malaya
and Singapore) and the Dutch (in the Netherlands East Indies).

De Gaulle naturally used the opportunity that the Japanese *coup*
presented to him to great effect. He openly challenged American,
and therefore Roosevelt's, anti-French sentiments. With French troops
actively engaged against Japanese forces de Gaulle was emboldened to
directly threaten the United States. He claimed that any further anti-
French or anti-French Indo-Chinese policies would push his fledgling
nation into the Soviet orbit for diplomatic assistance and protection.[17]

Yet despite the rapidly changing situation both within Europe and
Southeast Asia, no clear direction appeared forthcoming concerning
American policy. The State, War and Navy Committee still had no indi-
cation of the President's intentions and therefore sought once again to
clarify American policy towards Indo-China.[18] The State Department
naturally wanted to orchestrate American foreign policy and to construct a consistent and integrated approach towards both Europe and
Southeast Asia. But progress regarding American Indo-Chinese policy
remained blocked by Roosevelt. The control of American foreign policy
was therefore being contested by two rival architects with wildly differ-
ing visions towards the outlook for the post-war world. The momentum,
however, now appeared to swing towards the State Department and
away from Roosevelt. The President knew what he wanted to achieve
but his poor administrative skills meant that he did not know how he
was going to get there. Here the State Department held the advantage.
Its liaison with Hopkins, the War and Navy Departments, its count-
less policy memoranda and discussions, and its growing relationship
with the French Provisional Government enabled the State Department
to concoct a dual policy towards French Indo-China in opposition to

Roosevelt. In the State Department policy, France would be permitted to regain Indo-China, but it could also place the colony into voluntary trusteeship if it so desired – a sop to Roosevelt's original goal. However, the State Department naturally assumed that de Gaulle's France would not even consider undertaking the second step of voluntary trusteeship. This would be an alien concept contrary to French ideas of national rebirth.

This was the thinking behind the option of voluntary trusteeship (category c) that had been introduced by the State Department at the Yalta Conference.[19] Roosevelt may have thought at the time that this concept logically fitted with his flexible approach to foreign policy, but the European branch of the State Department later revealed to the British Government that their purpose for creating category c was 'to permit a climb down' from Roosevelt's entrenched position on Indo-China. By the time of the San Francisco Conference, the State Department had no qualms about demonstrating that Roosevelt had been far too zealous in his dealings about French Indo-China and that category c was an American 'face saver'.[20]

In the meantime, Roosevelt had been happy to accept the concept of voluntary trusteeship at the Yalta Conference. But if he had hoped that such amiability would stall further encroachments upon his trusteeship agenda, he would have been gravely disappointed. Throughout the spring of 1945, officials from both sides of the Atlantic continued to harass the President's position. Anglo-American naval discussion in Washington, between the British Admiral James Sommerville and the Commander in Chief of the American Navy Admiral Ernest King, had revealed to the British Government that the American Joint Chiefs of Staff was not in favour of Roosevelt's decision to exclude the French from Indo-China.[21] The American military establishment was opposed to the President's Indo-Chinese trusteeship policy and it was prepared to fight Roosevelt in the political arena. The Secretary of State for War, Stimson, felt empowered to challenge Roosevelt's control of the Indo-Chinese debate and even the Office of Strategic Services, which contained numerous anti-colonial stalwarts, was not now prepared to support the President on this particular issue. An Office of Strategic Services report that had been commissioned to re-evaluate American policy cautioned against the future use of trusteeship. It concluded that the 'unrest' and 'colonial disintegration' resulting from this policy would isolate the United States from its European allies, whose help was necessary to balance the United States against the growing power of the Soviet Union. Roosevelt's vision of the post-war world was based upon harmony and not equilibrium. But the Office of Strategic Services now favoured a more British approach to the post-war world, based upon the balance of power, and in doing so undermined Roosevelt still further.[22]

Roosevelt's death represented a tragic blow to American foreign policy. Its chief architect had been removed from the stage at a crucial moment in geopolitics. Within a month the war in the West would be over, and the San Francisco and Potsdam Conferences would be convened to usher in the post-war world order – a world order that Roosevelt had intended to dictate. For some time various elements within the British Government had noticed a sharp decline in the President's prowess. His obvious physical ailment at the Yalta Conference and his inability to chair complex negotiations clearly troubled Moran (Churchill's personal physician), Cadogan, Colville and Churchill.[23] Nonetheless, to assume that Roosevelt was mentally incapable of crafting and directing foreign policy during his final months would be to underestimate the strength of his inner feelings concerning the post-war world. Presidential musings about trusteeship and decolonisation had not diminished, even when faced with an alternative which was backed by most of the Washington establishment.

Nevertheless, Roosevelt's death ended the tense Washington stand off between the President and the State Department concerning the control of foreign policy. The American people genuinely mourned the loss of their Commander in Chief. A nation divided by segregation was united in grief; such was the respect and admiration for 'democracy's aristocrat'. Similarly, Churchill was deeply shocked when the news was conveyed to him.[24]

Therefore the President's death, before the San Francisco and Potsdam Conferences, appeared to stall American foreign policy at a crucial juncture – the dawning of the post-war world. But Roosevelt's death was also timely. Because Roosevelt's foreign policy was unique to himself, his death removed the sole obstacle to the State Department's dominance of American policy towards French Indo-China. In one fateful act, two contesting policies had become one. The State Department could now move into the foreign policy vacuum vacated by Roosevelt.

The day after Roosevelt's death, an initial special briefing dossier was presented to the new President by Stettinius. This was designed to bring Truman up to speed with American foreign policy and the broader context of international relations. The report highlighted British security fears and Britain's declining role within geopolitics 'to that of a junior partner of the Big Three'. It advised that 'The best interests of the United States require that every effort be made by this government to assist France, morally as well as physically, to regain her strength and influence'. The paper cautioned that 'in connection with Indo-China [France] showed unreasonable suspicions of American aims'. The State Department had thereby advocated a pro-French policy to the new President and neglected to mention Roosevelt's trusteeship plans.[25]

The rest of the Washington establishment was also moving quickly. On the same day the American Army spokesperson on the State, War and Navy Committee boldly voiced his misgivings about Roosevelt's policies. The development of two opposing policies towards French Indo-China was not in the military's interest. The representative criticised the policy vacuum. It was a 'serious embarrassment' for the military which was fighting alongside French and other European forces against Germany and Japan. The Committee agreed with his stance. Roosevelt's prohibition of the Indo-China debate would have to be immediately re-evaluated or restated.[26] This outburst was merely a foretaste of a more radical foreign policy *volte-face* as the State Department moved into the ascendancy, and in doing so aligned American and British policy concerning the future of French Indo-China.

Three days later a more detailed State Department policy manual was prepared for Truman. The dossier built upon the themes already set out in Stettinius' initial briefing paper. Although Britain and the United States were committed towards the 'progressive development of dependent peoples towards self-government' the paper described this in vague and uncertain future terms. It was made clear to Truman in a confident tone that 'The United States does not favour the impairment of British sovereignty over British colonial (i.e. not mandated) territory through the exercise of other than advisory functions by any international body'. Thus there would be no trusteeship for Hong Kong. American policy towards French colonial possessions was even clearer: 'Our policy has been to act in those areas in co-operation and agreement with the local French authorities and to respect French sovereignty'. The pro-French State Department policy promoted to Truman several days earlier had been reiterated. Again, the State Department failed to reveal Roosevelt's trusteeship policy or Roosevelt's embargo upon sustaining the French in Indo-China. Indeed, in the specific section dealing with Indo-China the manual stated that 'No final decisions have been made by this Government as to the future of Indo-China'. The language in the report gave the appearance of continuity and an already long-established government policy. But in reality Roosevelt's guiding principles were not being recapitulated or communicated to Truman. It was later confirmed that the State Department had deliberately misled the new President.[27]

Roosevelt had intended that the San Francisco Conference would not only herald the emergence of his world organisation but also the principles for future trusteeships.[28] In the event, however, the San Francisco Conference (April–June 1945) presented the State Department with the opportunity to resolve the Indo-Chinese dispute with France. At the conference the French Foreign Minister irately challenged Stettinius about trusteeship. Bidault made it very clear to the American Secretary of State that France did not propose to place Indo-China under any form of trusteeship, voluntary or otherwise. The hostile French response no doubt provoked a feeling of satisfaction from the State Department delegation. The original State Department policy of voluntary trusteeship had been designed with such a reaction in mind. Voluntary trusteeship was a sham, designed to allow for a withdrawal from Roosevelt's entrenched position.

In such circumstances, the Secretary of State's amnesia permitted both a full American climb down and for assurances to be made to France. Stettinius informed Bidault and Henri Bonnet, the French Ambassador to the United States, that 'the record is entirely innocent of any official statement of this Government questioning, even by implication, French sovereignty over Indo-China'.[29] Roosevelt's policy of trusteeship had been erased from the record. The United States needed amiable relationships with Britain and France for any possible future confrontation against the Soviet Union.[30] France's rehabilitation as a Great Power was complete. Roosevelt would have enacted far heavier terms upon the French. In his hands the substantial American veto in the post-war international organisation would have been far more ruthlessly deployed.[31] Roosevelt had never been shy about using his veto.[32] But Stettinius now held an olive branch aloft to the French delegation. The fifth permanent seat on the United Nations Security Council was being awarded to France: 'the United States welcomes this important step in the return of France to her rightful place in world affairs'.[33]

A lost opportunity

The origins of the Vietnam War have long fascinated historians, and the Vietnamese policies that Truman inherited from Roosevelt have become an area of intense academic debate.[34] Roosevelt may have known very little about Indo-China, but he was determined to liberate it from France. Indeed, he had expressed on a number of occasions that it was one of his principle war aims to remove Indo-China from the French Empire and to place it in some form of trusteeship in preparation for independence.[35] Roosevelt's death, before his plans had been realised, has caused historians to consider whether a power vacuum was created at a crucial moment in American foreign policy which fashioned a lost opportunity for the United States. The consequences of this lost opportunity would, in turn, lead to much suffering for France and the United States, and haunt the Vietnamese for generations.

In general therefore, historical debate surrounding the concept of a lost opportunity has focussed upon whether or not trusteeship died with Roosevelt. The historian Stein Tonnesson has clarified the historiography by categorising two distinct schools of thought concerning trusteeship analysis. The first category is a school of 'lost opportunity'. This consortium represents the views of those historians who either contest that trusteeship was never a serious, factual, presidential policy; or that trusteeship died with the President. The second category is a school of 'continuation'. This grouping consists of those historians content to argue that, as Roosevelt's policy of trusteeship was constantly being revised by the President as circumstances dictated, Truman's endorsement of French sovereignty represented a continuation of Roosevelt's own revisionism towards this issue.[36] To varying degrees, some advocates within both of these schools have tended to assume that American military necessity (in switching its focus away from China and towards the Pacific) and British imperial obduracy (as embodied by Churchill) contributed to the destruction of Roosevelt's original vision.[37] Others have argued that Roosevelt's ill-defined concept of trusteeship and his anti-French sentiments effectively prevented an early French return to Indo-China, and in so doing added to the post-war problems by producing a lost imperial opportunity for French colonialism.[38]

Roosevelt 'bluffed, infuriated and charmed contemporaries in much the same way that he has posterity'.[39] He was a juggler that was 'perfectly willing to mislead and tell untruths' in order to win the war.[40] In the words of Henry Stimson, the American Secretary for War, the President was 'a tough customer'.[41]

On the one hand Roosevelt treated trusteeship as a religious conviction. He was deeply ideologically committed to the notion of granting independence to colonial peoples. Despite the westward expansion of the United States and the later acquisition of the Philippines, Puerto Rico and Hawaii, Roosevelt shared popular American suspicions about old world imperialism. As a former British colony, the United States was engrained with deep anti-colonial feelings and Roosevelt could use trusteeship to prove to the American electorate that the United States was not fighting the Second World War merely to restore

British and French territories.[42] American anti-colonialism was actively
present in the popular subconscious between 1942 and 1945.[43] This
physically manifested itself in the high policy debate concerning the
future of French Indo-China and other European colonial possessions,
and Roosevelt had no problem finding allies within the Washington
establishment to support his grand vision of decolonisation through
trusteeship.

On the other hand Roosevelt was prepared to regard trusteeship
as a practical policy. It was just one of his more fluid foreign policies. Roosevelt kept Indo-Chinese trusteeship in constant revision as
he engaged in his daily power-play between the State Department
and other Allied governments on post-hostility planning. This suited
Roosevelt because he was not yet ready to commit to a final settlement,
and this would only be possible when he dictated the terms of the new
world order at the post-war peace conference.

Roosevelt was content to allow the ideological and the practical
aspects of trusteeship to operate independently of one another. This
increased policy fluidity. But the President was at his most dangerous
when he shrewdly chose to merge the ideological and the practical
together. It was in these moments that the British Foreign Office most
despaired.

By maintaining these two approaches towards trusteeship and not
committing himself to one hard and fast policy, Roosevelt created the
circumstances where – after his death – Truman struggled to grasp the
initiative in American foreign policy. Roosevelt's 'foreign policy had
been so personal to himself that it was doubtful whether Truman or
anyone he asked really appreciated what its "general line" had been'.[44]
This power vacuum enabled Americans in China Theatre and the Office
of Strategic Services to continue to apply Roosevelt's policies. Even after
Stettinius, on behalf of Truman, had personally reassured Bidault at
the San Francisco Conference about American support for the return
of France to Indo-China, the strongly anti-colonial Hurley was still
badgering Truman that such a move was contrary to Roosevelt's policy.[45]

Truman had certainly not helped himself regarding Hurley. Whilst
Truman was still coming to terms with American foreign policy he
had previously written to Hurley asking the Ambassador to 'continue
your efforts to accomplish the purposes outlined to you by President
Roosevelt'.[46] Hurley knew some of Roosevelt's thoughts about Indo-
Chinese trusteeship issues. However, because of the nature of Truman's
initial briefing by the State Department he assumed that his Indo-
Chinese policy was a natural continuation of Roosevelt's. Hurley was

not convinced that this was the case and sought to caution Truman that Britain was trying to use the debate 'to re-establish the prestige of imperialism'.[47] A further warning highlighted that Roosevelt had intended to remove Hong Kong from British control to which Churchill had replied 'over my dead body'.[48] As soon as the new President was able, Truman wrote to Hurley to assure him that such issues were receiving his full attention.[49] Hurley remained disgruntled, but there was little that he could actually do.[50]

Roosevelt's trusteeship policy had never anticipated the growth of Asian nationalism. Yet the potential American sponsorship of Asian independence from Japanese or Western imperialism was not without its appeal. The trusteeship argument was not lost on the leadership of the Vietnamese nationalist coalition, the Vietminh, or its main protagonist Ho Chi Minh. In July 1945, as Truman struggled with Roosevelt's legacy, the Vietminh requested France to provide for a Vietnamese postwar parliament under French tutelage and for full independence to be granted 'in a minimum of five years and a maximum of ten'.[51] Later, the Vietnamese declaration of independence in September 1945 dropped the call for trusteeship but still used symbolic imagery of freedom, as expressed in the American declaration of independence, to proclaim their freedom: 'All men are created equal. They are endowed by their creator with certain unalienable rights; among these are Life, Liberty and the pursuit of happiness'.[52]

Roosevelt's political cunning was embodied in trusteeship. Ideologically it resounded with the beliefs of the American people. Practically it remained fluid, in constant revision and adaptable to meet any challenge. By not formally integrating trusteeship into any formal American foreign policy, Roosevelt kept it pure, untainted by the State Department and available to be played with whenever he saw fit. But Roosevelt was not lacking in insight or intellectual prowess. Just as he was conscious of the wartime opportunities, so too did he understand the constraints. Roosevelt was well aware of the opposition within both Washington and London to his trusteeship policy.[53] He found it difficult to express any confidence in the British Foreign Office.[54] His frequent outbursts at the American Joint Chiefs of Staff were not merely anti-French or anti-British eruptions but also an attack on his own advisers who believed that trusteeship jeopardised American military and political policy concerning mandate territories and the future of the Japanese islands.

Roosevelt was able to ride such storms because of his dual approach to trusteeship and because he prevented outside interference by keeping its development to himself. At the same time Roosevelt was focussed upon his destination – the post-war peace conference. He had the foresight to understand that the United States would be the only major creditor that he held all of the main cards. This would be 'an American peace that belonged to him to dictate its organisation'.[55] Roosevelt therefore could be patient. He would choose when to confer about post-war planning and reconstruction. Roosevelt could clinically apply the threat of trusteeship when it was only absolutely necessary or, even more deviously, when he personally desired to toy with it. Thus Roosevelt's silences and inactivity, which have sometimes been construed as abandonment, were merely part of his political armoury. The only weakness in his armour – and one which he did not consider – was the possibility of his own death before peace could be realised.

The British Colonial Office and Foreign Office naturally opposed Roosevelt's trusteeship concept. British fears and criticisms were not eased by the breadth of weapons in the President's diplomatic arsenal which were arrayed against them. In Washington, Halifax witnessed first-hand Roosevelt's playful and disorganised manner. The President often chose to use conversation as others used 'a first draft on paper'.[56] Halifax had plenty of opportunities to observe Roosevelt's devious methods of getting things done. The President's fluid revisionism, his failure to integrate trusteeship within the broader context of American geopolitics and his reluctance to adopt a clearly defined stance upon trusteeship all resulted in particular disquiet in London. The conclusion in the Foreign Office was that 'The Americans do not wish us to recover our previous position in Asia, confuse this wish in their minds with the principle of self-determination (alias "freedom") and so see in every move to recover lost property a similar desire to enslave native peoples'.[57] Trusteeship was therefore an attack, based on the Atlantic Charter, upon the old European imperial system; and the Charter itself appeared to be stimulated by the potential for American economic gain.[58]

Roosevelt had to be careful in his commitment to national self-determination. On the one hand, trusteeship was his technique of nobly advancing indigenous peoples towards independence. It was thereby a means of convincing the American people that Roosevelt was not fighting the war merely to restore the bankrupt European colonial system. But on the other hand, Roosevelt had to avoid splitting the Allied cause by drawing the European powers together against the United States on this issue.

The balancing act that the President found himself in was not aided by the attitude of the Free French towards either Britain or the United

States. Roosevelt found de Gaulle arrogant and aloof. The French leader's 'autocratic temperament and his constant practice of playing off Britain against America' did not ingratiate him with the President. Roosevelt saw de Gaulle as representing 'acute and unconquerable nationalism' when France no longer possessed the status of a Great Power. Churchill enjoyed a bittersweet relationship with de Gaulle, but the Foreign Office was openly considerate of the Free French cause. The Foreign Office position clouded the Anglo-American relationship with the misconception that de Gaulle enjoyed the 'full' support of the British Government.[59] The Foreign Office was apprehensive that the French nation state's interests were being deliberately excluded from Allied decision-making by Roosevelt. A manoeuvre designed to punish France, for its capitulation to Germany and Japan, and to assist trusteeship. The Free French were equally (if not more) suspicious of American policy during the Second World War. Humiliated by the Germans and the Japanese, Free French pride was easily bruised by American impediment and added to their paranoia.

The Foreign Office correctly assumed that Roosevelt's plan of trusteeship for French Indo-China would create a blueprint for further decolonisation. Indeed, Britain feared permitting a precedent that could be eventually applied to Hong Kong being removed from the British Empire or Timor from Portugal.[60] Nevertheless, the President did little to calm British suspicions as he appeared willing to ignore previous American guarantees, including his own, in order to satisfy his trusteeship objective.[61]

As a result, Roosevelt had to be careful of not taking his trusteeship policy too far. This could have created a unified Allied block against his vision for the post-war world. Similarly, Churchill often sought to downplay Foreign Office zeal towards French Indo-China. Such Francophile fervour could endanger Churchill's special relationship with the President. Both leaders therefore chose at various stages of the debate to adopt a policy of silence to tone down the Anglo-American crisis over trusteeship. This served to cool heated passions on both sides of the Atlantic at crucial moments. Both statesmen were acutely aware of each others' sensitivities and personal feelings – this was, after all, a special relationship. Further confrontation would only have produced more problems and anxieties. The central issue, after all, would not be resolved until the post-war conferences.

In this context the voluntary trusteeship scheme (category c) agreed by the Allies at the Yalta Conference was not a victory for the European colonial powers against Roosevelt and trusteeship. The President was playing a long-term game. No doubt he viewed the agreement with some amusement. It was merely stalling the inevitable. The terms were vague enough for Roosevelt to ignore category c altogether. In the meantime, it would be the United Nations Security Council – led by the American President – which would have to construct the trusteeship machinery, and territorial decisions were not scheduled to be decided upon until the San Francisco Conference. Roosevelt later admitted as much to Hurley regarding Indo-China:

> The President said that in the coming San Francisco Conference there would be set up a United Nations trusteeship that [would] make effective the right of colonial people to choose the form of government [under] which they will live as soon as in the opinion of the United Nations they are qualified for independence.

Roosevelt could easily afford to be both hard-headed and high-minded. The United States would end the war as the main Allied creditor. It held the purse strings of a successful peace. American financial supremacy in European reconstruction and political authority in the United Nations would leave little room for dissent by Britain and France.[62]

In fact, Roosevelt's final thoughts about trusteeship before his death reveal that he had not changed his perspective. The President could afford to be vocally generous to both the British and the French. But his comments to Charles Taussig, the American Adviser on Caribbean Affairs, reveal that Roosevelt had not discarded his creed or dedication to colonial peoples: 'independence was the ultimate goal'.[63]

Churchill was equally conscious that changes would have to be made to the geopolitical map following the war. But Churchill was more concerned with the minutiae of actually fighting the war, and his special relationship with Roosevelt, than the details of post-war plans. On the whole, Churchill looked forward to United States playing a major role in the post-war world. A return to pre-war American isolationism was not desired. America's coming of age under British tutelage would create a powerful geopolitical force. A bilateral Anglo-American foreign policy would strengthen Britain's position as a Great Power and mitigate against its decline vis-à-vis the United States and the Soviet Union. This was the crux of Churchill's limited post-war thinking.

Nonetheless, whereas Churchill was prepared to put all of his eggs in one basket, the Foreign Office adopted a multifaceted approach. To a degree, this explains some of the Foreign Office's intransigence towards Churchill's blind commitment to Roosevelt. Foreign Office planning for the post-war world was far more advanced and lateral than Churchill could ever have been concerned with. The logic of recent European history indicated to the Foreign Office that a strong and rejuvenated France was crucial to Britain's future security – as both a partner and bulwark against Germany or Russia.[64] The balancing of Anglo-American and Anglo-French policies by the Foreign Office served to protect the illusion that Britain is still a Great Power. Foreign Office planning rituals added to this deception.

In reality the only voice that mattered was Roosevelt's. But even American policy demonstrated naiveties. Both Roosevelt's and to a lesser extent the State Department's post-war visions failed to consider European and extra-European economic networks as part of any meaningful debate.[65] Established economic ties would be vital components of any post-war reconstruction in either the European metropoles or their colonies. Thus the Foreign Office was defending all European and extra-European interests against the encroaching dollar imperialism of the American market empire by protecting French interests in Indo-China. The prospect of an American trusteeship of Indo-Chinese rubber, rice and coal was abhorrent.

Nevertheless, trusteeship became a lost opportunity. Roosevelt's death removed the key architect from the drawing board at the crucial moment when his plans could have been acted upon at the San Francisco and Potsdam Conferences. With Roosevelt's exit, Churchill's realignment with the Foreign Office and the State Department's management of Truman, the trusteeship debate concerning Indo-China – let alone Hong Kong or other colonial areas – was over. Roosevelt's post-war vision lay in tatters; although independence for colonial peoples became enshrined as article 73 of the United Nations Charter and symbolically the United States granted independence to its Southeast Asian colony – the Philippines – on 4 July 1946.[66] In the meantime violence had broken out in Vietnam. The Japanese surrender produced a power vacuum which was contested by the returning French colonial regime and Vietnamese nationalists of various hues.

Roosevelt's vision for trusteeship had never imagined the growth of Asian nationalism.[67] Nonetheless, the war had invigorated it and although it can be argued that things would have been very different if Roosevelt had lived, given his fluid and personal approach to foreign policy and Indo-China in particular, the President's response to such a challenge is impossible to guess. Strangely enough, Roosevelt was not against the notion of deploying either American or Chinese troops in Indo-China, and he had even requested for invasion plans to be drawn up to this effect.[68] How such forces would have fared is again impossible to deduce. The subsequent history of the Vietnam War would have been very different if this had been the case. But Roosevelt did not live to see his dreams realised and Britain appeared to attain a satisfactory closure to the wartime Indo-China debate.

Epilogue

In the immediate aftermath of the Potsdam Conference, British policy towards French Indo-China appeared victorious. Although Mountbatten had been forced to abandon his nebulous plans to include the whole of Indo-China within his operational sphere, Indo-China south of the 16 parallel was now officially included within the SEAC remit and Roosevelt's dream of trusteeship had been confined to the wards of history. British military planners initially expected the finale of the war against Japan to last for at least another year. To assist Britain's operations, within the now enlarged SEAC, the Potsdam Conference had approved the deployment of two French divisions against the Japanese – preferably in Indo-China.[1] At last the French were free to engage in the Asian military struggle and defend their honour in the Far East.

By this time Churchill had been removed from office by the British electorate and Roosevelt by fate. Nevertheless British policy towards French Indo-China continued undeterred across party lines.[2] The new Prime Minister and his Foreign Secretary, Clement Attlee and Ernest Bevin respectively, were oblivious to the finer details of Roosevelt and Churchill's Indo-Chinese trysts of the past three years. But they accepted the prevailing Whitehall rationale that Indo-China should be returned to France as soon as possible. After all, the re-establishment of the French Empire was synonymous with French national rebirth and American plans for the defence of Western Europe.[3]

The Far Eastern Section of the Foreign Office welcomed the conclusion of the war in Europe and the concentration of Allied policy upon Japan. A popular attitude within this section had accurately ascribed that for the last few years Eden had been prepared to sacrifice the Far East for European and American priorities; although it was also noted – with good grace – that in reality Eden had little choice in such matters.[4]

Now, however, the decay of the previous years could be swept aside. An expanded SEAC would protect French interests south of the 16 parallel and China Theatre would assume responsibility for the north.[5] Everything appeared to have reached its logical Whitehall conclusion. Yet in reality the British were ill-prepared for what followed.

Following the March 1945 Japanese *coup d'etat* against the Vichy French authorities in Indo-China, the Japanese had established indigenous nationalist regimes in Cambodia, Laos and Vietnam. These regimes were made up of volunteers from the middle and upper classes and represented the first attempt at Indo-Chinese self-government – albeit under Japanese tutelage and within Japanese greater Asia. In doing so, the Japanese had merely replaced the French as the resident imperial power. Yet under Japanese guidance Cambodian and Vietnamese nationalism began to evolve.[6] A number of Indo-Chinese exiles, who had been residing in Tokyo, were permitted to return to Indo-China. The Japanese established these 'independent' nationalists in prominent positions within their collaborator regimes.[7] At the same time a Vietnamese nationalist coalition, under the leadership of Ho Chi Minh, established a working relationship with the American Office of Strategic Services in China Theatre. The Vietminh, predominantly based in northern Vietnam, provided American officers with intelligence reports of Japanese activities and also rescued American pilots shot down over Indo-China, in return for a small amount of equipment and political support. The relationship proved to be of mutual benefit. Thus in July the Office of Strategic Services despatched a liaison team to the Vietminh headquarters located behind the Japanese lines.[8]

The dropping of atomic bombs on Hiroshima (6 August) and Nagasaki (9 August) abruptly ended the war in the Far East. In Tokyo the Japanese High Command sued for peace, but the Japanese army in Southeast Asia had not been defeated. Japanese forces throughout Indo-China felt betrayed. As a consequence they were reluctant to continue with their colonial duties whilst they waited for Allied forces to arrive and oversee their surrender. The functions of government therefore fell increasingly upon the puppet nationalists. In such circumstances, radical groups in Cambodia and Vietnam were prepared to gamble for true independence and to prevent the return of the French colonial regime. Unsurprisingly a power vacuum was rapidly developing. The Japanese no longer assumed administrative responsibility, but their puppet regimes had insufficient strength to manage Indo-China effectively. Cambodian and Vietnamese nationalism had been awakened, yet the local French population – prisoners of the Japanese since March – were eager to re-establish control before things got out of hand.

In Cambodia, the pro-Japanese nationalist Son Ngoc Thanh assumed control of the government.[9] He quickly recognised the regime of Ho Chi Minh in Vietnam and sent emissaries to the neighbouring states of Siam and China in order to achieve diplomatic recognition.[10] Within Cambodia pro-nationalist demonstrations were organised to demonstrate popular support for Thanh and a hastily arranged referendum provided a mandate in favour of independence.[11] An armed militia was raised to protect the fledgling nation.[12]

In Vietnam, the Vietminh gradually began to assume control of the country. On the same day that the atomic bomb was dropped on Hiroshima the Vietminh publicly declared its intention to disarm the Japanese before the arrival of any Allied Liberation Force and receive the Allied forces as the legitimate government of Vietnam.[13] At this stage the Vietminh was a loose coalition of Vietnamese nationalist parties, including the Indo-Chinese Communist Party led by Ho Chi Minh. Within a few years the communists would purge their competitors and assume direct control of the Vietminh movement.

Time was of the essence. A week after the detonation of the first atomic bomb, Allied forces had not arrived in Vietnam. The Supreme Allied Commander Southwest Pacific, American General Douglas MacArthur, had postponed liberation landings by Mountbatten until MacArthur had formally accepted the Japanese surrender. MacArthur was worried that without a formal surrender Allied troops could experience significant Japanese resistance.[14] No doubt this was unknown to Ho Chin Minh despite his access to American liaison officers. Nevertheless, Ho Chi Minh must have not believed his good fortune and the extra time that MacArthur's delay accorded. The National Committee of the Indo-Chinese Communist Party met on 13 August 1945 to consider its next move. Following its deliberations, a general insurrection was proclaimed by the Vietminh to seize the northern provincial capital of Hanoi and a massed rally was held in Hanoi on 17 August. The next day the Vietminh seized a large quantity of weapons and rapidly spread out from Hanoi to assume control of as much of Vietnam as possible. On 2 September, by coincidence the same day that the Allies received the formal Japanese surrender, Ho Chi Minh proclaimed the Vietnamese declaration of independence in Hanoi.[15] The stage was set for the tragic struggle of Vietnamese nationalism vis-à-vis Western imperialism.

Mountbatten was probably relieved with MacArthur's delay to Allied landings. He was not ready to assume peacekeeping duties in Cambodia and southern Vietnam. British planners were not prepared for South-east Asian liberation duties. Unlike the Americans they had very little knowledge as to the actual situation on the ground. In the same way, they were unaware of the logistical problems posed by American bombing of Japanese port and railway facilities during the final months of the war. In essence the British planners believed that because of the large French population they needed to prepare for some sort of European-style liberation where Allied troops would be welcomed as heroes. In consequence, they neglected the combined possibility of indigenous nationalist resistance to the return of colonial rule and a shortage of basic resources. Therefore, when the first British troops landed in southern Indo-China on 6 September, they found themselves ill-prepared to be peace enforcers rather than peacekeepers. Caught between the French antics for the reestablishment of imperialism, the frustrations of war-weary French colonists and the birth pangs of Cambodian and Vietnamese nationalism, a pitifully small number of British troops attempted to maintain some semblance of law and order, disarm the 75,000 plus Japanese forces and keep essential utilities working.[16] (War Office planners had believed that it would be possible to manage the Japanese surrender within French Indo-China with a SEAC force of 25,748 of which 803 were to be French colonial troops.)[17]

The tense situation between the newly arrived French administration, the French civilian population and the Cambodian and Vietnamese nationalists continued to degenerate towards anarchy. Faced with an increasingly dire humanitarian condition and the potential for extreme violence, the commander of the British forces, Major-General Sir Douglas Gracey, imposed a strict curfew and Mountbatten controversially rearmed 10,500 Japanese troops – who were by now officially Allied prisoners of war – to serve as additional peacekeepers.[18] Mountbatten repeatedly lobbied Attlee for additional troops.[19] The requests were made in vain. The Prime Minister considered the demobilisation of British imperial forces a greater political priority than the firestorms in Saigon or Phnom Penh.[20] These foreign fields were not Britain's to rebuild and therefore not worthy of greater entanglement.

Nonetheless Britain could neither escape its surrender responsibilities nor withdraw from Indo-China until adequate French forces had arrived. Trapped between the rebirth of French imperialism and the dawn of Cambodian and Vietnamese nationalism the British-led Allied Liberation Forces were caught in a conflict in which they behaved more like conquerors than liberators – burning houses and carrying out other counterinsurgency duties.[21] The Second World War may have been officially over but Allied casualties continued to accumulate. Between 10 October 1945 and 21 January 1946 the British Indian Army suffered 988 casualties in policing French Indo-China. Japanese casualties were higher at 1303 whilst the French numbered 2700.[22]

Even when sufficient French troops had arrived in Indo-China and Britain's duties regarding the Japanese were deemed to have been sufficiently completed, Britain still found itself entangled by Indo-China. The main British Allied Liberation Force managed to withdraw in January 1946, but small numbers of British observers continued to operate in Vietnam and Cambodia as part of post-Second World War liberation obligations. It was not until the successful conclusion of the Siamese-Cambodian border dispute in late November 1946 that Britain became the first Western power to extricate itself from what would eventually be known as the Vietnam War.[23]

Conclusion

During the Second World War, the seemingly innocuous and often neglected territory of French Indo-China was not only fundamental to Britain's regional objectives within Southeast Asia but it was also crucial within the larger context of British imperial war aims, both for the war itself and for the configuration of the post-war world. The future of French Indo-China was an important aspect of Allied high policy debate with the potential to create hostility to, and possibly fatally damage, the Anglo-American special relationship – the crux of Churchill's wartime strategy. Grave implications were also evident for the future of the British Empire. Washington's, and in particular Roosevelt's, enthusiasm for international trusteeship fashioned a dangerous precedent for decolonisation and American global hegemony. The dangers that this created were compounded twofold. Firstly, because the British Prime Minister had put all of his eggs into the American basket, Churchill was willing to sacrifice French Indo-China for the sake of his all-important special relationship with Roosevelt even though Indo-China was the President's primary test case for trusteeship. Secondly, Churchill's leadership priorities were not conducive to the giving of adequate attention to the structure of the post-war world.

Roosevelt regarded war as the pursuit of politics by other means. In this regard the President was a wily character. Roosevelt's approach towards wartime high policy and post-war structures was always highly fluid and in constant revision. But it would be a mistake to assume that the President did not possess clear post-war objectives. Roosevelt knew his direction of travel even if the route taken sometimes appeared illogical or even contradictory. The President was not naïve in his approach. Above all, Roosevelt was an experienced puppet master rather than a skilled administrator. The President's discussions with Stalin at the Tehran Conference about the merits of French colonial rule and also his desire to elevate China to the status of a Great Power – and at the same time a dependent ally – demonstrated his ability to stack the deck in his favour. In addition, French collaboration with Nazi Germany and capitulation to Japan in the Far East did little to validate French colonial authority. International opinion was a powerful tool. There can be little doubt that Roosevelt's vocal criticism of the French colonial record indirectly influenced de Gaulle's Brazzaville Declaration and later fed the French development of the *Fonds d'Investissements pour le Developpement Economique et Social* – a colonial development and welfare programme commonly known as *FIDES*.

Yet it would be a mistake to assume that Roosevelt had everything his own way. Even in Washington opposition existed to the President's navigation of foreign policy. On the specific issue of French Indo-China, the American position was complicated because the President had failed to unify his administration behind his plans for international trusteeship. Many of Roosevelt's anti-imperial sycophants were fervent supporters of his plans. They were more than prepared to carry on such manoeuvrings after the President's death. But even during Roosevelt's lifetime opposition towards the President's plans became more vocal from both State Department Europeanists and senior members of the American armed forces, all of whom regarded a strong France as vital to post-war American interests. Even Roosevelt loyalists had the ability to confound and confuse both American and British thinking in relation to colonial issues. For example, Winant, the American Ambassador to Britain, subtly substituted the words 'social and economic development' for the word 'independence' in dealing with colonial subjects and certainly added to further Anglo-American misunderstandings and suspicion. But ultimately, in Washington, foreign policy was the President's personal fiefdom. The post-war world would be beaten into shape by this zealous anti-imperialist who was determined not to see a repeat of the disappointment of the 1919 Versailles Conference – a failure to fashion the world in the American image. Roosevelt believed that he had the leverage to achieve this. The United States would finish the war as the main Allied creditor nation. American finance was Roosevelt's ultimate weapon. The President could use the post-war peace conference, the four policemen – Britain, China, Russia and the United States (three if Britain objected) – and the United Nations to prevent a return to the pre-war status quo. As the Tehran Conference demonstrated, Stalin would have been happy to side with China and the United States against the old colonial powers. Roosevelt was ruthless enough to commit political adultery against Churchill. Short-term diplomatic niceties such as the Anglo-American special relationship could easily be up-ended in the dawning of the new American age.

In contrast to Roosevelt, Churchill was uxorious towards the President. The Prime Minister also gave very little thought to post-war problems. Instead Churchill let himself become consumed by the micromanagement of the war. His public appearances dressed in army, air force and naval uniforms betrayed his love for battle. The eternal man of action appeared most content when he was visiting the troops, playing with military hardware, arguing with his generals about strategy or poring over military minutiae. This micromanagement of military affairs meant that Churchill simply could not keep abreast of everything else that was going on. It also made the Prime Minister vulnerable prey to those with clear post-war objectives.

Churchill's decision not to bother reading all of the telegrams concerning the Lend-Lease Agreement was perhaps understandable. But the Prime Minister's admission that he did not keep up to date with Indo-Chinese issues was an astonishing revelation considering the explosive nature of the subject. Certainly, Indo-China was of less relevance to other wartime problems. Yet to ignore it altogether, knowing the direction of Roosevelt's travel, was an enormous gamble.

As Churchill's special relationship drifted from equilibrium to dependency upon the United States, Churchill's susceptibility to American post-war strategy increased; a point not lost upon Roosevelt. Churchill's inability to get key issues concerning France discussed at the second Quebec Conference (1944), or indeed afterwards with Roosevelt at his family home in Hyde Park, demonstrated the Prime Minister's subservience to the agenda of the American President. Yet it should also be noted that the failure to discuss French Indo-China – intentionally or otherwise – at Quebec probably avoided any damaging Allied disagreements and produced one of the most successful wartime conferences.

Nonetheless it would be unfair to imply that the Prime Minister had merely lost the plot with reference to French Indo-Chinese affairs. Churchill may have been myopic. But the Prime Minister was certainly no simpleton and the special relationship-Indo-Chinese conundrum was undoubtedly a complicated affair. Yes Churchill chose to indulge in the micromanagement of the war effort, and failed to keep fully abreast of post-war issues, but he was also acutely aware of some of the President's domestic limitations. Likewise, Roosevelt was just as aware of some of the domestic constraints that Churchill faced. The President was certainly not an admirer of the British Foreign Office. The solitude of leadership and the irritations of bureaucracy unquestionably produced a common bond between the two Allied leaders. This mutual appreciation shaped a degree of subtlety towards each other's position that was sometimes lost by others on both sides of the Atlantic. Therefore, although Churchill's silences, stalling techniques and periodic ramblings reflected just how isolated the Prime Minister had become within his own government concerning French Indo-China, at times these tactics also demonstrated a deeper appreciation of the fluidity of Roosevelt's domestic situation – for example the anti-colonial rhetoric surrounding the 1944 presidential election.

Consequently the understanding of Churchill's position towards the special relationship was far more complicated than his contemporaries, or indeed some historians, comprehended. The Prime Minister was definitely not totally immature in his dealings with Roosevelt. But Churchill's insightful interpretation of the domestic workings of the American President therefore made Churchill's Indo-Chinese policy incoherence far less forgivable. The Prime Minister must have understood Roosevelt's ardent anti-imperialism, the Franco-phobia and the desire to overthrow the failings of the old world economic order. Churchill naturally assumed a large degree of equality between the bride and the groom within his marriage of convenience. Churchill believed that this was an Anglo-Saxon union based upon a common racial superiority and civilising mission, and he therefore supposed that the United States would wish to reciprocate his affections upon his terms. What Churchill failed to observe was that Roosevelt had his eyes upon the dowry of empire. Nevertheless, when the chips were down Churchill knew on which side his bread was buttered. The Prime Minister was willing, time and again, to sacrifice French Indo-China for the sake of his special relationship with Roosevelt. The President clearly held the upper hand. Churchill assumed that the Anglo-American connection had to be preserved at all costs. It was a dangerous gamble; international trusteeship for French Indo-China created a precedent for decolonisation that could result in Britain losing Hong Kong, India and other valuable territories at the whim of an American president and to the benefit of American economic interests.

Churchill's ability to be love struck by romantic visions of an Anglo-Saxon special relationship was not replicated by others in the British Government. Eden, for one, was not amused by either the machinations or the methods of the American President. If Churchill was guilty in his failure to address post-war issues, Eden emerged from the Indo-China debate with the reputation of a seer. A Foreign Office defence of French Indo-China was vitally important to prevent multiple imperial and foreign policy denouements. The Foreign Office naturally opposed Churchill's reluctance to address Indo-Chinese issues and Roosevelt's anti-imperialism. If the Foreign Office could have forced Churchill to take a more decisive and earlier stand against the President, then much of the political drift that resulted would have been avoided – but at what price? Churchill regarded the special relationship as indispensible.

Throughout the Second World War, the Foreign Office had maintained the consistent approach of France maintaining its hold on French Indo-China. This centred upon a Foreign Office desire to maintain France as a Great Power – a policy that served as a natural, if inferior, counterweight to Churchill's blind Anglo-Saxonism. After all, the logic of recent history had already proved that the future shape of Western Europe was of grave concern to Britain's national security. In addition, a strong imperial France was more likely to support Britain vis-à-vis the United States and Russia in the post-war global hierarchy. The prospect of Britain's continued representation – supported by France and the other colonial powers – at the top table of world affairs was a tantalising lure. Nevertheless not everyone within the British Government was unified behind the Foreign Office approach. These internal divisions demonstrated that tensions over colonial policy were not merely confined to disagreements over the future of Britain's own colonial territories.

Neither Churchill nor the Foreign Office was aided in the Indo-Chinese dispute by Mountbatten. Steeped in reverence for the British royal family, Mountbatten was Churchill's preferred choice for the command of SEAC. But Mountbatten's manipulation of Churchill, Brooke and Roosevelt in relation to his ambiguous Gentleman's Agreement with Chiang Kai-Shek further complicated the Indo-Chinese high policy debates in London and Washington and also strained local Allied operations in Southeast Asia.

At times the Foreign Office approach towards French Indo-China could be hopelessly optimistic. Yet the ruthless ability of Eden and others to pursue a unified approach – often in opposition to Churchill – with the COS, the Colonial Office and others revealed the importance of the Indo-Chinese debate to Britain's imperial future. Indeed the decision to involve the Dominion Governments on the debate concerning the future of the French territories just in case they sided with Roosevelt confirmed the depth of Foreign Office anxiety. But even this approach was fraught with difficulties for the Foreign Office. Britain's failures in the war in the Far East meant that Australia and New Zealand had begun to turn towards the United States for military protection and diplomatic leadership. The Pacific War Council – based in Washington – served as a useful tool to rally Australia, Canada, China, New Zealand and the Philippines towards Roosevelt's view that Britain should avoid making statements about the restoration of the French Empire.

The Foreign Office was certainly not aided in its approach to Anglo-American, colonial or post-war issues by Smuts. In the South African Prime Minister, Churchill found an enthusiastic ally. Smuts enjoyed his own unique relationship with Churchill. The two former military men mutually benefited from their natural bond and indulged in their respective camaraderie. Churchill needed little encouragement to develop his romantic affiliation with Roosevelt and Smuts openly advocated that Churchill needed to deepen his very special rapport with the American President against any domestic British opposition – notably the Foreign Office. Smuts was fully aware of Roosevelt's ardent anti-colonial agenda. But the South African Prime Minister believed that nothing should be allowed to detract from the Churchill–Roosevelt partnership. In his opinion this was Britain's most valuable asset. This was something that Churchill unsurprisingly wholeheartedly agreed with.

On occasion Churchill's rhetoric concerning colonial and post-war concerns could be just as confusing as others involved in this debate – for example Winant. The Prime Minister regularly sought to avoid any dangerous British commitments regarding not just the future of the British colonies but also the Dominions. Was this just evidence of Churchill's mid-Victorian language concerning the empire or a reaction to more recent events such as Canada's growing intimacy with the United States? In the light of Churchill's approach to macro-management issues and the future structure of the post-war world it was more probable that the Prime Minister just had not grasped how much had actually changed in the nature of Anglo-Dominion relations as a direct result of the war; a charge that directly paralleled his failure to keep abreast with the Indo-China debate.

Ultimately the Japanese *coup* in March 1945 and Roosevelt's death in April permitted Churchill the face-saving opportunity of aligning himself with Eden and the Foreign Office. Roosevelt clearly had it as one of his principle war aims to place French Indo-China into some form of international trusteeship. Had it not been for Roosevelt's death, then the resolution of the trusteeship debate would have been very different. This would have been fraught with difficulties for Britain's post-war imperial ambitions. A dangerous precedent for decolonisation would have been established.

Select Chronology

1941
August   Atlantic Conference (Atlantic Charter)
December–January   Washington Conference
December   Japanese attack Pearl Harbor

1942
June   Churchill visits Roosevelt at his private home at
                    Hyde Park
                    Washington Conference
October   Eleanor Roosevelt visits Britain
November   British War Cabinet accepts the principles of the
                    Four-Power Plan

1943
January   Casablanca Conference
                    Churchill and Roosevelt travel together to Marrakesh
March   Eden visits Washington
May   Washington Conference
July   Oliver Stanley's speech on colonial self-government
August   Churchill visits Roosevelt at Hyde Park
                    Quebec Conference
October–November   Moscow Conference
October   Mountbatten's Gentleman's Agreement with Chiang
                    Kai-Shek
November   Cairo Conference
                    Tehran Conference

1944
January   Wide-ranging discussion by Roosevelt and Halifax on
                    the future of French Indo-China and other colonial
                    possessions
                    Australia and New Zealand Conference to discuss
                    regional concerns
April   Dominions Prime Ministers Conference in London
August–September   Dumbarton Oaks Conference
September   Quebec Conference
                    Churchill visits Roosevelt at Hyde Park
October   Churchill, Eden and Mountbatten meet for discussions
                    in Cairo

1945
January–February   Malta Conference
February   Yalta Conference agrees the role of the United Nations
                    Trusteeship Council

	British aircraft shot down by American fighters over French Indo-China
March	Japanese *coup d'etat* in French Indo-China
	Brazzaville Declaration by the French Government
April–June	San Francisco Conference
April	Death of Roosevelt
June	United Nations Charter established at San Francisco
July–August	Potsdam Conference
July	Churchill loses the British general election
August–September	Cambodia and Vietnam declare independence from France
September	British liberation forces arrive in Vietnam and Cambodia

Select Personalia

Britain

Attlee. Clement Attlee. Lord President of the Council and Deputy Prime Minister 1943–45; Prime Minister 1945–51.

Bennett. John Sterndale Bennett. Head of Far Eastern Department, Foreign Office 1944–46.

Bevin. Ernest Bevin. Foreign Secretary 1945–51.

Brooke. General Sir Alan Brooke (Field Marshal 1944). Chief of the Imperial General Staff 1941–46.

Cadogan. Sir Alexander Cadogan. Permanent Under-Secretary of State, Foreign Office 1938–45.

Carton de Wiart. Lt.-General Sir Adrian Carton de Wiart. Churchill's personal representative to China.

Churchill. Winston Churchill. Prime Minister and Minister of Defence 1940–45.

Colville. John Colville. Assistant Private Secretary to Churchill 1940–41 and 1943–45.

Cooper. Duff Cooper. Ambassador to France 1944–47.

Cranborne. Lord Cranborne (Robert Gascoyne-Cecil). Secretary of State for the Dominions 1943–45.

Dening. Maberly Esler Dening. Chief Political Adviser to the Supreme Allied Commander of SEAC 1943–46.

Dill. Field Marshal Sir John Dill. Head of the British Joint Service Mission Washington 1941–44.

Dixon. Pierson Dixon. Principal Private Secretary to Eden 1943–45 and Bevin 1945–48.

Eden. Anthony Eden. Foreign Secretary 1940–45.

Gracey. Major-General Sir Douglas Gracey. Allied Liberation Force Commander southern Indo-China 1945–46.

Halifax. Lord Halifax (Edward Wood). Ambassador to US 1941–46.

Harvey. Sir Oliver Harvey. Assistant Under-Secretary, Foreign Office 1943–46.

Hollis. Major-General Leslie Hollis. War Cabinet Secretariat 1939–46.

Ismay. General Hastings Ismay. Chief of Staff to Churchill in his role as Minister of Defence 1940–45 and Deputy Secretary to the War Cabinet 1940–45.

Jacob. Brigadier Ian Jacob. Assistant Secretary to the War Cabinet 1939–46.

Killearn. Lord Killearn (Sir Miles Lampson). Ambassador to Egypt 1936–46.

Macmillan. Harold. Special Minister in North Africa 1942–45.

Moran. Lord Moran (Sir Charles Wilson). Churchill's personal doctor.

Morrison. Herbert Morrison. Home Secretary 1940–45.

Mountbatten. Admiral Lord Louis Mountbatten. Supreme Allied Commander of SEAC 1943–46.

Stanley. Colonel Oliver Stanley. Secretary of State for the Colonies 1942–45.

Wilson. Field Marshal Sir Henry (Jumbo) Wilson. Head of British Joint Service Mission, Washington 1944–47.

Wood. Sir Kingsley Wood. Chancellor of the Exchequer 1940–43.

Woolton. Lord Woolton (Frederick Marquis). Minister for Food 1940–43; Minister of Reconstruction 1943–45; Lord President of the Council 1945.

France

Alessandri. General Marcel Alessandri. Commander of the French retreat in Indo-China March 1945.

Baudet. Philippe Baudet. Chief of the Asia-Oceania Section of the Foreign Ministry.

Bidault. Georges Bidault. Foreign Minister 1944–46.

Blaizot. General Roger Blaizot. Head of the Military Mission to SEAC.

Bonnet. Henri Bonnet. Ambassador to the United States 1944–54.

Boucher de Crevecoeur. Lt.-Colonel Jean Boucher de Crevecoeur (later promoted to General). Commander of French troops seconded to SOE work in SEAC 1943–45.

de Gaulle. General Charles de Gaulle. Free French Leader London 1940–43; Head of the French Committee of National Liberation 1943; President of the French Provisional Government 1944–46.

Darlan. Admiral Jean-Francois Darlan. Vichy Vice President and Foreign Minister 1941–42.

Giraud. General Henri-Honore Giraud. Prisoner of War in Germany 1940–42; High Commissioner North Africa 1942–43; Commander in Chief Land and Air Forces 1942–44; Inspector-General of the Army 1944–45.

Massigli. René Massigli. Ambassador to Britain.

Pechkoff. General Zinovi Pechkoff. Head of de Gaulle's military mission to Chiang Kai-Shek.

Petain. Marshal Henri Philippe Petain. Head of Vichy France 1940–44.

United States

Chennault. Major-General Claire Chennault. Head of the American Air Force attached to China Theatre.

Connally. Thomas Connally. Chair of the Senate Foreign Relations Committee 1941–47.

Donovan. Major-General Bill Donovan. Head of the Office for Strategic Services 1942–45 (the forerunner of the Central Intelligence Agency).

Eisenhower. General Dwight Eisenhower. Supreme Allied Commander for North Africa (Operation Torch) 1942–43.

Harriman. William Averell Harriman. Personal diplomatic representative of President Roosevelt 1941–43; Ambassador to Russia 1943–46.

Hopkins. Harry Hopkins. Personal diplomatic representative of President Roosevelt and President Truman.

Hull. Cordell Hull. Secretary of State 1933–44.

Hurley. General Patrick Hurley. Ambassador to China 1944–45.

Ickes. Harold Ickes. Secretary of the Interior 1933–46.

Leahy. Admiral William Leahy. Chief of Staff to the Commander in Chief (Roosevelt and then Truman) 1942–49.

MacArthur. General Douglas MacArthur. Supreme Allied Commander Southwest Pacific.

Marshall. General George Marshall. Army Commander in Chief 1939–45.

Morgenthau. Henry Morgenthau. Secretary of the Treasury 1934–45.

Murphy. Robert Murphy. Presidential diplomatic envoy to North Africa.

Patti. Major Archimedes Patti. Head of the Office for Strategic Services Mission to Indo-China 1945.

Roosevelt. Franklin Delano Roosevelt. President 1933–45.

Roosevelt. Theodore Roosevelt. President 1901–09.

Stettinius. Edward Stettinius. Secretary of State 1944–45.

Stilwell. Lt.-General Joseph Stilwell. Commander in Chief of American forces in China and Chief of Staff to Chiang Kai-Shek 1942–44.

Stimson. Henry Stimson. Secretary of War 1940–45.

Taussig, Charles William Taussig. Presidential advisor on Caribbean affairs.

Truman. Harry Truman. Vice-President 1944–45; President 1945–52.

Wallace. Henry Wallace. Vice-President 1941–44.

Wedemeyer. Lt.-General Albert Wedemeyer. Deputy Chief of Staff SEAC 1944; Commander in Chief of American forces in China 1945–46.

Welles. Sumner Welles. Under-Secretary of State 1937–43.

Willkie. Wendell Willkie. Republican presidential candidate 1940.

Wilson. Woodrow Wilson. President 1913–21.

Winant. John Winant. Ambassador to Britain 1941–46.

Others

Chiang Kai-Shek. President of China 1928–49; President of Taiwan 1949–75.

Curtin. John Curtin. Prime Minister of Australia 1941–45.

Fraser. Peter Fraser. Prime Minister of New Zealand 1940–49.

Ho Chi Minh. Leader of the Vietminh; Leader of the Indo-Chinese Communist Party 1945–69; President of the Democratic Republic of Vietnam 1945–69; Prime Minister 1945–55.

King. William Mackenzie King. Prime Minister of Canada 1935–48.

Smuts. Field Marshal Jan Smuts. Prime Minister of South Africa 1939–48.

Son Ngoc Thanh. Pro-Japanese Cambodian Nationalist; Foreign Minister 1945; Prime Minister 1945.

Notes

Introduction

1. J. Charmley, *Churchill's Grand Alliance: The Anglo-American Special Relationship 1940–57*, London, 1995, p. 3.
2. H. Kissinger, *Diplomacy*, London, 1994, p. 395.
3. S. Tonnesson, *The Vietnamese Revolution of 1945: Roosevelt, Ho Chi Minh and De Gaulle in a World at War*, London, 1991, p. 63; W. R., Louis, *Imperialism at Bay: The United States and the Decolonisation of the British Empire 1941–5*, New York, 1978, p. 26, citing E. R. Stettinius Jr, *Roosevelt and the Russians: The Yalta Conference*, New York, 1949, p. 237.
4. Kissinger, *Diplomacy*, p. 395.
5. L. D. Epstein, *Britain: An Uneasy Ally*, Chicago, 1954, p. 209.
6. Louis, *Imperialism at Bay*, p. 14.
7. D. C. Watt, *Succeeding John Bull, America in Britain's Place, 1900–1975*, Cambridge, 1984, p. 195.
8. The Cadbury Research Library, Birmingham University, Papers of Anthony Eden (hereinafter AP), AP 20/11/13B, Roosevelt to Churchill, 31 December 1943.
9. J. M. Siracusa, 'The United States, Viet-Nam and the Cold War: A Reappraisal', *Journal of Southeast Asian Studies*, vol. 5, 1974, p. 85.
10. Ibid., p. 87; AP 20/10/184, Eden to Churchill, PM/43/184, 25 June 1943.
11. AP 20/10/314B, Paraphrase of State Department to Ambassador Winant, 8 October 1943.
12. AP 20/11/484, Eden to Churchill, PM/44/486, 2 July 1944.
13. C. Thorne, *Allies of a Kind: The United States, Britain and the War against Japan, 1941–1945*, London, 1979; Louis, *Imperialism at Bay*.

1 Churchill's Conundrum

1. R. S. Churchill, *Winston S. Churchill, Volume 2: Young Statesman 1901–1914*, London, 1967, p. 283.
2. Press Conference of President Roosevelt on the USS Quincy, 23 February 1945, A. B. Cole (Ed.), *Conflict in Indochina and International Repercussions: A Documentary History, 1945–1955*, New York, 1956, p. 48.
3. Charmley, *Churchill's Grand Alliance*, pp. 3–4.
4. Orders, 'Adjusting to a New Period in World History: Franklin Roosevelt and European Colonialism', in D. Ryan and V. Pungong (Eds), *The United States and Decolonization: Power and Freedom*, Basingstoke, 2000, pp. 4–5; Kissinger, *Diplomacy*, p. 34.
5. Charmley, *Churchill's Grand Alliance*, p. 5.

6. W. La Feber, 'The American View of Decolonization, 1776–1920: An Ironic Legacy', in Ryan and Pungong (Eds), *The United States and Decolonization*, p. 29; M. H. Hunt, 'Conclusions: the Decolonization Puzzle in US Policy – Promise versus Performance', in Ryan and Pungong (Eds), *The United States and Decolonization*, p. 212.

7. Hunt, Ibid., p. 211.

8. J. M. Burns, *Roosevelt: The Lion and The Fox*, New York, 1956, pp. 24–9.

9. Charmley, *Churchill's Grand Alliance*, pp. 4–5.

10. Burns, *Roosevelt: The Lion and The Fox*, pp. 47, 54, 57.

11. La Feber, 'The American View of Decolonization, 1776–1920: An Ironic Legacy', in Ryan and Pungong (Eds), *The United States and Decolonization*, p. 36.

12. Charmley, *Churchill's Grand Alliance*, p. 5.

13. Kissinger, *Diplomacy*, pp. 30, 52.

14. Lord Halifax, *Fulness of Days*, London, 1957, pp. 249, 253–4, 258, 260.

15. Thorne, *Allies Of A Kind*, p. 283; M. Viorst, *Hostile Allies: FDR and Charles De Gaulle*, New York, 1965, p. 191.

16. Charmley, *Churchill's Grand Alliance*, p. 13.

17. Burns, *Roosevelt: The Lion and The Fox*, pp. 373–4.

18. Eden, *The Memoirs of Anthony Eden, Earl of Avon: The Reckoning*, Boston, 1965, (second printing), p. 433.

19. Charmley, *Churchill's Grand Alliance*, p. 136.

20. Halifax, *Fulness of Days*, p. 261.

21. J. Lacouture, *De Gaulle: The Rebel: 1890–1944*, London, 1993, p. 333.

22. G. R. Hess, *The United States' Emergence as a Southeast Asian Power, 1940–1950*, New York, 1987, p. 56; Roosevelt to Churchill, R559, 12 June 1944, W. F. Kimball (Ed.), *Churchill and Roosevelt: The Complete Correspondence: Alliance Declining, 1944–1945*, Princeton, 1984, pp. 180–2.

23. AP 20/10/230A, 896 Circular to Washington, 14 June 1943.

24. Burns, *Roosevelt: The Lion and The Fox*, pp. 84, 380.

25. Halifax, *Fulness of Days*, p. 293.

26. E. Waugh, *Brideshead Revisited: The Sacred and Profane Memoirs of Captain Charles Ryder*, London, 2000, p. 283.

27. A. Roberts, *The Holy Fox: The Life of Lord Halifax*, London, 1997, p. 287.

28. Franklin D. Roosevelt Library, Hyde Park, New York (hereinafter FDRL), Welles Papers, Box 151, Atlantic Charter Folder, Memorandum of Conversation, 11 August 1941; Record of Conversation, 11 August 1941.

29. FDRL, Roosevelt Papers, President's Secretary's Files, Box 1, Atlantic Charter Folder, Welles to Roosevelt, 21 October 1941.

30. FDRL, Roosevelt Papers, President's Secretary's Files, Box 1, Atlantic Charter Folder, First British Draft, 10 August 1941.

31. FDRL, Roosevelt Papers, President's Secretary's Files, Box 1, Atlantic Charter Folder, For Delivery to the Press, 14 August 1941.

32. FDRL, Roosevelt Papers, The Republican National Committee Papers, Box 46, Atlantic Charter Folder, *Associated Press* release, 14 August 1941; *Daily Mail*, 14 August 1941; *International News*, 17 August 1941.

33. FDRL, Welles Papers, Box 151, Atlantic Charter Folder, Roosevelt to Congress, 21 August 1941.

34. C. Hull, *The Memoirs of Cordell Hull Volume 2*, London, 1948, p. 1485.

35. J. M. Lee and M. Petter, *The Colonial Office, War, and Development Policy: Organisation and the Planning of a Metropolitan Initiative 1939–1945*, London, 1982, p. 113.
36. FDRL, Roosevelt Papers, President's Secretary's File, Box 1, ABCD Folder, Message From HMS Duke of York, 18 December 1941.
37. W. S. Churchill, *The Second World War: Volume 3 The Grand Alliance*, London, 1950, p. 590.
38. Lord Moran, *Winston Churchill: The Struggle for Survival 1940–1965* (hereinafter *Moran Diary*) London, 1966, 14 January 1942, p. 22; 17 January 1942, p. 24.
39. AP 20/53/107, British Embassy Washington to Eden, 5 January 1942.
40. M. Gilbert, *Winston Spencer Churchill, Volume 7: The Road to Victory 1941–1945*, London, 1986, pp. 36, 43.
41. J. W. Wheeler-Bennett, *King George VI: His Life and Reign*, London, 1958, p. 535.
42. M. Gilbert, *Churchill: A life*, London, 1991, p. 715.
43. J. Harvey (Ed.), *The War Diaries of Oliver Harvey 1941–1945* (hereinafter *Harvey Diary*), London, 1978, 11 January 1942, p. 86; 18 July 1942, p. 141.
44. Eden, *The Reckoning*, p. 370.
45. D. Dilks (Ed.), *The Diaries of Sir Alexander Cadogan 1938–1945* (hereinafter *Cadogan Diary*), London, 1971, 4 January 1942, p. 428.
46. M. Gilbert, *Churchill and America*, London, 2006, pp. 252–3.
47. Roosevelt to Churchill, R106, 18 February 1942, Kimball (Ed.), *Churchill and Roosevelt: The Complete Correspondence: Alliance Emerging 1933–1942*, Princeton, 1984, pp. 362–4; *Cadogan Diary*, Editorial Note, 4 February 1942, pp. 431–2.
48. Churchill to Roosevelt, C30, 20 February 1942, Kimball (Ed.), *Churchill and Roosevelt: The Complete Correspondence: Alliance Emerging*, p. 364.
49. Gilbert, *Churchill and America*, pp. 256–7; *Moran Diary*, pp. 27–8, 31; Gilbert, *Churchill*, p. 719.
50. W. S. Churchill, *The Second World War: Volume 4 The Hinge of Fate*, London, 1951, p. 193; Roosevelt to Churchill, R172, 29 July 1942, Kimball (Ed.), *Churchill and Roosevelt: The Complete Correspondence: Alliance Emerging*, pp. 546–50.
51. W. F. Kimball, *The Juggler: Franklin Roosevelt as Wartime Statesman*, Princeton, 1991, p. 133.
52. Churchill, *The Second World War: Volume 4*, p. 126.
53. *Harvey Diary*, 18 July 1942, p. 141.
54. Danchev and D. Todman (Eds), *War Diaries 1939–1945: Field Marshal Lord Alan Brooke* (hereinafter *Brooke Diary*), London, 2001, 10 March 1942, pp. 237–8; 31 March 1942, p. 243; 15 April 1942, pp. 248–9; 26 May 1942, p. 272; pp. 268, 273.
55. Churchill, *The Second World War: Volume 4*, p. 387.
56. Lee and Petter, *The Colonial Office, War And Development Policy*, p. 121.
57. L. J. Butler, *Industrialisation and the British Colonial State: West Africa 1939–1951*, London, 1997, p. 104.
58. Kissinger, *Diplomacy*, p. 402.
59. Lee and Petter, *The Colonial Office, War And Development Policy*, p. 244.

60. Lord Ismay, *The Memoirs of General the Lord Ismay*, London, 1960, pp. 250–7; Gilbert, *Churchill*, pp. 722–4; Gilbert, *Churchill and America*, p. 259.
61. CO 825/35/4, f253, Minutes of the Colonial Office Committee on Post-War Problems, 2 April 1942, A. J. Stockwell (Ed.), *British Documents on the End of Empire, Series B, Volume 3: Malaya, Part1, The Malayan Union Experiment 1942–1948*, London, 1995, p. 7; Eden, *The Reckoning*, p. 401.
62. *Harvey Diary*, 7 July 1942, pp. 138–9; 9 July 1942, p. 139.
63. K. Sainsbury, *Churchill and Roosevelt at War: The War They Fought and the Peace They Hoped to Make*, London, 1994, p. 117.
64. *Brooke Diary*, 9 July 1942, p. 278.
65. *Harvey Diary*, 14 September 1942, p. 156.
66. Eden, *The Reckoning*, p. 394.
67. *Harvey Diary*, 15 October 1942, p. 168; 19 October 1942, p. 170.
68. Gilbert, *Winston Spencer Churchill, Volume 7*, pp. 240–1; *Harvey Diary*, 23 October 1942, p. 171.
69. Churchill, *The Second World War: Volume 4*, p. 504.
70. Wheeler-Bennett, *King George VI*, pp. 549–52.
71. *Harvey Diary*, 3 November 1942, pp. 175–6.
72. *Cadogan Diary*, 3 November, 1942, p. 488.
73. J. Charmley, *Churchill the End of Glory: A Political Biography*, Orlando, 1994, p. 514; Gilbert, *Churchill*, p. 734; Gilbert, *Winston Spencer Churchill, Volume 7*, pp. 254–5.
74. *Harvey Diary*, 16 November 1942, pp. 186–7.
75. Gilbert, *Winston Spencer Churchill, Volume 7*, p. 254.
76. *Harvey Diary*, 24 November 1942, p. 192.
77. *Cadogan Diary*, p. 488.
78. Churchill, *The Second World War: Volume 4*, p. 566; *Harvey Diary*, 14 November 1942, pp. 182–5; 1 December 1942, pp. 194–5; 7 December 1942, pp. 196–7; 12 December 1942, p. 199; 20 December 1942, pp. 201–2; 23 December 1942, pp. 202–3.
79. *Cadogan Diary*, 28 December, 1942, pp. 500–1.
80. Gilbert, *Winston Spencer Churchill, Volume 7*, p. 292.
81. *Harvey Diary*, 2 January 1943, p. 209; 7 January 1943, pp. 209–10.
82. The National Archives, Public Record Office, London (hereinafter TNA), CO 323/1858/23, Note by Sir A. Rumbold, FO, 14 January 1943.
83. TNA, CAB 122/812, Eden to Halifax, no. 8996, 29 December 1943.
84. Gilbert, *Winston Spencer Churchill, Volume 7*, pp. 304–5.
85. *Cadogan Diary*, 17 January 1943, p. 504.
86. *Moran Diary*, 22 January 1943, pp. 80–1; 24 January 1943, pp. 81–2.
87. H. Macmillan, *War Diaries* (hereinafter *Macmillan Diary*), London, 1984, 26 January 1943, pp. 6–11.
88. Sir J. Colville (Ed.), *The Fringes of Power: The Downing Street Diaries, 1939–1955* (hereinafter *Colville Diary*), London, 1985, pp. 752–3; Gilbert, *Winston Spencer Churchill, Volume 7*, pp. 308–9.
89. *Moran Diary*, 19 January 1943, pp. 79–80.
90. *Brooke Diary*, 20 January 1943, p. 304; p. 363.
91. Gilbert, *Winston Spencer Churchill, Volume 7*, pp. 309–10.
92. Kimball, *The Juggler*, p. 83.
93. Hess, *The United States' Emergence as a Southeast Asian Power*, pp. 71–2.

2   Churchill's Conceit

1. *Moran Diary*, 24 January 1943, pp. 81–3.
2. TNA, PREM 4/42/9, Attlee and Eden to Churchill, no. 314, 27 January 1943.
3. *Harvey Diary*, 28 January 1943, p. 215; 8 February 1943, pp. 217–18.
4. TNA, PREM 4/27/9, Halifax to Churchill, 5 February 1943.
5. TNA, CAB 119/50, Le Mesurier to Director of Plans Adm, Air, WO, 6 February 1943.
6. Hess, *The United States' Emergence as a Southeast Asian Power*, pp. 71–2.
7. L. C. Gardner, *Approaching Vietnam: From World War Two Through Dienbienphu*, London, 1988, p. 47.
8. W. C. Gibbons, *The U.S. Government and the Vietnam War Part 1: 1945–1960*, Princeton, 1986, p. 9.
9. TNA, CAB 65/33, WM (43) 30, 15 February 1943.
10. *Harvey Diary*, 13 February 1943, pp. 219–20; 25 February 1943, pp. 223–4.
11. TNA, FO 371/35917/F1589/877/61, *The Times*, 5 March 1943.
12. Louis, *Imperialism at Bay*, pp. 251–2.
13. Marquess of Linlithgow to Leo Amery, 8 March 1943, N. Mansergh (Ed.), *Constitutional Relations Between Britain and India: The Transfer of Power 1942–7: Volume 3: Reassertion of Authority, Gandhi's Fast and the Succession of the Viceroyalty 21 September 1942–12 June 1943*, London, 1971, pp. 772–6.
14. *Harvey Diary*, 11 March 1943, pp. 227–8; 29 March 1943, pp. 239–40.
15. Eden, *The Reckoning*, p. 430.
16. *Harvey Diary*, 13 March 1943, pp. 228–9; 16 March 1943, pp. 231–3; 28 March 1943, pp. 238–9.
17. Thorne, *Allies of a Kind*, p. 283, citing *Stimson Diary*, 28 March 1943.
18. Eden, *The Reckoning*, p. 433.
19. *Cadogan Diary*, 21 March 1943, p. 515.
20. TNA, FO 371/35917/F1851/877/G1, Conversations between Welles and Halifax, 25 March 1943.
21. TNA, PREM 4/42/9, Halifax to Churchill, no. 1470, T. 397/3, 28 March 1943.
22. Eden, *The Reckoning*, p. 440.
23. Churchill College Cambridge, Papers of the Rt Hon. Earl of Halifax (microfilm) (hereinafter Halifax), HLFX2, A4/410/4/15, Speech by Eden, 26 March 1943.
24. *Cadogan Diary*, 30 March 1943, p. 517.
25. Charmley, *Churchill the End of Glory*, p. 486.
26. Halifax, *Fulness of Days*, p. 257.
27. *Cadogan Diary*, 30 March 1943, p. 517.
28. TNA, CAB 65/38, WM (43) 53, Conclusions, 13 April 1943.
29. Thorne, *Allies of a Kind*, pp. 274, 277.
30. Halifax to Eden, 1 April 1943, R. D. Crockatt (Ed.), *British Documents on Foreign Affairs: Reports and Papers from the Foreign Office Confidential Print: Series C, North America, Part 3: Volume 3, April 1943–December 1943*, University Publications of America, 1999, pp. 8–13.
31. TNA, CAB 65/38, WM (43) 53, Conclusions, 13 April 1943.
32. AP 20/40/25, Cranborne to Eden, 26 April 1943.
33. TNA, FO 371/35927/F2116/1953/61, Paper by Wint, revised version, 19 May 1943.

34. *Harvey Diary*, 23 April 1943, pp. 248–9.
35. *Moran Diary*, p. 96.
36. *Harvey Diary*, 21 May 1943, pp. 259–60.
37. American-British luncheon meeting, 22 May 1943, British Embassy, *Foreign Relations of the United States: Diplomatic Papers: Department of State Publication* (hereinafter *FRUS*), *The Conferences at Washington and Quebec 1943*, Washington D.C., 1970, pp. 166–72; J. M. Blum (Ed.), *The Price of Vision: The Diary of Henry A. Wallace 1942–1946* (hereinafter *Wallace Diary*), Boston, 1973, 22 May 1943, pp. 201–2.
38. *Brooke Diary*, 12 May 1943, p. 402.
39. Roosevelt-Churchill luncheon meeting, 24 May 1943, White House, *FRUS, The Conferences at Washington and Quebec 1943*, pp. 188–9; *Wallace Diary*, 24 May 1943, pp. 207–12.
40. *Harvey Diary*, 25 May 1943, p. 261; 24 May 1943, pp. 260–1.
41. *Moran Diary*, 25 May 1943, p. 97; 28 May 1943, pp. 99, 103.
42. *Cadogan Diary*, 18 June 1943, p. 537.
43. *Harvey Diary*, 12 July 1943, p. 273; P. M. Dunn, *The First Vietnam War*, London, 1985, pp. 71–2.
44. Hess, *The United States' Emergence as a Southeast Asian Power*, p. 78; Louis, *Imperialism at Bay*, p. 277.
45. TNA, FO 371/35930/F4023/4023/61G, Minute by Hudson, 26 July 1943.
46. AP 20/10/184, Eden to Churchill, 26 June 1943.
47. AP 20/10/314B, Paraphrase of message from the State Department to Winant, 8 October 1943.
48. W. F. Kimball, 'Wheel Within a Wheel: Churchill, Roosevelt, and the Special Relationship', in R. Blake and W. R. Louis (Eds), *Churchill*, Oxford, 1993, p. 300.
49. *Harvey Diary*, 13 July 1943, pp. 273–4.
50. CO 323/1858/9, Memorandum by Carstairs 15 June 1943, S. R. Ashton and S. E. Stockwell (Eds), *British Documents on the End of Empire, Series A, Volume 1: Imperial Policy and Colonial Practice 1925–1945: Part 2: Economic Policy, Social Policies and Colonial Research,* London, 1996, pp. 157–65.
51. Stanley 13 July 1943, A. N. Porter and A. J. Stockwell (Eds), *British Imperial Policy and Decolonializisation, Volume 1, 1938–1951*, London, 1987, pp. 156–67.
52. TNA, DO 35/1620, Unidentified minute, 2 May 1946.
53. TNA, FO 371/35930/F4023/4023/G61, Minute by Bromley, 7 August 1943.
54. TNA, FO 371/35930/F4023/4023/G61, Minute by Clarke, 11 August 1943.
55. W. A. Harriman and E. Abel, *Special Envoy to Churchill and Stalin 1941–1946*, New York, 1975, p. 222.
56. Memorandum by Pavolosky, 10 August 1943, *FRUS, The Conferences at Washington and Quebec 1943*, pp. 681–2.
57. Thorne, *Allies of a Kind*, p. 274.
58. Gilbert, *Churchill: A Life*, p. 751.
59. TNA, FO 371/35921/F4646/1422/61, Minute by Butler, 21 August 1943.
60. *Cadogan Diary*, 22 August 1943, pp. 553–4.
61. TNA, CAB 122/1065, Note to Dwyer, 7 August 1943; Memorandum, COS (Q) 9 (Revise), 10 August 1943; Memorandum, COS (Q) 9 (Final), 15 August 1943.

62. TNA, CAB 122/1065, Quadrant 2nd Meeting, 23 August 1943.
63. Combined Chiefs of Staff, Roosevelt and Churchill Meeting, 23 August 1943, *FRUS, The Conferences at Washington and Quebec 1943*, p. 947.
64. *Brooke Diary*, 14 May 1943, pp. 403–4; 15 August 1943, p. 441.
65. TNA, DO 35/1731, Dominions Office to Australia, Canada, New Zealand and South Africa, 9 September 1943.
66. Harriman and Abel, *Special Envoy*, pp. 226–8.
67. Campbell to Eden, 16 September 1943, Crockatt (Ed.), *British Documents on Foreign Affairs: Reports and Papers from the Foreign Office Confidential Print: Series C, North America, Part 3: Volume 3*, pp. 210–11.
68. *Moran Diary*, 7 September 1943, p. 118.
69. Churchill to Roosevelt, 13 September 1943, *FRUS, The Conferences at Washington and Quebec 1943*, pp. 1336–7.
70. Gilbert, *Churchill and America*, pp. 287, 281.
71. *Harvey Diary*, 6 September 1943, pp. 290–1; 6 October 1943, pp. 304–5.
72. *Brooke Diary*, 23 August 1943, p. 447; 8 October 1943, p. 459.
73. Eden, *The Reckoning*, p. 470.
74. *Brooke Diary*, 13 September 1943, p. 452.
75. TNA DO 35/1618, Dening's Terms of Reference, 5 October 1943.
76. Southampton University Library, Papers of Admiral Lord Louis Mountbatten Earl of Burma (hereinafter MB), MB 1/C50/13, Mountbatten to Brooke, 3 February 1944.
77. P. Ziegler, *Mountbatten*, Glasgow, 1985, pp. 242–3.
78. TNA, CAB 122/1067, Mountbatten to COS, 837/SEACOS, 9 November 1943.
79. P. Ziegler (Ed.), *The Personal Diaries of Admiral, the Lord Louis Mountbatten, Supreme Commander Southeast Asia 1943–1946* (hereinafter *Mountbatten Diary*), London, 1988, 19 October 1943, pp. 16–17.
80. TNA, PREM 3/90/3, Mountbatten to Roosevelt, 23 October 1943; MB 1/C205, Roosevelt to Mountbatten, 8 November 1943; TNA, WO 203/5131, Mountbatten to Sommervell, SC5/602/S, 17 March 1945.
81. TNA, PREM 3/90/3, Mountbatten to Roosevelt, 23 October 1943.
82. TNA, PREM 3/90/3, Mountbatten to Churchill, 23 October 1943; MB 1/C50/2, Mountbatten to Brooke, 23 October 1943.
83. MB 1/C205, Roosevelt to Mountbatten, 8 November 1943.
84. TNA, CAB 122/1065, Memorandum by American Joint Chiefs of Staff, CCS 308/7, 24 November 1943; CAB 99/25 COS 5th Meeting, 26 November 1943.
85. TNA, WO 203/5068, Dill to India, COSSEA 6, 8 November 1943.
86. TNA, CAB 122/1065, Memorandum by American Joint Chiefs of Staff, CCS 308/7, 24 November 1943.
87. TNA, FO 371/41798/F4292/100/23, Mountbatten to COS, SEACOS 231, 14 September 1944.
88. TNA, CAB 99/25, Memorandum by Mountbatten, COS 11, 25 November 1943.
89. TNA, CAB 99/25, COS 22, 29 November 1943; COS 23, 29 November 1943; FO 371/41720/F4930/9/61G, Hollis to Churchill, 13 October 1944.
90. G. Bordinier (Ed.), *La Guerre D'Indochine 1945–54: Textes et Documents, Volume 1, Le Retour de la France en Indochine 1945–1946*, Vincennes, 1987, p. 19.

91. TNA, PREM 3/180/7, Campbell to Foreign Office, no. 4658, 14 October 1943.
92. Hess, *The United States' Emergence as a Southeast Asia Power*, p. 80.
93. TNA, PREM 3/180/7, Campbell to Foreign Office, no. 4658, 14 October 1943.
94. TNA, PREM 3/180/7, Minute by Churchill, 16 October 1943.
95. TNA, FO 371/35921/F5379/14222/61, Minute by Clarke, 18 October 1943.
96. TNA, PREM 3/180/7, Cadogan to Churchill, PM 43/343, 21 October 1943.
97. TNA, PREM 3/180/7, Minute by Churchill, 22 October 1943.
98. Wheeler-Bennett, *King George VI*, p. 594.
99. Hull, *The Memoirs of Cordell Hull Volume 2*, p. 1596.
100. B. Fall, *The Two Vietnams*, London, 1963, p. 52.
101. Thorne, *Allies of a Kind*, p. 274.
102. TNA, PREM 3/180/7, Cadogan to Churchill, 3 November 1943; M. Thomas, 'Free France, the British Government and the Future of French Indo-China 1940–45', *Journal of Southeast Asian Studies*, vol. 28, no. 1, 1997, pp. 148–9.
103. TNA, CAB 122/1065, Combined Chiefs of Staff Memorandum by the British COS, CCS 308/6, 8 November 1943, Annex II.
104. TNA, PREM 3/180/7, Minute by Churchill, 19 November 1943.
105. TNA, PREM 3/180/7, Minute by Churchill, 22 November 1943.
106. TNA, FO 371/35935/F6582/6582/61G, Brief for Cadogan, 22 November 1943.
107. TNA, PREM 3/180/7, Minute by Churchill, 17 December 1943.
108. T. Evans (Ed.), *The Killearn Diaries 1943–1946* (hereinafter *Killearn Diary*), London, 1972, 21 November 1943, pp. 261–2.
109. *Brooke Diary*, 21 November 1943, pp. 476–7.
110. W. S. Churchill, *The Second World War, Volume 5 Closing The Ring*, London, 1952, p. 289.
111. The Middle East Centre Archive, St Anthony's College Oxford, Papers of Sir Miles Lampson, Lord Killearn (hereinafter Lampson), Lampson 5/2, 23 November 1943, p. 252.
112. *Moran Diary*, 16–17 November 1943, pp. 126–9.
113. *Brooke Diary*, 22 November 1943, p. 477; 23 November 1943, pp. 477–80; 24 November 1943, p. 480.
114. Roosevelt dinner for Chiang Kai-Shek, Cairo, 23 November 1943, *FRUS, The Conferences at Cairo and Tehran 1943*, Washington D.C., 1961, p. 325.
115. *Killearn Diary*, 24 November 1943, pp. 263–4.
116. *Moran Diary*, 24 November 1943, p. 131.
117. *Killearn Diary*, 24 November 1943, pp. 263–4.
118. Lampson 5/2, 25 November 1943, p. 254; Eden, *The Reckoning*, p. 491.
119. *Brooke Diary*, 25 November 1943, p. 481.
120. Eden, *The Reckoning*, p. 493.
121. *Cadogan Diary*, pp. 577–8.
122. *Moran Diary*, 24 November 1943, p. 131.
123. Lampson 5/2, 26 November 1943, pp. 254–5.
124. A. Horne, *Macmillan: 1894–1956 Volume 1 of the Official Biography*, London, 1988, p. 207.

125. Sainsbury, *Churchill and Roosevelt at War*, pp. 170, 173–4.
126. *Mountbatten Diary*, 27 November 1943, p. 36.
127. TNA, FO 800/461/FE/46/9, Dening to Bevin, no. 46, 29 January 1946.
128. *Moran Diary*, 28 November 1943, pp. 133–4.
129. R. Edmunds, 'Churchill and Stalin', in Blake and Louis (Eds), *Churchill*, pp. 317–8.
130. Roosevelt and Stalin exchange views on France and Indo-China, Tehran Conference, 28 November 1943, A. W. Cameron (Ed.), *Viet-Nam Crisis, A Documentary History, Volume 1, 1940–1956*, New York, 1971, pp. 10–11.
131. D. C. Watt, *Succeeding John Bull, America in Britain's Place, 1900–1975*, Cambridge, 1984, p. 199.
132. Harriman and Abel, *Special Envoy*, pp. 265–6.
133. *Moran Diary*, 29 November 1943, pp. 136–41; *Cadogan Diary*, p. 582.
134. TNA, PREM 3/178/2, Attlee to Churchill, no. 1050, 30 November 1943.
135. TNA, PREM 3/178/2, Churchill to Attlee, no. 554, 1 December 1943.
136. *Brooke Diary*, 30 November 1943, pp. 486–7; *Moran Diary*, 30 November 1943, pp. 141–4.
137. *Macmillan Diary*, 5 December 1943, pp. 317–9.
138. *Moran Diary*, 11 December–27 December 1943, pp. 148–56; Gilbert, *Churchill: A Life*, p. 763.
139. TNA, CAB 65/40, WM (43) 169, Conclusions, 13 December 1943; Watt, *Succeeding John Bull*, p. 199.
140. TNA, CO 323/1858/23, Benson to Eastwood, 6 December 1943.
141. Declaration of the French Committee of National Liberation, 8 December 1943, Cameron (Ed.), *Vietnam Crisis, A Documentary History, Volume 1*, pp. 11–12.
142. Eden, *The Reckoning*, p. 441.
143. TNA, PREM 3/178/2, Eden to Churchill, no. 699, 20 December 1943.
144. TNA, PREM 3/178/2, Churchill to Eden, no. 769, 21 December 1943.
145. TNA, PREM 3/178/2, Eden to Churchill, no. 786, 24 December 1943.
146. TNA, PREM 3/178/2, Minute by Churchill, 25 December 1943; CAB 122/812, Eden to Halifax, 29 December 1943.
147. TNA, FO 371/35930/F6441/4023/G61, Clarke to Peterson, 17 December 1943.
148. TNA, FO 371/35935/F6582/6582/G61, Brief for Cadogan, 22 November 1943.
149. TNA, CAB 122/812, Halifax to FO, 3 January 1944.
150. TNA, FO 371/35921/F6656/1422/61, Minute by Cavendish Bentinck, 22 December 1943.
151. TNA, FO 371/35921/F6656/1422/61, Minute by Clarke, 21 December 1943.
152. TNA, FO 371/35930/F6808/4023/G61, Minute by Eden, 26 December 1943; FO 371/35921/F6656/1422/61, Minute by Butler, 21 December 1943.
153. TNA, FO 371/35930/F4461/4023/61G, Minute by Hudson, 27 December 1943.
154. TNA, FO 660/44, Duncannon to Reilly, 9 December 1943.
155. AP 20/11/13B, Roosevelt to Churchill, 31 December 1943.
156. *Macmillan Diary*, 23 December 1943, pp. 334–5; 25 December 1943, pp. 337–9.

3   Churchill's Isolation

1. *Brooke Diary*, 1 January 1944, p. 509.
2. Halifax, HLFX2, A4/410/4/16, Cadogan to Halifax, 10 January 1944.
3. Ziegler, *Mountbatten*, pp. 242–3, 284–5.
4. TNA, WO 203/4414, FO to SAC, no. 1302, 8 January 1944.
5. TNA, FO 371/41723/F478/66/10, Record of the French Administration in Indo-China, 8 January 1944.
6. G. Smith, *American Diplomacy During The Second World War 1941–1945*, New York, 1965, p. 92.
7. M. Jacobson, 'Winston Churchill and the Third Front', *Journal of Strategic Studies*, vol. 14, no. 3, September 1991, p. 349.
8. CAB 98/41, Stanley to Cabinet, CMB (44) 3, 14 January 1944, Stockwell (Ed.), *British Documents on the End of Empire, Series B, Volume 3: Malaya: Part1: The Malayan Union Experiment 1942–1948*, pp. 64–70.
9. CO 852/587/2, Memorandum by the Colonial Office, no. 1, CEAC (44) 14, 13 February 1944, Ashton and Stockwell (Eds), *British Documents on the End of Empire, Series A, Volume 1: Imperial Policy and Colonial Practice 1925–1945: Part 2: Economic Policy, Social Policies and Colonial Research*, pp. 182–4.
10. CO 852/588/111, Memorandum by Stanley, no. 10, WP (44) 643, 15 November 1944, Ashton and Stockwell (Eds), *British Documents on the End of Empire, Series A, Volume 1: Imperial Policy and Colonial Practice 1925–1945: Part 2: Economic Policy, Social Policies and Colonial Research*, pp. 203–5.
11. TNA, PREM 3/178/2, Eden to Churchill, no. 1312, 11 January 1944.
12. TNA, PREM 3/178/2, Churchill to Eden, no. 1255, 12 January 1944.
13. Hess, *The United States' Emergence as a Southeast Asian Power*, pp. 79, 86, 99–101, 105, 126–7.
14. TNA, CAB 122/812, Halifax to Foreign Office, 3 January 1944; PREM 3/178/2, Halifax to FO, no. 258, 18 January 1944.
15. TNA, FO 371/41723/F980/66/61G, Minute by Cadogan, 2 February 1944.
16. TNA, FO 371/41723/F980/66/61G, Minute by Eden, undated.
17. TNA, FO 371/40369/W376/15/E74, Faller for Hood to Taylor, 20 January 1944.
18. TNA, PREM 3/160/7, COS (44) 48th Meeting (0), 14 February 1944.
19. TNA, WO 203/444, Foreign Office to Supreme Allied Commander, no. 1302, 8 January 1944.
20. TNA, PREM 3/160/7, Dening to Foreign Office, 17 February 1944.
21. AP 20/11/44A, Churchill to Mountbatten, 15 February 1944; 20/11/74A, Churchill to Roosevelt, 15 February 1944.
22. Roosevelt to Hull, 24 January 1944, Cameron (Ed.), *Viet-Nam Crisis, A Documentary History, Volume 1*, p. 13.
23. F. E. Pollock and W. R. Kimball, 'In Search of Monsters to Destroy: Roosevelt and Colonialism', in Kimball, *The Juggler*, pp. 144–5.
24. Louis, *Imperialism at Bay*, pp. 28, 43.
25. TNA, DO 35/1214, WR227/8/1, Australia and New Zealand to Britain, 25 January 1944.
26. TNA, DO 35/1214, WR227/11, Speech by Fraser, 17 January 1944.
27. TNA, DO 35/1912, Boyd Shannon to Bottomley, 15 October 1946.

28. TNA, DO 35/1214, WR227/8/1, Australia and New Zealand to Britain, 25 January 1944.

29. Roberts, *The Holy Fox*, pp. 294–5.

30. Halifax, HLFX2, A4/410/4/15, Eden to Halifax, 10 February 1944.

31. Halifax, HLFX2, A4/410/4/19, Cranborne to Halifax, 9 February 1944.

32. L. Neal, *The Washington Ambassadorship of Lord Halifax 1941–1946*, MLitt thesis, Oxford, 1985, p. 118.

33. *The Pentagon Papers, The Defense Department History of United States Decision Making on Vietnam*, Volume 1, Gravel Edition, Boston, 1971, p. 11.

34. House of Commons Statement by Churchill, 22 February 1944, *Hansard House of Commons Parliamentary Debates*, Volume 397, Column 700.

35. TNA, CAB 81/45, Post-Hostilities Planning Sub-Committee, PHP (44) 2 (0) Final, 22 January 1944.

36. TNA, CAB 66/47, Memorandum by Eden, WP (44) 111, 16 February 1944.

37. TNA, PREM 3/178/2, WM (44) 25th, Conclusions, 24 February 1944; CAB 65/41, WM (44) 25th, Conclusions, 24 February 1944.

38. AP 20/12/116, Churchill to Eden and Cranborne, M. 266/4, 11 March 1944.

39. TNA, PREM 3/178/2, Cranborne to Churchill, 31 March 1944.

40. TNA, PREM 3/178/2, Minute by Churchill, 1 April 1944.

41. TNA, FO 371/41719/F1911/9/61, Cabinet to Clarke, 19 April 1944; Minute by Clarke, 1 May 1944; Minute by Allen, 2 May 1944.

42. TNA, PREM 4/31/4, Memorandum by Cranborne, WP (44) 211, 18 April 1944.

43. TNA, FO 371/41720/F4348/9/61G, Memorandum by Eden, 10 September 1944; Thorne, *Allies of a Kind*, p. 469.

44. AP 20/12/416, Churchill to Eden, M. 886/4, 19 July 1944.

45. Louis, *Imperialism at Bay*, p. 36.

46. FO 461/3, AN 1538/16/45, Memorandum: 'British Foreign Policy Towards the United States', 21 March 1944, R. D. Crockatt (Ed.), *British Documents on Foreign Affairs: Reports and Papers from the Foreign Office Confidential Print: Series C, North America, Part 3: Volume 4, January 1944–December 1944*, University Publications of America, 1999, pp. 137–9.

47. FO 461/3, AN 1346/325/45, Halifax to Eden, no. 316, 24 March 1944, Crockatt (Ed.), *British Documents on Foreign Affairs: Reports and Papers from the Foreign Office Confidential Print: Series C, North America, Part 3: Volume 4, January 1944–December 1944*, pp. 177–9.

48. FO 461/3, AN 1577/16/45, British Embassy in Washington to the Foreign Office, 1 May 1944, Crockatt (Ed.), *British Documents on Foreign Affairs: Reports and Papers from the Foreign Office Confidential Print: Series C, North America, Part 3: Volume 4, January 1944–December 1944*, pp. 199–252.

49. *Colville Diary*, 28 April 1944, p. 486; 29 April 1944, p. 486; 1 May 1944, p. 487.

50. *Brooke Diary*, 9 May 1944, p. 545.

51. *Colville Diary*, 13 May 1944, p. 489.

52. TNA, PREM 3/180/7, Mountbatten to COS, SEACOS 136, 13 April 1944.

53. TNA, PREM 3/180/7, Hollis to Churchill, 23 April 1944.

54. TNA, PREM 3/180/7, Minute by Churchill, 4 May 1944.

55. TNA, CAB 120/708, Ismay to Peterson, 6 May 1944.

56. TNA, FO 371/41723/F2223/66/61G, Minute by Cadogan, 12 May 1944.

57. TNA, PREM 3/180/7, Selborne to Churchill and Eden, 12 May 1944.
58. TNA, PREM 3/180/7, Eden to Churchill, PM. 44/349, 18 May 1944.
59. TNA, PREM 3/180/7, Churchill to Eden, M. 580/4, 21 May 1944; AP 20/12/116, Churchill to Eden and Cranborne, M. 266/4, 11 March 1944.
60. *Harvey Diary*, 31 May 1944, p. 341.
61. *Cadogan Diary*, 5 June 1944, pp. 634–5; 9 May 1944, p. 627.
62. TNA, CAB 81/45, Post-Hostilities Planning Sub-Committee, PHP (44) 4 (0) Final, 26 April 1944.
63. TNA, CAB 120/708, Mountbatten to COS, 1 June 1944.
64. TNA, PREM 3/180/7, Minute by Churchill, 2 June 1944.
65. TNA, CAB 120/708, Hollis to Churchill, 2 June 1944.
66. TNA, FO 371/41719/F2703/9/61, Draft Minute by Eden, 6 June 1944.
67. TNA, PREM 3/180/7, Churchill to Hollis, D. 190/4, 11 June 1944.
68. TNA, CAB 120/708, Hollis to Churchill, 12 June 1944; PREM 3/180/7, COS to Mountbatten, COSSEA 113, 12 June 1944.
69. AP 20/12/744, Bracken to Eden, 9 June 1944.
70. AP 20/12/416, Churchill to Eden, M. 886/4, 19 July 1944.
71. Roosevelt to Churchill, no. 559, 12 June 1944, Kimball (Ed.), *Churchill and Roosevelt: The Complete Correspondence: Alliance Declining, 1944–1945*, pp. 180–1.
72. TNA, CAB 122/812, Halifax to Foreign Office, no. 3475, 27 June 1944.
73. AP 20/41/26, Dixon to Eden, 14 August 1944.
74. Eden, *The Reckoning*, p. 528; AP 20/12/744, Bracken to Eden, 9 June 1944.
75. *Cadogan Diary*, 7 July 1944, pp. 645–6.
76. AP 20/12/47, Churchill to Eden, M. 887/4, 20 July 1944.
77. *Harvey Diary*, 15 July 1944, pp. 346–8.
78. *Macmillan Diary*, 5 June 1944, p. 455; 21 June 1944, pp, 470–1; Eden, *The Reckoning*, pp. 515, 519–20, 526.
79. *Cadogan Diary*, 23 July 1944, p. 650; 3 August 1944, pp. 653–4.
80. *Brooke Diary*, 10 July 1944, p. 568; 17 July 1944, p. 570; 26 July 1944, pp. 574–5.
81. *Moran Diary*, 4 August 1944, p. 162; 20 August 1944, p. 171.
82. G. Rosie, *The British in Vietnam*, London, 1970, p. 33.
83. J. J. Norwich (Ed.), *The Duff Cooper Diaries 1915–1951* (hereinafter *Cooper Diary*), London, 2005, 12 July 1944, p. 315.
84. TNA, FO 371/41724/F3020/66/61G, Untitled, 22 June 1944.
85. TNA, FO 371/41724/F3020/66/61G, Minute by Cadogan, 27 June 1944; AP 20/11/484, Eden to Churchill, PM/44/486, 2 July 1944.
86. TNA, PREM 3/180/7, War Cabinet COS Committee, COS (44) 668 (0), 28 July 1944.
87. TNA, HS 1/321, Memorandum by Force 136, 20 June 1944; CAB 120/708, Ismay to Churchill, COS 1340/4, 2 August 1944; PREM 3/180/7, Minute by Churchill, 3 August 1944.
88. TNA, FO 371/41720/F4930/9/61G, Hollis to Churchill, 13 October 1944.
89. TNA, WO 193/195, COS to Joint Service Mission, COS (W) 228, 4 August 1944.
90. TNA, WO 193/195, War Office to Cabinet, no. 7532, 25 August 1944.
91. TNA, FO 371/41719/F3948/9/61, Sterndale Bennett to Hollis, 19 August 1944.

92. TNA, FO 371/41720/F4119/9/61, Minute by Foulds, 6 September 1944.
93. TNA, WO 193/195, Joint Service Mission to COS, JSM 227, 30 August 1944.
94. TNA, PREM 3/180/7, Halifax to Foreign Office, no. 4685, 30 August 1944; Joint Service Mission to AMSSO, JSM 228, 31 August 1944; Roosevelt to Hull, 28 August 1944, *FRUS, The Conference at Quebec 1944*, Washington D.C., 1972, pp. 251–2.
95. P. Clarke, *The Last Thousand Days of the British Empire: Churchill, Roosevelt and the Birth of the Pax Americana*, New York, 2008, p. 47.
96. TNA, FO 371/41724/F3677/66/61G, Minute by Foulds, 9 August 1944.
97. TNA, FO 371/41719/F3948/9/6, Mountbatten to Eden, 16 August 1944.
98. TNA, CAB 65/43, WM (44) 106th, Conclusions, 14 August 1944; PREM 3/178/2, WM (44) 106th, Conclusions, 14 August 1944.
99. TNA, FO 371/41719/F4028/9/61, Meeting between Eden and Massigli, 24 August 1944; FO 371/41720/F4348/9/61G, Memorandum by Eden, 10 September 1944.
100. TNA, FO 371/ 41719/F4018/9/61, Foreign Office to Dening, no.166, 4 September 1944.
101. *Brooke Diary*, 8 September 1944, p. 589; 9 September 1944, p. 590; 10 September 1944, p. 590.
102. *Colville Diary*, 12 September 1944, p. 513.
103. TNA, PREM 3/180/7, Colville, Defence Office Aide Memoire, 12 September 1944.
104. TNA, PREM 3/180/7, Colville to Lawford, 26 September 1944; FO 371/41720/F4681/9/61G, Sterndale Bennett to Churchill, 7 October 1944.
105. TNA, PREM 3/180/7, Lawford to Colville, undated; Gilbert, *Winston Spencer Churchill, Volume 7*, pp. 964–70.
106. D. R. Drachman, *United States Policy Towards Vietnam 1940–45*, New Jersey, 1970, p. 51.
107. TNA, FO 371/41720/F4348/9/61G, Memorandum by Eden, 19 September 1944.
108. TNA, FO 371/41724/F4140/66/61G, Minute by Foulds, 12 September 1944.
109. TNA, FO 371/41720/F4348/9/61, Minute by Eden, 22 September 1944.
110. TNA, CAB 120/708, Mountbatten to COS, SEACOS no. 231, 14 September 1944; WO 193/195, Dening to Foreign Office, no. 134, 6 September 1944.
111. TNA, CAB 120/708, Minute by Churchill, 16 September 1944; COS to Vice-COS, no. 206, 16 September 1944.
112. TNA, CAB 122/1067, COS (44) 336th Meeting (0), 12 October 1944.
113. TNA, FO 371/41720/F4495/9/61G, Dening to Foreign Office, no. 165, 30 September 1944.
114. TNA, FO 371/41720/F4495/9/61G, Minute by Eden, undated.
115. TNA, WO 203/5068, Mountbatten to Eden, SC4/1579/F, 2 October 1944; FO 371/41719/F3948/9/61, Mountbatten to Eden, 16 August 1944; MB 1/C96, Eden to Mountbatten, 5 May 1944.
116. Thomas, 'Free France, the British Government and the Future of French Indo-China 1940–45', p. 153.
117. TNA, FO 371/41720/F4681/9/61G, Sterndale Bennett to Churchill, 7 October 1944; FO 371/41720/F4495/9/61G, Foreign Office to Paris, no. 211, 8 October 1944.

118. TNA, FO 371/41720/F4681/9/61G, Minute by Eden, 8 October 1944.
119. TNA, WO 193/195, COS (44) 345th Meeting (0), 23 October 1944.
120. AP 20/12/486, Churchill to Eden, M. (Tof1) 4/4, 11 October 1944.
121. TNA, PREM 3/180/7, Sterndale Bennett to Dixon, no. 3688, 14 October 1944.
122. TNA, FO 371/41720/F4930/9/61G, Hollis to Churchill, 13 October 1944.
123. TNA, FO 371/41720/F4930/9/61, Eden to Churchill, 20 October 1944.
124. TNA, FO 371/41721/F5303/9/61, Minute by Sterndale Bennett, 4 November 1944.
125. TNA, PREM 3/180/7, Note by Martin, 20 October 1944; *Mountbatten Diary*, 20 October 1944, pp. 142–4.
126. TNA, WO 203/5068, Supreme Allied Commander 18th Meeting (0), 25 October 1944.
127. TNA, PREM 3/180/7, Churchill to Ismay, 20 October 1944.
128. TNA, PREM 3/180/7, Ismay to Churchill, 20 October 1944.
129. TNA, PREM 3/180/7, Eden to Churchill, 20 October 1944; CAB 120/708, Cabinet to Dening, Hearty 256, 21 October 1944; PREM 3/180/7, Churchill to Eden, M. (Tol) 16/4, 21 October 1944.
130. TNA, FO 371/41724/F5016/66/61G, Minute by Foulds, 30 October 1944.
131. TNA, PREM 3/180/7, Memorandum by American Joint Chiefs of Staff, CCS 708, 6 October 1944, Enclosure A, Fenard to Washington to Commander in Chief American Fleet, no. 389, 19 September 1944, Appendix, 19 September 1944.
132. TNA, PREM 3/180/7, Colville to Mottershead, 20 December 1944.
133. TNA, PREM 3/180/7, First Sea Lord to Churchill, 22 December 1944.
134. TNA, PREM 3/180/7, Minute by Churchill, no. 1251/4, 31 December 1944.
135. TNA, CAB 65/49, WM (45) 7th, Conclusions, 22 January 1945; Tonnesson, *The Vietnamese Revolution of 1945*, p. 206.
136. TNA, HW 1/3314, Spanish Embassy in Washington to Ministry of Foreign Affairs Madrid, no. 138127, 8 November 1944.
137. TNA, CAB 79/89, COS (44) 62 Meeting, 25 June 1944; Ziegler, *Mountbatten*, pp. 242–3, 284–5.
138. TNA, FO 371/41799/F330/100/23, Sterndale Bennett to Lawford, no. 466, 11 November 1944.
139. TNA, CAB 122/1066, Mountbatten to COS, SEACOS 247, 27 October 1944.
140. TNA, FO 371/41719/F4036/9/61, Joint Service Mission to COS, JSM 227, 30 August 1944.
141. *Brooke Diary*, 31 May 1944, p. 552; 8 November 1944, p. 619; 16 November 1944, p. 626; 22 November 1944, p. 627; 7 December 1944, p. 633; Gilbert, *Winston Spencer Churchill, Volume 7*, p. 951.
142. TNA, FO 371/41721/F5303/9/61, Minute by Sterndale Bennett, 4 November 1944.
143. TNA, FO 371/41721/F5303/9/61, Minute by Eden, 8 November 1944.
144. *Harvey Diary*, 11 November 1944, pp. 364–6.
145. TNA, CAB 120/708, War Cabinet COS Committee, COS (44) 968 (0), 13 November 1944; Annex, Draft, Price to Halifax, 13 November 1944.
146. *The Pentagon Papers, The Defense Department History of United States Decision Making on Vietnam*, Volume 1, p. 11.

147. Hess, *The United States' Emergence as a Southeast Asian Power*, p. 128.
148. J. Sbrega, *Anglo American Relations and Colonialism in East Asia 1941–5*, London, 1983, p. 90.
149. Thorne, *Allies of a Kind*, p. 592.
150. Louis, *Imperialism at Bay*, p. 425.
151. Kissinger, *Diplomacy*, p. 371.
152. Hess, *The United States' Emergence as a Southeast Asian Power*, p. 128.
153. TNA, PREM 4/31/4, Memorandum by Stanley, APW (44) 124, 7 December 1944.
154. *Cadogan Diary*, 7 December 1944, p. 685.
155. *Brooke Diary*, 12 December 1944, pp. 634–5; 13 December 1944, p. 635.
156. PREM 4/31/4, Memorandum by Attlee, WP (44) 738, 16 December 1944, S. R. Ashton and S. E. Stockwell (Eds), *British Documents on the End of Empire, Series A, Volume 1: Imperial Policy and Colonial Practice 1925–1945: Part 1: Metropolitan Reorganisation, Defence and International Relations, Political Change and Constitutional Reform*, London, 1996, pp. 198–215.
157. *Cadogan Diary*, 20 December 1944, pp. 688–9; *Colville Diary*, 25 November 1944, p. 528; 30 November 1944, pp. 529–30, 21 December 1944, p. 537.
158. AP 20/12/718, Churchill to Eden, M. 1257/4, 31 December 1944.
159. PREM 4/31/4, Eden to Churchill, PM/45/11, 8 January 1945, Ashton and Stockwell (Eds), *British Documents on the End of Empire, Series A, Volume 1: Imperial Policy and Colonial Practice 1925–1945: Part 1: Metropolitan Reorganisation, Defence and International Relations, Political Change and Constitutional Reform*, pp. 215–18.
160. PREM 4/31/4, Churchill to Martin, 10 January 1945, Ashton and Stockwell (Eds), Ibid.
161. PREM 4/31/4, Martin to Churchill, 10 January 1945, Ashton and Stockwell (Eds), Ibid.
162. PREM 4/31/4, Eden to Churchill, PM/45/51, 24 January 1945, Ashton and Stockwell (Eds), Ibid.
163. TNA, WO 203/5561B, Dening to Foreign Office, no. 35, 19 January 1945.
164. TNA, FO 371/41721/F6155/9/61, Halifax to Foreign Office, no. 6888, 28 December 1944.
165. TNA, CAB 80/91, Memorandum by COS Committee, COS (45) 64 (0), 21 January 1945, Annex 2, Halifax to Foreign Office, no. 32, 2 January 1945.
166. TNA, FO 371/46304/F85/11/61/G, Minute by Foulds, 4 January 1945.
167. TNA, FO 371/46325/F234/127/61, Minute by Scott, 13 January 1945; Minute by Thyme Henderson 14 January 1945.
168. TNA, CAB 80/91, Memorandum by COS Committee, COS (45) 64 (0), 21 January 1945, Annex 3, Halifax to Foreign Office, no. 168, 9 January 1945.
169. TNA, CAB 80/91, COS (45) 64 (0), Memorandum by COS Committee, 21 January 1945, Annex 4, Dening to FO, no.14, 6 January 1945; CAB 121/741, Memorandum by COS Committee, COS (45) 64 (0), 21 January 1945, Annex 3, Halifax to Foreign Office, no. 168, 9 January 1945.
170. TNA, CAB 121/741, Memorandum by COS Committee, COS (45) 64 (0), 21 January 1945; COS (45) 27th Meeting, 25 January 1945; Eden to Hollis, undated.

171. TNA, CAB 80/91, Memorandum by COS Committee, COS (45) 64 (0), 21 January 1945, Annex 3, Halifax to Foreign Office, no. 168, 9 January 1945.
172. TNA, CAB 80/91, Memorandum by COS Committee, COS (45) 96 (0), 4 February 1945, Annex, Dening to Foreign Office, no. 44, 29 January 1945.
173. TNA, CAB 80/91, Memorandum by COS Committee, COS (45) 96 (0), 4 February 1945.
174. Roosevelt to Stettinius, 1 January 1945, Cameron (Ed.), *Viet–Nam Crisis, A Documentary History, Volume 1*, pp. 18–19.
175. Hess, *The United States' Emergence as a Southeast Asian Power*, p. 133.
176. Thorne, *Allies of a Kind*, p. 1.

4   Churchill's Realignment

1. Gilbert, *Winston Spencer Churchill, Volume 7*, p. 1140.
2. TNA, PREM 3/185/4, Eden to Churchill, PM/45/32, 16 January 1945.
3. Thomas, 'Free France, the British Government and the Future of French Indo-China 1940–45', p. 155.
4. TNA, PREM 3/185/4, Churchill to Eden, 19 January 1945.
5. TNA, PREM 3/185/4, Eden to Churchill, PM/45/50, 23 January 1945; Churchill to Eden, M 113/5, 25 January 1945.
6. *Harvey Diary*, 18 January 1945, p. 374; 24 January 1945, p. 374.
7. Churchill College Cambridge, Papers of Duff Cooper, Viscount Norwich (hereinafter DUFC), DUFC 4/5, Cooper to Cadogan, 29 January 1945.
8. TNA, WO 193/195, Dening to Foreign Office, no. 32, 16 January 1945.
9. TNA, CAB 121/741, Dening to Bennett, no. 1339, 2 February 1945.
10. TNA, FO 371/46304/F956/11/G61, Sterndale Bennett to Garrett, 17 February 1945.
11. Gilbert, *Churchill and America*, p. 325.
12. Eden, *The Reckoning*, pp. 590, 592.
13. *Moran Diary*, 3 February 1945, pp. 218–9; Eden, *The Reckoning*, p. 593; *Cadogan Diary*, 7 February 1945, p. 705; 20 February 1945, p. 717.
14. Sainsbury, *Churchill and Roosevelt at War*, p. 15.
15. Eden, *The Reckoning*, p. 593.
16. Louis, *Imperialism at Bay*, pp. 457–60; TNA, PREM 3/178/3, Churchill to Eden, M (Arg) 9/5, 13 February 1945.
17. Eden, *The Reckoning*, pp. 227–8; *Moran Diary*, 9 February 1945, pp. 227–8.
18. TNA, PREM 4/31/4, Churchill to Attlee, M 190/5, 10 March 1944.
19. Sainsbury, *Churchill and Roosevelt at War*, pp. 123–4.
20. J. Sbrega, 'The Anti-Colonial Policies of Franklin D. Roosevelt: A Reappraisal', *Political Science Quarterly*, vol. 101, no. 1, 1986, p. 77.
21. Tonnesson, *The Vietnamese Revolution of 1945*, p. 211; Hess, *The United States' Emergence as a Southeast Asian Power*, pp. 135–6.
22. Memorandum, 9 February 1945, *FRUS: The Conferences at Malta and Yalta 1945*, Washington D.C., 1955, p. 858; Report by the Foreign Ministers, 9 February 1945, pp. 858–60.
23. Louis, *Imperialism at Bay*, pp. 457–60; TNA, PREM 3/178/3, Churchill to Eden, M (Arg) 9/5, 13 February 1945.

24. TNA, FO 371/46304/F986/11/G61, Note by Dixon, 15 February 1945.
25. M. Thomas, 'Silent Partners: SOE's French Indo-China Section 1943–1945', *Modern Asian Studies*, vol. 34, no. 4, 2000, p. 944.
26. *Moran Diary*, 4 February 1945, pp. 222–3.
27. Roosevelt to Stalin, 8 February 1945, *FRUS: The Conferences at Malta and Yalta 1945*, pp. 766–71.
28. Roosevelt to Stalin, 8 February 1945, Cole (Ed.), *Conflict in Indochina and International Repercussions*, p. 47.
29. Press Conference by Roosevelt, 23 February 1945, Cole (Ed.), *Conflict in Indochina and International Repercussions*, p. 48.
30. TNA, FO 371/46304/F1269/11/61G, Dening to Sterndale Bennet, 16 February 1945.
31. MB 1/C280, Wedemeyer to Mountbatten, 29 January 1945.
32. TNA, FO 371/46304/F163/11/G61, Minute by Sterndale Bennett, 9 January 1945.
33. TNA, CAB 80/91, Memorandum by COS Committee, COS (45) 96 (0), 4 February 1945.
34. N. Smart, *Biographical Dictionary of British Generals of the Second World War*, Barnsley, 2005, pp. 58–9.
35. MB 1/C42/62, Carton de Wiart to Mountbatten, 7 February 1945.
36. Thomas, 'Free France, the British Government and the Future of French Indo-China 1940–45', p. 140; A. Short, *The Origins of the Vietnam War*, London, 1989, p. 58, footnote 28, citing Dunn, *The First Vietnam War*.
37. MB 1/C42/62, Carton de Wiart to Mountbatten, 7 February 1945; MB 1/C42/66/4, Minute by Air Vice-Marshall Whitworth-Jones, 22 February 1945.
38. MB 1/C42/66/6, Air Vice-Marshal Whitworth-Jones to Mountbatten, 27 February 1945; MB 1/C42/66/4, Minute by Air Vice-Marshale Whitworth-Jones, 22 February 1945.
39. MB 1/C280, Wedemeyer to Mountbatten, 10 February 1945.
40. TNA, FO 371/46325/F1154/127/61G, Seymour to Sterndale Bennett, no. 160, 9 February 1945.
41. Thomas, 'Silent Partners: SOE's French Indo-China Section 1943–1945', pp. 944–7; J. Boucher De Crevecoeur, *La Liberation Du Laos 1945–46*, Vincennes, 1985, p. 15.
42. TNA, PREM 3/178/3, Carton de Wiart to Churchill, T 211/5, 22 February 1945.
43. TNA, CAB 120/708, Churchill to Eden, M (ARG) 9/5, 13 February 1945.
44. TNA, HW 1/3527, Secret 157, 8 February 1945; Minute by Churchill, 20 February 1945.
45. TNA, CAB 80/92, Memorandum by COS Committee, COS (45) 120 (0), 21 February 1945.
46. Halifax, HLFX2, A4/410/4/15, Halifax to Eden, 25 August 1944; G. C. Herring, 'The Truman Administration and the Restoration of French Sovereignty in Indochina', *Diplomatic History*, vol. 1, no. 2, spring 1977, p. 106; C. Thorne, 'Indochina and Anglo-American Relations 1942–5', *Pacific Historical Review*, vol. 45, 1976, p. 75.
47. J. M. Burns, *Roosevelt: The Soldier Of Freedom 1940–1945*, San Diego, 1970, pp. 591–3; Pollock, and Kimball, 'In Search of Monsters to Destroy:

Roosevelt and Colonialism', p. 154; Butler, *Industrialisation and the British Colonial State*, p. 138.

48. TNA, CAB 120/708, Ismay to Churchill, 27 February 1945.
49. TNA, CAB 120/708, Wilson to Ismay, FMW 14, 9 March 1945.
50. TNA, CAB 120/708, Ismay to Churchill, 12 March 1945; Minute by Churchill 18 March 1945.
51. TNA, CAB 80/92, COS (45) 143 (0), Annex 2, Dening to Foreign Office, no. 73, 26 February 1945.
52. TNA, CAB 121/741, Churchill to Eden and Ismay for COS, 1 March 1945.
53. TNA, CAB 80/92, Memorandum by COS Committee, COS (45) 143 (0), 3 March 1943, Foreign Office to COS, 2 March 1945, Annex 1; CAB 80/91, Memorandum by COS Committee, COS (45) 64 (0), 21 January 1945, Annex 2, Halifax to Foreign Office, no. 32, 2 January 1945.
54. AP 20/13/60, Eden to Churchill, PM/45/81, 4 March 1945; Minute by Churchill, 6 March 1945.
55. TNA, CAB 80/92, Memorandum by COS Committee, COS (45) 143 (0), 3 March 1943, Foreign Office to COS, 2 March 1945, Annex 1.
56. TNA, CAB 121/741, COS (45) 59th Meeting, 5 March 1945.
57. D. Lancaster, *The Emancipation of French Indochina*, London, 1961, pp. 104–7; B. Kiernan, *How Pol Pot Came to Power, a History of Communism in Kampuchea, 1930–1975*, London, 2004, p. 49.
58. AP 20/13/73, Eden to Churchill, PM/45/99, 11 March 1945.
59. TNA, CAB 121/741, Joint Service Mission Washington to AMSSO, no. 595, 12 March 1945.
60. TNA, PREM 3/178/2, Churchill to Ismay, D 72/5, 12 March 1945.
61. TNA, PREM 3/178/3, Eden to Cooper, draft, 12 March 1945.
62. TNA, CAB 121/741, COS (45) 171 (0), 14 March 1945.
63. AP 20/13/229, Churchill to Roosevelt, 17 March 1945.
64. TNA, CAB 121/741, JIC (45) 91 (0), 18 March 1945.
65. TNA, CAB 121/741, COS to Mountbatten, COSSEA 216, Draft, undated, Annex 3.
66. TNA, CAB 120/708, Wilson to COS, FMW 23, 18 March 1945.
67. Meeting of the CCS with Roosevelt and Churchill, 23 August 1943, Item 7, *FRUS: The Conferences at Washington and Quebec 1943*, pp. 941–9.
68. TNA, CAB 120/708, COS to Wilson, 1746, 19 March 1945; Churchill to COS, 20 March 1945.
69. TNA, WO 203/5068, Mountbatten to COS, SEACOS 337, 21 March 1945.
70. TNA, WO 203/5131, Mountbatten to Somervell, SC5/602/S, 17 March 1945.
71. TNA, PREM 3/178/3, Churchill to Eden and Ismay for COS, M 237/5, 19 March 1945.
72. TNA, CAB 120/708, Ismay to Churchill, 19 March 1945; FO 371/46305/F1790/11/G61, Minute by Eden, undated.
73. TNA, CAB 121/741, COS to Joint Service Mission, COS (W) 686, 19 March 1945.
74. TNA, PREM 3/178/3, Churchill to Ismay for COS, 20 March 1945.
75. TNA, PREM 3/178/3, Wilson to Churchill and COS, FMW 24, T 307/5, 20 March 1945.
76. R. H. Spector, *Advice and Support: The Early Years of the United States Army in Vietnam 1941–1960*, Washington D.C., 1983, pp. 31, 34; TNA, WO

208/670, Sitrep 3, 15 March 1945; Sitrep 4, 15 March 1945; JBS/172, 14 March 1945; JBS/180, 19 March 1945; Noiret to Montgomery, 19 March 1945; Sitrep 5, 16 March 1945; Sitrep 13, 27 March 1945; Sitrep 17, 27 March 1945; Sitrep 19, 30 March 1945; Sitrep 20, 31 March 1945; Sitrep 21, 2 April 1945; Thomas, 'Silent Partners: SOE's French Indo-China Section 1943–1945', p. 947.

77. TNA, CAB 121/741, Mountbatten to COS, SEACOS 339, 22 March 1945.
78. TNA, CAB 121/741, 'Support for French Resistance Forces in Indo-China', CCS 644/21, 29 March 1945, Enclosure B, Fenand to Combined Chiefs of Staff, no. 17 MN/SE 12 TS, 27 March 1945; Enclosure C, Fenand to Combined Chiefs of Staff, no. 18 MN/SE 124 TS, 27 March 1945.
79. TNA, CAB 121/741, Joint Service Mission to Cabinet, JSM 646, 30 March 1945.
80. TNA, CAB 121/741, Sterndale Bennett to Air Commodore Beaumont, 30 March 1945.
81. Thorne, *Allies of a Kind*, p. 631.
82. TNA, FO 371/46306/F2065/11/61G, Wilson to COS, FMW 40, 30 March 1945.
83. TNA, FO 371/46306/F2065/11/61G, Wilson to COS, FMW 39, 30 March 1945.
84. TNA, PREM 3/178/3, Roosevelt to Churchill, no. 724, T 324/5, 22 March 1945.
85. TNA, CAB 120/708, Wilson to COS, FMW 25, 20 March 1945.
86. TNA, FO 371/46305/F1829/11/G61, Minute by Sterndale Bennett, 24 March 1945.
87. TNA, PREM 3/178/3, Wilson to Ismay, FMW 33, 27 March 1945.
88. TNA, CAB 120/708, Ismay to Churchill, 19 March 1945.
89. TNA, CAB 21/1027, Minute by Churchill, M 270/5, 30 March 1945.
90. TNA, PREM 3/159/12, Foreign Office brief, 28 March 1945, Annex 1, 'Hurley', 28 March 1945.
91. TNA, PREM 3/159/12, Foreign Office brief, 28 March 1945, Annex 6, 'Indo-China', 28 March 1945.
92. TNA, PREM 3/159/12, Churchill to Colville, 17 March 1945; Minute by Churchill, 11 April 1945; Louis, *Imperialism at Bay*, p. 7; *Brooke Diary*, 6 April 1945, p. 682; 11 April 1945, p. 682.
93. TNA, PREM 3/178/3, Churchill to Hollis, D 92/5, 31 March 1945.
94. TNA, PREM 3/178/3, Churchill to Hollis, D 93/5, 3 April 1945.
95. *Colville Diary*, 6 April 1945, p. 574.
96. TNA, CAB 120/708, Mountbatten to COS, SEACOS 359, 8 April 1945.
97. Memorandum by the Assistant to the President's Naval Aide (G. M. Elsey), undated, *FRUS: The Conference at Berlin 1945 (The Potsdam Conference) Volume 1*, Washington D.C., 1960, pp. 915–21.
98. TNA, PREM 3/178/3, Churchill to Roosevelt, no. 943, T 438/5, 11 April 1945.
99. *Cooper Diary*, 13 April 1945, p. 361.
100. TNA, PREM 3/178/3, Truman to Churchill, no. 4, T 478/5, 14 April 1945.
101. TNA, CAB 121/741, Churchill to Ismay, 15 April 1945; Price to Brooke, CAS, First Sea Lord, ref. COS 563/5, 15 April 1945.
102. TNA, CAB 120/708, Ismay to Churchill, 19 April 1945.

103. TNA, CAB 120/708, Churchill to Truman, no. 9, T 537/5, 20 April 1945.
104. Hess, *The United States' Emergence as a Southeast Asian Power*, p. 151.
105. TNA, PREM 3/180/7, Churchill to Cadogan, M 339/5, 15 April 1945.
106. TNA, CAB 120/708, COS to Mountbatten, COSSEA no. 249, 25 April 1945.
107. TNA, PREM 4/31/4, Churchill to Attlee, M 190/5, 10 March 1944.
108. TNA, FO 371/46325/F2144/127/61G, Minute by Sterndale Bennett, 5 April 1945.
109. TNA, FO 371/46325/F2144/127/61G, Minute by Scott, 7 April 1945.
110. Declaration of the Provisional French Government Concerning Indo-China, 24 March 1945, Cole (Ed.), *Conflict in Indochina and International Repercussions*, pp. 5–7.
111. DUFC 4/5, Cooper to Campbell, 30 April 1945.
112. Caffrey to State Department, 24 March 1945, *FRUS: 1945: Volume 6: The British Commonwealth, The Far East*, Washington D.C., 1969, p. 302.
113. TNA, FO 371/46306/F2348/11/G61, Minute by Cadogan, 9 April 1945.
114. TNA, FO 371/46306/F2909/11/G61, Hollis to Sterndale Bennett, 7 May 1945; Minute by Sterndale Bennett, undated.
115. TNA, DO 35/1213/WR208/3/6, Stephenson to Machtig, 5 March 1945; Cranborne to Churchill, 23 March 1945.
116. TNA, DO 35/1912, Boyd Shannon to Bottomley, 15 October 1946.
117. TNA, DO 35/1904, Amery to Wavell, 5 March 1945.
118. TNA, FO 371/46304/F1269/11/61G, Sterndale Bennet to Dening, 14 April 1945.
119. CAB 81/46, PHP (45) 29 (0) Final, 29 June 1945, Ashton and Stockwell (Ed.), *British Documents on the End of Empire, Series A, Volume 1: Imperial Policy and Colonial Practice 1925–1945: Part 1: Metropolitan Reorganisation, Defence and International Relations, Political Change and Constitutional Reform*, pp. 231–44.
120. *Colville Diary*, 23 April 1945, p. 591; 24 April 1945, p. 592; 26 April 1945, p. 592; 14 May 1945, p. 599; 23 May 1945, pp. 601–2.
121. Memorandum by the Assistant to the President's Naval Aide (G.M. Elsey), undated, *FRUS: The Conference at Berlin 1945 (The Potsdam Conference) Volume 1*, pp. 915–21.
122. TNA, CAB 120/708, Wilson to COS, FMW 84, 10 May 1945; CAB 119/205, JP (45) 90 (Final), 24 April 1945.
123. MB 1/C280, Wedemeyer to Mountbatten, 12 May 1945.
124. MB 1/C280, Mountbatten to Wedemeyer, 21 May 1945.
125. TNA, PREM 3/178/3, Wilson to COS and Mountbatten, FMW 95, 29 May 1945.
126. TNA, PREM 3/178/3, Wilson to COS, FMW 100, 1 June 1945; Spector, *Advice and Support*, p. 49.
127. TNA, CAB 122/1177, Marshall to Wilson, 5 June 1945; WO 203/5239, Aung San to Mountbatten, 14 June 1945, Enclosure, 28 May 1945, H. Tinker (Ed.), *Burma: The Struggle For Independence 1944–1948: Documents From Official And Private Sources: Volume 1: From Military Occupation to Civil Government 1 January 1944 to 31 August 1946*, London, 1983, pp. 326–31.
128. TNA, CAB 122/1177, Wilson to COS, FMW 106, 8 June 1945.
129. TNA, PREM 3/178/3, COS to Wilson, Cypher 3681, 11 June 1945.

130. TNA, FO 371/46307/F3492/11/G61, Minute by Sterndale Bennett, 22 May 1945; Minute by Eden, 27 May 1945.
131. TNA, WO 203/5291, War Office to Mountbatten, 97099 Cypher CA 4, 29 May 1945; WO 203/4452, Anderson to Joubert, CA 4/BM/75, 16 March 1945; A. Patti, *Why Vietnam?*, Berkley, 1980, pp. 58, 67, 102, 125–9.
132. TNA, CAB 119/205, COS (45) 161st Meeting, 26 June 1945.
133. TNA, CAB 119/205, COS to Joint Service Mission, COS (W) 12, 5 July 1945.
134. TNA, CAB 122/1066, Minute by Churchill, 19 July 1945.
135. TNA, CAB 119/205, Foreign Office to Terminal, no. 38, 16 July 1945.
136. TNA, CAB 21/1027, Halifax to Foreign Office, 25 June 1945.
137. TNA, CAB 119/205, Foreign Office to Terminal, no. 37, 16 July 1945; no. 36, 16 July 1945.
138. TNA, FO 371/46307/F240/11/G61, Minute by Butler, 10 July 1945.
139. AP 20/13/217, Eden to Churchill, Halifax, no. 3345, 14 May 1945; Eden, *The Reckoning*, p. 632; *Cadogan Diary*, 24 May 1945, p. 745; Louis, *Imperialism at Bay*, p. 534; Herring, 'The Truman Administration and the Restoration of French Sovereignty in Indochina', *Diplomatic History*, p. 104; NA FO 461/5, Halifax to Eden, U4416/12/70, 30 May 1945, Enclosure, no. 2, Address by Stettinius, 28 May 1945, R. D. Crockatt (Ed.), *British Documents on Foreign Affairs: Reports and Papers from the Foreign Office Confidential Print: Series C, North America, Part 3: Volume 5, January 1945–December 1945*, University Publications of America, 1999, pp. 97–103.
140. Halifax, HLFX2, A4/410/4/22, United Nations Draft Charter, 25 June 1945; Adopted Charter, 26 June 1945.
141. MB 1/C206, Draft record of a conversation with Truman, 24 July 1945.
142. *Brooke Diary*, 7 August 1945, p. 715.
143. Neal, *The Washington Ambassadorship of Lord Halifax 1941–1946*, p. 127.
144. *Moran Diary*, 22 July 1945, p. 279.
145. TNA, PREM 8/33, Foreign Office to Terminal, no. 259, 28 July 1945; Terminal to Foreign Office, no. 324, T 12/45, 1 August 1945.
146. TNA, CAB 119/205, COS Terminal (45) 6th Meeting, 20 July 1945; Cadogan to Hollis, 22 July 1945; T. O. Smith, 'Britain and Cambodia, September 1945–November 1946: A Reappraisal', *Diplomacy and Statecraft*, vol. 17, no. 1, 2006, p. 73; see T. O. Smith, *Britain and the Origins of the Vietnam War: UK Policy in Indo-China 1943–50*, London, 2007, for an analysis of British post-war policy towards Vietnam.

5 Trusteeship's Denouement

1. J. L. Gormly, *From Potsdam to the Cold War; Big Three Diplomacy 1945–7*, Delaware, 1990, pp. 12–14.
2. Charmley, *Churchill's Grand Alliance*, p. 9.
3. Gardner, *Approaching Vietnam*, p. 47; Hess, *The United States' Emergence as a Southeast Asian Power*, p. 99.
4. Kimball, *The Juggler*, p. 7.
5. Hess, *The United States' Emergence as a Southeast Asian Power*, pp. 79, 86; Tonnesson, *The Vietnamese Revolution of 1945*, p. 64.

6. Hess, *The United States' Emergence as a Southeast Asian Power*, pp. 126–7; Short, *The Origins of the Vietnam War*, p. 36.
7. Dunn, *The First Vietnam War*, p. 86.
8. Hess, *The United States' Emergence as a Southeast Asian Power*, p. 94; W. La Feber, 'Roosevelt, Churchill and Indochina 1942–5', *American Historical Review*, vol. 80, 1975, p. 1289.
9. Short, *The Origins of the Vietnam War*, p. 36.
10. Hess, *The United States' Emergence as a Southeast Asian Power*, p. 128.
11. Herring, 'The Truman Administration and the Restoration of French Sovereignty in Indochina', p. 99; R. E. Sherwood, *Roosevelt and Hopkins: An Intimate History*, New York, 1948, pp. 834–5.
12. Hess, *The United States' Emergence as a Southeast Asian Power*, p. 134.
13. *Cadogan Diary*, Cadogan to Halifax, undated, pp. 586–7.
14. *Harvey Diary*, 29 March 1943, pp. 239–40.
15. Thorne, *Allies of a Kind*, pp. 501, 631.
16. S. Tonnesson, 'The Longest Wars: Indochina 1945–75', *Journal of Peace Research*, vol. 22, no. 1, 1985, p. 11.
17. Thorne, *Allies of a Kind*, p. 622.
18. Spector, *Advice and Support*, p. 43.
19. Hess, *The United States' Emergence as a Southeast Asian Power*, pp. 135–6, 145.
20. TNA, FO 371/46307/F4240/11/61G, Minute by Butler, 10 July 1945.
21. Thorne, *Allies of a Kind*, p. 631.
22. Louis, *Imperialism at Bay*, p. 489; Thorne, *Allies of a Kind*, p. 600; Kissinger, *Diplomacy*, p. 395.
23. *Moran Diary*, 4 February 1945, pp. 222–3; *Cadogan Diary*, 6 February 1945, p. 704; 7 February 1945, p. 705; 20 February 1945, p. 717; *Colville Diary*, 19 February 1945, pp. 560–1; Gilbert, *Churchill: A life*, pp. 817, 825; Gilbert, *Winston Spencer Churchill, Volume 7*, pp. 1167, 1169, 1170, 1175.
24. Gilbert, *Churchill and America*, pp. 341–4; Burns, *Roosevelt: The Soldier of Freedom 1940–1945*, pp. 601–6.
25. Harry S. Truman Library, Independence, Missouri (hereinafter HSTL), Truman Papers, President's Secretary's Files, Box 138, Stettinius to Truman, 13 April 1945.
26. Thorne, *Allies of a Kind*, p. 629.
27. HSTL, Truman Papers, President's Secretary's Files, Box 138, Policy Manual, 16 April 1945; S. Tonnesson, 'Franklin D. Roosevelt, Trusteeship and Indochina: A Reassessment', in M. A. Lawrence and F. Logevall (Eds), *The First Vietnam War: Colonial Conflict and Cold War Crisis*, Massachusetts, 2007, pp 68–9.
28. Memorandum, 9 February 1945, *FRUS: The Conferences at Malta and Yalta 1945*, p. 858; Report by the Foreign Ministers, 9 February 1945, pp. 858–60; HSTL, Truman Papers, Map Room File 1945, Box 1, Hurley to Truman, 28 May 1945.
29. Herring, 'The Truman Administration and the Restoration of French Sovereignty in Indochina', p. 104; Grew to Caffrey, 9 May 1945, Cameron (Ed.), *Viet-Nam Crisis: A Documentary History. Volume 1*, p. 36.
30. Thorne, 'Indochina and Anglo-American Relations 1942–5', p. 96.
31. Burns, *Roosevelt: The Soldier of Freedom 1940–1945*, p. 609.
32. *Harvey Diary*, 18 January 1945, p. 374.

33. FO 461/5, Halifax to Eden, U4416/12/70, 30 May 1945, Enclosure, no. 2, Address by Stettinius, 28 May 1945, Crockatt (Ed.), *British Documents on Foreign Affairs: Reports and Papers from the Foreign Office Confidential Print: Series C, North America, Part 3: Volume 5*, pp. 97–103.

34. Tonnesson, 'Franklin D. Roosevelt, Trusteeship and Indochina: A Reassessment', pp. 57–60.

35. TNA, CAB 122/812, Halifax to Foreign Office, 3 January 1944; PREM 3/178/2, Halifax to FO, no. 258, 18 January 1944; Roosevelt to Hull, 24 January 1944, Cameron (Ed.), *Viet-Nam Crisis, A Documentary History, Volume 1*, p. 13; TNA, PREM 3/180/7, Churchill to Eden, M. 580/4, 21 May 1944.

36. Tonnesson, *The Vietnamese Revolution of 1945*, pp. 13–19; La Feber, 'Roosevelt, Churchill and Indochina 1942–5', p. 1277.

37. *The Pentagon Papers, The Defense Department History of United States Decision Making on Vietnam, Volume 1*, p. 2.

38. Short, *The Origins of the Vietnam War*, p. 38.

39. Charmley, *Churchill's Grand Alliance*, p. 11.

40. Kimball, *The Juggler*, p. 7.

41. Viorst, *Hostile Allies*, p. 191.

42. House of Commons Statement by Churchill, 22 February 1944, *Hansard House of Commons Parliamentary Debates*, Volume 397, Column 700.

43. FO 461/5, American Relations with the British Empire, AN 1577/16/45, 1 May 1944, Crockatt (Ed.), *British Documents on Foreign Affairs: Reports and Papers from the Foreign Office Confidential Print: Series C, North America, Part 3: Volume 4*, pp. 199–252.

44. Charmley, *Churchill's Grand Alliance*, p. 159.

45. HSTL, Truman Papers, Map Room File 1945, Box 1, Hurley to Truman, 28 May 1945.

46. HSTL, Truman Papers, Map Room File 1945, Box 2, Truman to Hurley, 12 May 1945.

47. HSTL, Truman Papers, Map Room File 1945, Box 1, Hurley to Truman, 20 May 1945.

48. HSTL, Truman Papers, Map Room File 1945, Box 1, Hurley to Truman, 28 May 1945.

49. HSTL, Truman Papers, Map Room File 1945, Box 2, Truman to Hurley, 4 June 1945.

50. HSTL, Truman Papers, Map Room File 1945, Box 1, Hurley to Grew, 1 June 1945.

51. Vietnamese Aide-Memoire, July 1945, Cole (Ed.), *Conflict In Indochina and International Repercussions*, p. 17.

52. Declaration of Independence of the Republic of Vietnam, 2 September 1945, Cole (Ed.), *Conflict In Indochina and International Repercussions*, pp. 19–21.

53. Thorne, *Allies Of A Kind*, pp. 600, 629, 631.

54. Joint Chiefs of Staff Meeting, 7 January 1943, *FRUS: The Conferences at Washington 1941–2, and Casablanca 1943*, Washington D.C., 1968, pp. 505–14.

55. Viorst, *Hostile Allies*, p. 155, citing General Charles de Gaulle, *Memoirs de Guerre, Vol.2, L'Unite 1942–1944*, Paris, 1956, p. 80.

56. Halifax, *Fulness of Days*, p. 253.

57. TNA, FO 371/46325/F234/127/61, Minute by J. Thyme Henderson, 14 January 1945.
58. S. M. Habibuddin, 'Franklin D. Roosevelt's Anti-colonial Policy Towards Asia. Its Implications for India, Indo-china and Indonesia 1941–5', *Journal of Indian History*, vol. 53, 1975, p. 498.
59. AP 20/10/230A, 896 Circular to Washington, 14 June 1943; Lacouture, *De Gaulle: The Rebel*, p. 333.
60. Siracusa, 'The United States, Viet-Nam and the Cold War: A Re-appraisal', pp. 85, 87; AP 20/10/184, Eden to Churchill, PM/43/184, 25 June 1943.
61. AP 20/11/484, Eden to Churchill, PM/44/486, 2 July 1944; TNA, PREM 3/187, Roosevelt to Churchill, T139/2, 29 January 1942.
62. Memorandum, 9 February 1945, *FRUS: The Conferences at Malta and Yalta 1945*, p. 858; Report by the Foreign Ministers, 9 February 1945, pp. 858–60; HSTL, Truman Papers, Map Room File 1945, Box 1, Hurley to Truman, 28 May 1945; F. R. Dulles and G. Ridinger, 'The Anti-colonial policies of Roosevelt', *Political Science Quarterly*, vol. LXX, 1955, pp. 1, 10.
63. Thorne, *Allies Of A Kind*, p. 630; Sbrega, 'The Anti-Colonial Policies of Franklin D. Roosevelt: A Re-appraisal', p. 77; Memorandum of a Conversation by Taussig, 15 March 1945, *FRUS: 1945: Volume 1: General: The United Nations*, Washington D.C., 1967, pp. 121–4.
64. Thorne, *Allies Of A Kind*, p. 466.
65. S. Bills, *Empire and the Cold War: The Roots of United States-Third World Antagonism*, London, 1990, p. 73.
66. *The Pentagon Papers, The Defense Department History of United States Decision Making on Vietnam, Volume 1*, p. 16; R. Blum, *Drawing the line*, Berkley, 1979, p. 105.
67. G. R. Hess, 'Franklin D. Roosevelt and French Indochina', *Journal of American History*, vol. 59, no. 2, September 1972, p. 366.
68. D. G. Marr, *Vietnam 1945: The Quest For Power*, Berkley, 1995, p. 269; Tonnesson, *The Vietnamese Revolution of 1945*, pp. 168–70, 213–14.

Epilogue

1. Meeting of the Combined Chiefs of Staff, 24 July 1945, *FRUS: The Conference at Berlin 1945 (The Potsdam Conference) Volume 2*, Washington D.C., 1960, p. 377.
2. For an analysis of the seamless transition of British foreign policy from the Conservative to Labour Governments following the 1945 general election, see J. Saville, *The Politics of Continuity: British Foreign Policy and the Labour Government 1945–1946*, London, 1993.
3. N. Tarling, 'Some Rather Nebulous Capacity: Lord Killearn's Appointment in Southeast Asia', *Modern Asian Studies*, vol. 20, no. 3, 1986, pp. 559–600; Thorne, 'Indochina and Anglo-American Relations 1942–5', p. 96.
4. TNA, WO 203/5655, Dening to Mountbatten, 7 August 1945.
5. TNA, PREM 8/33, Foreign Office to Terminal, no. 259, 28 July 1945; Terminal to Foreign Office, no. 324, T 12/45, 1 August 1945.
6. D. P. Chandler, *A History of Cambodia*, Washington D.C., 1999, p. 170.

7. M. Vickery, *Kampuchea: Politics, Economics and Society*, London, 1986, p. 8; Patti, *Why Vietnam*, pp. 58, 453.
8. Bills, *Empire and the Cold War*, pp. 83–4.
9. Chandler, *A History of Cambodia*, p. 171.
10. V. M. Reddi, *A History of the Cambodian Independence Movement 1863–1955*, Triupati, 1973, p. 108; Centre des Archives d'Outre-Mer, Aix-en-Provence (hereinafter CAOM): Governement Generale d'Indochine, GGI/65498, 'Etudes sur thes movements rebelles au Cambodge 1942–1952', Annex, 'Le Nationalisme Khmer', pp. 19–21.
11. Chandler, *A History of Cambodia*, p. 171.
12. CAOM, Governement Generale d'Indochine, GGI/65498, 'Etudes sur thes movements rebelles au Cambodge 1942–1952', Annex, 'Le Nationalisme Khmer', p. 3; TNA, WO 172/7009, Secret War Diary Headquarters Allied Liberation Force Phnom Penh, 9–31 October 1945, 4 November 1945; WO 208/636, Telegram no. 14569, 12 November 1945.
13. R. E. M. Irving, *The First Indochina War, French and American Policy 1945–1954*, London, 1975, p. 16, citing B. Fall, *Street Without Joy*, p. 26.
14. S. Tonnesson 'Filling The Vacuum: 1945 in French Indochina, the Netherlands East Indies and British Malaya', in H. Antlov and S. Tonnesson (Eds), *Imperial Policy and Southeast Asian Nationalism 1930–1957*, Surrey, 1995, pp. 123–5.
15. Dunn, *The First Vietnam War*, p. 16; R. B. Smith, *Viet-Nam and the West*, London, 1968, p. 111; Saville, *The Politics of Continuity*, p. 178; Dunn, *The First Vietnam War*, pp. 18, 123.
16. TNA, WO 203/5025, Director Intelligence to Mountbatten, 26 January 1946.
17. TNA, WO 203/1934, Inter Service Topographical Department, 26 August 1945, Appendix H.
18. TNA, WO 203/2185, Allied Liberation Force French Indo-China, Summary of Operations up to 8 November 1945.
19. Dunn, *The First Vietnam War*, pp. 241–2; Ziegler, *Mountbatten*, p. 332; TNA, PREM 8/63, Mountbatten to Cabinet, SEACOS 489, 24 September 1945; WO 172/1790, Mountbatten to WO, Signal SAC 27379, 3 November 1945.
20. TNA, PREM 8/63, Defence Committee, DO(45)7th Meeting, 5 October 1945.
21. Rosie, *The British in Vietnam*, pp. 57–86, 138–9; M. A. Lawrence, *Assuming the Burden: Europe and the American Commitment to War in Vietnam*, London, 2005, pp. 105, 111; G. Hughes, 'A 'Post-war' War: The British Occupation of French-Indochina, September 1945–March 1946', *Small Wars & Insurgencies*, vol. 17, no. 3, 2006, pp. 263–86; C. Bayly and T. Harper, *Forgotten Wars: The End of Britain's Asian Empire*, London, 2008, pp. 145–58.
22. TNA, WO 162/ 277, Far East – Army and Navy Casualties, 4th Edition.
23. For detailed accounts of British policy towards Vietnam and Cambodia, see Smith, *Britain and the Origins of the Vietnam War*, and P. Neville, *Britain in Vietnam: Prelude to Disaster 1945–46*, London, 2008.

Bibliography

Archival Sources

Britain

The National Archives, Public Record Office, London:

Admiralty:

ADM 119 Accountant General's Department
ADM 199 War History Cases and Papers
ADM 223 Naval Intelligence Papers

Air Ministry:

AIR 8 Department of the Chief of Air Staff
AIR 23 Overseas Commands
AIR 40 Directorate of Intelligence and other Intelligence Papers

Cabinet Office:

CAB 21 Registered Files 1916–65
CAB 65 War Cabinet Minutes
CAB 66 War Cabinet Memoranda
CAB 69 War Cabinet Defence Committee (Operations)
CAB 79 War Cabinet Chiefs of Staff Committee Minutes
CAB 80 War Cabinet Chiefs of Staff Committee Memoranda
CAB 81 War Cabinet Chiefs of Staff Committee and Sub-Committees
CAB 84 War Cabinet Joint Planning Committees
CAB 99 War Cabinet Commonwealth and International Conferences
CAB 119 Joint Planning Staff Files
CAB 120 Minister of Defence: Secretariat Files
CAB 121 Special Secret Information Centre
CAB 122 British Joint Staff Mission: Washington Office Files
CAB 128 Cabinet Minutes 1945–72
CAB 129 Cabinet Memoranda 1945–72
CAB 134 Cabinet Miscellaneous Committees: Minutes and Papers

Colonial Office:

CO 323 Colonies: General Original Correspondence
CO 537 Confidential General and Confidential Original Correspondence
CO 825 Eastern Original Correspondence
CO 968 Defence Department and Successors: Original Correspondence

Dominions Office:

DO 35 Commonwealth Relations Office

Foreign Office:

FO 115 Embassy and Consulates, United States of America: General Correspondence
FO 371 Political Departments: General Correspondence
FO 660 Offices of Various Political Representatives, Second World War: Papers
FO 930 Foreign Publicity Files
FO 950 Claims Department: Correspondence and Claims
FO 953 Information Policy Department and Regional Information Departments
FO 954 Private Office Papers of Sir A. Eden

Special Operations Executive:

HS 1 Far East: Registered Files
HS 7 Histories and War Diaries

Government Communications Headquarters:

HW 1 Government Code and Cipher School: Signals Intelligence Passed to the Prime Minister, Messages and Correspondence

Ministry of Agriculture and Food:

MAF 83 Supply Department
MAF 97 Establishment Department: British Food Mission, Washington

Prime Minister:

PREM 3 Prime Minister's Papers 1940–45
PREM 4 Prime Minister's Papers 1940–45
PREM 8 Prime Minister's Papers 1945–51

War Office:

WO 32 Registered Papers General Series
WO 106 Directorate of Military Operations and Intelligence
WO 162 Adjutant General
WO 172 SEAC War Diaries
WO 193 Directorate of Military Operations
WO 203 Far East Forces
WO 208 Directorate of Military Intelligence
WO 220 Directorate of Civil Affairs
WO 252 Surveys, Maps and Reports
WO 311 War Crimes Files

The Cadbury Research Library, Birmingham University:

Papers of Anthony Eden, Lord Avon

Churchill College Cambridge:

Papers of Sir Alexander Cadogan
Papers of Sir Winston Spencer Churchill
Papers of Duff Cooper, Viscount Norwich
Papers of the Rt Hon. Earl of Halifax (microfilm)

Southampton University Library:

Papers of Admiral Lord Louis Mountbatten Earl of Burma

The Middle East Centre Archive, St Anthony's College, Oxford:

Papers of Sir Miles Lampson, Lord Killearn

University of East Anglia Library, Norwich:

Papers of Sir Winston Spencer Churchill (microfilm)

France

Centre des Archives d'Outre-Mer, Aix-en-Provence:

Governement General de L'Indochine

America

Franklin D. Roosevelt Library, Hyde Park, New York:

Papers of President Franklin D. Roosevelt
  Map Room Papers
  Official File
  President's Secretary's Files
  Private Secretary's File
  President's Speeches Files
Papers of Adolf A. Berle
Papers of Harry A. Hopkins
Papers of Alexander Sachs
Papers of Sumner Welles
Papers of the Republican National Committee

Harry S. Truman Library, Independence, Missouri:

Papers of President Harry S. Truman
  Map Room Papers
  Naval Aide's File
  Official File
  President's Secretary's File
  Private Secretary's Files
  Post-Presidential File
  White House Confidential File
Papers of Dean Acheson

Papers of Clark M. Clifford
Papers of George M. Elsey

Published Primary Sources

British Documents on the End of Empire, Series A, Volume 1 : Ashton, S. R., and Stockwell, S.E. (Eds),
> *Imperial Policy and Colonial Practice 1925–1945: Part 1: Metropolitan Reorganisation, Defence and International Relations, Political Change and Constitutional Reform,* London, 1996.
> *Imperial Policy and Colonial Practice 1925–1945: Part 2: Economic Policy, Social Policies and Colonial Research,* London, 1996.
British Documents on the End of Empire, Series A, Volume 2: Hyam, R.(Ed.),
> *The Labour Government and the End of Empire 1945–1951: Part 1: High Policy,* London, 1991.
> *The Labour Government and the End of Empire 1945–1951: Part 2: Economics and International Relations,* London, 1991.
> *The Labour Government and the End of Empire 1945–1951: Pari 3: Strategy, Policies and Constitutional Change,* London, 1991.
> *The Labour Government and the End of Empire 1945–1951: Part 4: Race Relations and the Commonwealth,* London, 1991.
British Documents on the End of Empire, Series B, Volume 3: Stockwell, A. J. (Ed.),
> *Malaya: Parti: The Malayan Union Experiment 1942–1948,* London, 1995.
British Documents on Foreign Affairs: Reports and Papers from the Foreign Office Confidential Print: Series C, North America, Part 3: Crockatt, R. D. (Ed.),
> *Volume 2: January 1942–March 1943,* University Publications of America, 1999.
> *Volume 3: April 1943–December 1943,* University Publications of America, 1999.
> *Volume 4: January 1944–December 1944,* University Publications of America, 1999.
> *Volume 5: January 1945–December 1945,* University Publications of America, 1999.
British Imperial Policy and Decolonializisation, Volume 1, 1938–1951, Porter, A. N. and Stockwell, A. J. (Eds), London, 1987.
Burma: The Struggle for Independence 1944–1948: Documents from Official and Private Sources: Tinker, H. (Ed.),
> *Volume 1: From Military Occupation to Civil Government 1 January 1944 to 31 August 1946,* London, 1983.
Churchill and Roosevelt : The Complete Correspondence: Kimball, W. (Ed.),
> *Alliance Emerging, 1933–1942,* Princeton 1984.
> *Alliance Forged, 1942–1944,* Princeton, 1984.
> *Alliance Declining, 1944–1945,* Princeton, 1984.
Conflict In Indochina and International Repercussions: A Documentary History, 1945–1955, Cole, A. B. (Ed.), New York, 1956.
Constitutional Relations Between Britain and India: The Transfer of Power 1942–7: Mansergh, N. (Ed.),
> *Volume 3: Reassertion of Authority, Gandhi's Fast and the Succession of the Viceroyalty 21 September 1942–12 June 1943,* London, 1971. *Volume 4:*

The Bengal Famine and the New Viceroyalty 15 June 1943–31 August 1944, London, 1973.

Volume 5: The Simla Conference: Background and Proceedings 1 September 1944–28 July 1945, London, 1974.

Volume 6: The Post War Phase: New Moves by the Labour Government I August 1945–22 March 1946, London, 1976.

Documents on British Policy Overseas Series 1:
Butler, R., and Pelly, M. (Eds), *Volume 1: The Conference at Potsdam, 1945*, London, 1984.

Documents Relating to British Involvement in the Indochina Conflict 1945–65, London, 1965.

Foreign Relations of the United States: Diplomatic Papers: Department of State Publication:
The Conferences at Washington 1941–2, and Casablanca 1943, Washington D.C., 1968.

The Conferences at Washington and Quebec 1943, Washington D.C, 1970.

The Conferences at Cairo and Tehran 1943, Washington D.C., 1961. *1943: Volume 3: The British Commonwealth, Eastern Europe, The Far East*, Washington D.C., 1963.

The Conference at Quebec 1944, Washington D.C., 1972.

The Conferences at Malta and Yalta 1945, Washington D.C., 1955.

The Conference at Berlin 1945 (The Potsdam Conference) Volume 1, Washington D.C., 1960.

The Conference at Berlin 1945 (The Potsdam Conference) Volume 2, Washington D.C., 1960.

1945: Volume 1: General: The United Nations, Washington D.C., 1967.

1945: Volume 6: The British Commonwealth, The Far East, Washington D.C., 1969.

Hansard House of Commons Parliamentary Debates, 1943–1945, Volumes 386–412, London, 1943–1945.

La Guerre D'Indochine 1945–54: Textes et Documents, Volume 1, Le Retour de la France en Indochine1945–1946, Bordinier, G.(Ed.), Vincennes, 1987.

The Pentagon Papers, The Defense Department History of United States Decision Making on Vietnam, Volume 1, Gravel Edition, Boston, 1971.

Viet-Nam Crisis: A Documentary History. Volume 1, 1940–1956, Cameron, A.W. (Ed.), New York, 1971.

Vietnam, the Definitive Documentation of Human Decisions. Volume 1, Porter, G. (Ed.), Philadelphia, 1979.

Published Memoirs and Diaries

Blum, J.M. (Ed.), *The Price of Vision: The Diary of Henry A. Wallace 1942–1946*, Boston, 1973.

Boucher De Crevecoeur, J., *La Liberation Du Laos 1945–46*, Vincennes, 1985.

Churchill, W. S., *The Second World War: Volume 3 The Grand Alliance*, London, 1950.

Churchill, W. S., *The Second World War: Volume 4 The Hinge of Fate*, London, 1951.

Churchill, W. S., *The Second World War: Volume 5 Closing The Ring*, London, 1952.

Churchill, W. S., *The Second World War: Volume 6 Triumph and Tragedy*, London, 1954.

Colville, Sir. J. (Ed.), *The Fringes of Power: The Downing Street Diaries, 1939–1955*, London, 1985.

D' Argenlieu, G. T., *Chronique D'Indochine 1945–1947*, Paris, 1985.

Danchev, A., and Todman, D. (Eds), *War Diaries 1939–1945: Field-Marshal Lord Alan Brooke*, London, 2001.

Dilks, D. (Ed.), *The Diaries of Sir Alexander Cadogan 1938–1945*, London, 1971.

Dixon, P., (Ed.), *Double Diploma: The Life of Sir Pierson Dixon*, London, 1968.

Eden, A., *The Memoirs of Anthony Eden, Earl of Avon: The Reckoning*, Boston, 1965, (second printing).

Evans, T. (Ed.), *The Killearn Diaries 1943–1946*, London, 1972.

Halifax, Lord., *Fulness of Days*, London, 1957.

Harriman, W. A., and Abel E., *Special Envoy to Churchill and Stalin 1941–1946*, New York, 1975.

Harvey, J. (Ed), *The War Diaries of Oliver Harvey 1941–1945*, London, 1978.

Hull, C, *The Memoirs of Cordell Hull Volume 2*, London, 1948.

Ismay, Lord., *The Memoirs of General the Lord Ismay*, London, 1960.

Macmillan, H., *War Diaries*, London, 1984.

Moran, Lord., *Winston Churchill: The Struggle for Survival 1940–1965*, London, 1966.

Norwich, J. J. (Ed.), *The Duff Cooper Diaries 1915–1951*, London, 2005.

Patti, A., *Why Vietnam?* Berkley, 1980.

Sainteny, J., *Histoire d'une Paix Manquee: Indochine 1945–1947*, Paris, 1967.

Sainteny, J., *Ho Chi Minh and His Vietnam: A Personal Memoir*, Translated By H. Briffault, Chicago, 1972.

Sihanouk, N., *Souvenirs Doux et Amers*, Paris, 1981.

Wedemeyer, A. C., *Wedemeyer Reports*, New York, 1958.

Ziegler, P. (Ed.), *The Personal Diaries of Admiral, the Lord Louis Mountbatten, Supreme Commander Southeast Asia 1943–1946*, London, 1988.

Secondary Sources

Adamthwaite, A., 'Britain and the World 1945–9: The View From The Foreign Office', *International Affairs*, vol. 61, no. 2, Spring 1985, pp. 223–35.

Aldrich, R., 'Imperial Rivalry: British and American Intelligence in Asia 1942–6', *Intelligence and National Security*, vol. 3, no. 1, January 1988, pp. 5–55.

Ambrose, S. E., 'Churchill and Eisenhower in the Second World War', in Blake, R., and Louis, W. R. (Eds), *Churchill*, Oxford, 1993.

Antlov, H.; and Tonnesson, S. (Eds), *Imperial Policy and Southeast Asian Nationalism 1930–1957*, Surrey, 1995.

Bayly, C., and Harper, T., *Forgotten Armies: Britain's Asian Empire and The War With Japan*, London, 2005.

Bayly, C., and Harper, T., *Forgotten Wars: The End of Britain's Asian Empire*, London, 2008.

Beloff, M., 'Churchill and Europe', in Blake, R., and Louis, W. R. (Eds), *Churchill*, Oxford, 1993.

Bills, S., *Empire and the Cold War: The Roots of United States-Third World Antagonism*, London, 1990.

Blake, R., and Louis, W. R. (Eds), *Churchill*, Oxford, 1993.

Blum, R., *Drawing the Line*, New York, 1979.

Brown, K. E., 'The Interplay of Information and Mind in Decision Making; Signals Intelligence and Franklin D. Roosevelt's Policy Shift on Indochina', *Intelligence and National Security*, vol. 13, no. 1, 1998, pp. 109–31.

Bullock, A., *Ernest Bevin Foreign Secretary 1945–51*, London, 1983.

Burns, J. M., *Roosevelt: The Lion and the Fox*, New York, 1956.

Burns, J. M., *Roosevelt: The Soldier of Freedom 1940–1945*, San Diego, 1970.

Butler, L. J., *Industrialisation and the British Colonial State: West Africa 1939–1951*, London, 1997.

Butler, L. J., *Britain and Empire: Adjusting to a Post-Imperial World*, London, 2002.

Butler, L. J., 'British Decolonization', in Thomas, M., and Moore, B., and Butler, L., J., *Crises of Empire: Decolonization and Europe's Imperial States, 1918–1975*, London, 2008.

Buttinger, J., *Vietnam: A Dragon Embattled Volume 1*, London, 1967.

Chandler, D. P., 'The Kingdom of Kampuchea, March–October 1945: Japanese Sponsored Independence in Cambodia in World War Two', *Journal of Southeast Asian Studies*, vol. 17, no. 1, March 1986, pp. 80–93.

Chandler, D. P., *A History of Cambodia*, Washington D.C., 1999.

Charmley, J., *Duff Cooper*, London, 1986.

Charmley, J., *Churchill the End of Glory: A Political Biography*, Orlando, 1994.

Charmley, J., *Churchill's Grand Alliance: The Anglo-American Special Relationship 1940–57*, London, 1995.

Chen, K. C., *Vietnam and China 1938–54*, Princeton, 1969.

Churchill, R.S., *Winston S. Churchill, Volume 2: Young Statesman 1901–1914*, London, 1967.

Clarke, P., *The Last Thousand Days of the British Empire: Churchill, Roosevelt and the Birth of the Pax Americana*, New York, 2008.

Colbert, E., 'The Road Not Taken: Decolonialisation and Independence in Indonesia and Indochina', *Foreign Affairs*, vol. 51, April 1973, pp. 608–28.

Colbert, E., *Southeast Asia in International Politics 1941–1956*, London 1977.

Cruickshank, C., *SOE in the Far East*, Oxford, 1983.

D' Este, C., *Warlord: A Life of Winston Churchill at War, 1874–1945*, New York, 2008.

Day, D., 'Promise and Performance: Britain's Pacific Pledge 1943–5', *War and Society*, vol. 4, no. 2, September 1988, pp. 71–93.

Donnison, F. S. V., *British Military Administration in the Far East 1943–1946*, London, 1956.

Drachman, E. R., *United States Policy Towards Vietnam 1940–45*, New Jersey, 1970.

Duiker, W. J., *China and Vietnam: The Roots of Conflict*, Berkley, 1986.

Dulles, F. R., and Ridinger, G., 'The Anti-colonial Policies of Roosevelt', *Political Science Quarterly*, vol. XX, 1955, pp. 1–18.

Duncanson, D., *Government and Revolution in Vietnam*, London, 1968.

Dunn, P. M., *The First Vietnam War*, London, 1985.

Edmonds, R., 'Churchill and Stalin', in Blake, R., and Louis, W. R. (Eds), *Churchill*, Oxford, 1993.

Epstein, L. D., *Britain: An Uneasy Ally*, Chicago, 1954.

Fall, B., *Last Reflections on a War*, New York, 1967.

Fall, B., *The Two Vietnams*, London, 1963.

Gardner, L. C., *Approaching Vietnam: From World War Two Through Dienbienphu*, London, 1988.

Gardner, L. C., 'How We Lost Vietnam 1940–54', in Ryan, D., and Pungong, V. (Eds), *The United States and Decolonization, Power and Freedom*, Basingstoke, 2000.

Garrett, C. W., 'In Search of Grandeur: France in Vietnam 1940–1946', *The Review of Politics*, vol. 29, no. 3, July 1967, pp. 303–23.

Gibbons, W. C., *The U.S. Government and the Vietnam War, Part 1: 1945–1960*, Princeton, 1986.

Gilbert, M., *Winston Spencer Churchill, Volume 7: The Road to Victory 1941–1945*, London, 1986.

Gilbert, M, *Winston Spencer Churchill, Volume 8: Never Despair 1945–1965*, London, 1988.

Gilbert, M., *Churchill: A Life*, London, 1991.

Gilbert, M., *Churchill and America*, London 2006.

Gormly, J. L., *From Potsdam to the Cold War; Big Three Diplomacy 1945–7*, Delaware, 1990.

Goscha, C. E., and Ostermann, C. (Eds), *Connecting Histories: Decolonization and the Cold War in Southeast Asia, 1945–1962*, Stanford, 2009.

Gupta, P. S., *Imperialism and the British Labour Movement 1914–1965*, London, 1975.

Habibuddin, S. M., 'Franklin D. Roosevelt's Anti-colonial Policy Towards Asia. Its Implications for India, Indo-china and Indonesia 1941–5', *Journal of Indian History*, vol. 53, 1975, pp. 497–522.

Hammond, R. J., *Food Arid Agriculture in Britain 1939–1945*, London, 1954.

Hastings, M., *Winston's War: Churchill 1940–1945*, London, 2010.

Herman, A., *Gandhi and Churchill: The Epic Rivalry That Destroyed an Empire and Forged Our Age*, New York, 2009.

Herring, G. C., 'The Truman Administration and the Restoration of French Sovereignty in Indochina', *Diplomatic History*, vol. 1, no. 2, spring 1977, pp. 97–117.

Hess, G. R., 'Franklin D. Roosevelt and French Indochina', *Journal of American History*, vol. 59, no. 2, September 1972, pp. 353–68.

Hess, G. R., 'United States Policy and the Origins of the Vietminh War 1945–1946', *Peace and Change*, 3, Summer and Fall, 1975, pp. 24–33.

Hess, G. R., *The United States' Emergence as a Southeast Asian Power, 1940–1950*, New York, 1987.

Hesse-D'Alzon, C., *Presence Militaire Française En Indochine 1940–1945*, Vincennes, 1985.

Homberger, E., and Charmley, J. (Eds), *The Troubled Face of Biography*, New York, 1988.

Horne, A., *Macmillan: 1894–1956 Volume 1 of the Official Biography*, London, 1988.

Hughes, G., 'A 'Post-war' War: The British Occupation of French-Indochina, September 1945–March 1946', *Small Wars & Insurgencies*, vol. 17, no. 3, 2006, pp. 263–86.

Hunt, M. H., 'Conclusions: the Decolonization Puzzle in US Policy – Promise versus Performance', in Ryan, D., and Pungong V. (Eds), *The United States and Decolonization: Power and Freedom*, Basingstoke, 2000.

Hutton, C., *A Policy of Neglect: British Diplomacy Towards French Indochina 1943–45*, PhD thesis, UEA, 1995.

Hyam, R., *Britain's Declining Empire: The Road to Decolonisation 1918–1968*, Cambridge, 2006.

Irving, R. E. M., *The First Indochina War, French and American Policy 1945–1954*, London, 1975.

Jacobson, M, 'Winston Churchill and the Third Front', *Journal of Strategic Studies*, vol. 14, no. 3, September 1991, pp. 337–62.

Johnson, D., 'Churchill and France', in Blake, R., and Louis, W. R. (Eds), *Churchill*, Oxford, 1993.

Keegan, J., 'Churchill's Strategy', in Blake, R., and Louis, W. R. (Eds), *Churchill*, Oxford, 1993.

Kent, J., 'Anglo-French Co-operation 1939–49', *Journal of Imperial and Commonwealth History*, vol. 17, no. 1, 1988, pp. 55–82.

Kiernan, B., *How Pol Pot came to Power: A History of Communism in Kampuchea, 1930–75*, London, 2004.

Kimball, W. F., *The Juggler: Franklin Roosevelt as Wartime Statesman*, Princeton, 1991.

Kimball, W. F., 'Wheel Within a Wheel: Churchill, Roosevelt, and the Special Relationship', in Blake, R., and Louis, W. R. (Eds), *Churchill*, Oxford, 1993.

Kissinger, H., *Diplomacy*, London, 1994.

La Feber, W., 'Roosevelt, Churchill and Indochina 1942–5', *American Historical Review*, vol. 80, 1975, pp. 1277–95.

La Feber, W., 'The American View of Decolonization, 1776–1920: An Ironic Legacy, in Ryan, D., and Pungong V. (Eds), *The United States and Decolonization: Power and Freedom*, Basingstoke, 2000.

Lacouture, J., *De Gaulle: The Rebel: 1890–1944*, London, 1993.

Lacouture, J., *De Gaulle: The Ruler: 1945–1970*, London, 1993.

Lancaster, D., *The Emancipation of French Indochina*, London, 1961.

Lawrence, Atwood, M., 'Transnational Coalition Building The Making of the Cold War in Indochina', *Diplomatic History*, vol. 26, no. 3, Summer 2002, pp. 453–80.

Lawrence, Atwood, M., *Assuming The Burden: Europe and the American Commitment to War in Vietnam*, London, 2005.

Lawrence, Atwood, M., and Logevall, F. (Eds), *The First Vietnam War: Colonial Conflict and Cold War Crisis*, Massachusetts, 2007.

Lee, J. M., and Petter, M., *The Colonial Office, War, And Development Policy: Organisation and the Planning of A Metropolitan Initiative 1939–1945*, London, 1982.

Louis, W. R., *Imperialism at Bay: The United States and the Decolonisation of the British Empire 1941–5*, New York, 1978.

Machiavelli, N., *The Prince*, London, 2003.

Marr, D. G, 'Vietnam 1945: Some Questions', *Vietnam Forum*, vol. 6, Summer 1985, pp. 155–93.

Marr, D. G., *Vietnam 1945: The Quest For Power*, Berkley, 1995.

McLane, C. B., *Soviet Strategies in South-East Asia*, Princeton, 1966.

Merrill, D., 'The Ironies of History: The United States and the Decolonization of India', in Ryan, D., and Pungong V. (Eds), *The United States and Decolonization: Power and Freedom*, Basingstoke, 2000.

Morgan, D. J., *The Official History of Colonial Development Volume 2, Developing British Colonial Resources 1945–1951*, London, 1980.

Munro, D., *The Four Horsemen: The Flames of War in the Third World*, New Jersey, 1987.

Neal, L., *The Washington Ambassadorship of Lord Halifax 1941–1946*, MLitt thesis, Oxford, 1985.

Neilson, K., and Otte, T. G., *The Permanent Under-Secretary for Foreign Affairs, 1854–1946*, New York, 2009.

Neville, P., *Britain in Vietnam: Prelude to Disaster 1945–46*, London, 2008.

Nitz, K., 'Independence without Nationalists? The Japanese and Vietnamese Nationalism during the Japanese period 1940–5', *Journal of Southeast Asian Studies*, vol. 15, no. 1, March 1984, pp. 108–33.

Nong Van Dan., *Churchill, Eden and Indo-China, 1951–1955*, London, 2010.

Orders, P., 'Adjusting to a New Period in World History: Franklin Roosevelt and European Colonialism', in Ryan, D., and Pungong V. (Eds), *The United States and Decolonization: Power and Freedom*, Basingstoke, 2000.

Palleson, E. S., *United States Policy Toward Decolonialization in Asia 1945–50*, DPhil thesis, Oxford, 1995.

Pollock, F. E., and Kimball, W. F., 'In Search of Monsters to Destroy: Roosevelt and Colonialism', in Kimball, W. F., *The Juggler: Franklin Roosevelt as Wartime Statesman*, Princeton, 1991.

Pungong, V., 'The United States and the International Trusteeship System', in Ryan, D., and Pungong V. (Eds), *The United States and Decolonization: Power and Freedom*, Basingstoke, 2000.

Reddi, V. M., *A History of the Cambodian Independence Movement 1863–1955*, Triupati, 1973.

Rhodes James, R., 'Churchill the Parliamentarian, Orator and Statesman', in Blake, R., and Louis, W. R (Eds), *Churchill*, Oxford, 1993.

Roberts, A., *The Holy Fox: The Life of Lord Halifax*, London, 1997.

Roberts, A., *Masters and Commanders: How Roosevelt, Churchill, Marshall and Alanbrooke Won the War in the West*, London, 2008.

Robinson, R., 'Imperial Theory as a Question of Imperialism after Empire', *Journal of Imperial and Commonwealth History*, vol. 12, January 1984, pp. 42–54.

Rosie, G., *The British in Vietnam*, London, 1970.

Ryan, D., 'The United States, Decolonization and the World System', in Ryan, D., and Pungong V. (Eds), *The United States and Decolonization: Power and Freedom*, Basingstoke, 2000.

Ryan, D., and Pungong V. (Eds), *The United States and Decolonization: Power and Freedom*, Basingstoke, 2000.

Rydell, R. W., and Kroes, R., *Buffalo Bill in Bologna: The Americanization of the World, 1869–1922*, Chicago, 2005.

Sainsbury, K., *Churchill and Roosevelt at War: The War They Fought and the Peace They Hoped to Make*, London, 1994.

Saville, J., *The Politics of Continuity: British Foreign Policy and the Labour Government 1945–1946*, London, 1993.

Sbrega, J., *Anglo American Relations and Colonialism in East Asia 1941–5*, London, 1983.

Sbrega, J., 'First Catch Your Hare: Anglo-American Perspectives on Indochina during the Second World War', *Journal of Southeast Asian Studies*, vol. 14, no. 1, August 1984, pp. 63–78.

Sbrega, J., 'Determination Versus Drift: The Anglo-American Debate over the Trusteeship Issue 1941–5', *Pacific Historical Review*, vol. 55, no. 2, May 1986, pp. 256–80.

Sbrega, J., 'The Anti-Colonial Policies of Franklin D. Roosevelt: A Re-appraisal', *Political Science Quarterly*, vol. 101, no. 1, 1986, pp. 65–84.

Sherwin, M. J., *A World Destroyed: The Atomic Bomb and the Grand Alliance*, New York, 1975.

Sherwood, R. E., *Roosevelt and Hopkins: An Intimate History*, New York, 1948.

Shiraishi, T., and Furuta, M. (Eds), *Indochina in the 1940s and 1950s*, New York, 1992.

Short, A., *The Origins of the Vietnam War*, London, 1989.

Siracusa, J. M., 'The United States, Viet-Nam and the Cold War: A Re-appraisal', *Journal of Southeast Asian Studies*, 1974, pp. 82–101.

Smart, N., *Biographical Dictionary of British Generals of the Second World War*, Barnsley, 2005.

Smith, C., *England's Last War Against France: Fighting Vichy 1940–1942*, London, 2009.

Smith, G., *American Diplomacy During The Second World War 1941–1945*, New York, 1965.

Smith, R. B., *Viet-Nam and the West*, London, 1968.

Smith, R. B., 'The Japanese Period in Indochina and the Coup of 9 March 1945', *Journal of Southeast Asian Studies*, September 1978, pp. 268–301.

Smith, T. O., 'Britain and Cambodia, September 1945–November 1946: A Reappraisal', *Diplomacy and Statecraft*, vol. 17, no. 1, 2006, pp. 73–91.

Smith, T. O., 'Europe, Americanization and Globalization', Review Article, *European History Quarterly*, vol. 37, no. 2, 2007, pp. 301–9.

Smith, T. O., *Britain and the Origins of the Vietnam War: UK policy in Indo-China 1943–50*, London, 2007.

Smith, T. O., 'Resurrecting the French Empire: British Military Aid to Vietnam 1945–7', *University of Sussex Journal of Contemporary History*, vol. 11, 2007, pp. 1–13.

Smith, T. O., 'Major-General Sir Douglas Gracey: Peacekeeper or Peace-Enforcer, Saigon 1945?', *Diplomacy and Statecraft*, vol. 21, no. 2, 2010, pp. 226–39.

Smith, T. O., 'Lord Killearn and British Diplomacy Regarding French Indo-Chinese Rice Supplies 1946–48' *History* (forthcoming).

Sockeel-Richarte, P., Le Problème De La Soverainte Française Sur L'Indochine', in Institut Charle De Gaulle, *General De Gaulle Et L'Indochine 1940–61*, Actes Etablis par G. Pilleul, Paris, 1982.

Soustelle, J., 'Indochina and Korea: One Front', *Foreign Affairs*, vol. 29, 1950, pp. 56–66.

Spector, R. H., 'Allied Intelligence and Indochina 1943–45', *Pacific Historical Review*, vol. 51, 1982, pp. 23–50.

Spector, R. H., *Advice and Support: The Early Years of the United States Army in Vietnam 1941–1960*, Washington D.C., 1983.

Stockwell, A. J., 'The United States and Britain's Decolonization of Malaya, 1942–57', in Ryan, D., and Pungong V. (Eds), *The United States and Decolonization: Power and Freedom*, Basingstoke, 2000.

Tarling, N., 'Some Rather Nebulous Capacity: Lord Killearn's Appointment in Southeast Asia', *Modern Asian Studies*, vol. 20, no. 3, 1986, pp. 559–600.

Tarling, N., *Britain, Southeast Asia and the onset of the Cold War 1945–1950*, Cambridge, 1998.

Thomas, M., 'Free France, the British Government and the Future of French Indochina 1940–45', *Journal of Southeast Asian Studies*, vol. 28, no. 1, 1997, pp. 137–60.

Thomas, M., 'Silent Partners: SOE's French Indo-China Section 1943–1945', *Modern Asian Studies*, vol. 34, no. 4, 2000, pp. 943–76.

Thomas, M., 'French Decolonization', in Thomas, M, and Moore, B., and Butler, L. J., *Crises of Empire: Decolonization and Europe's Imperial States, 1918–1975*, London, 2008.

Thomas, M., and Moore, B., and Butler, L. J., *Crises of Empire: Decolonization and Europe's Imperial States, 1918–1975*, London, 2008.

Thomas, M., 'Processing Decolonization: British Strategic Analysis of Conflict in Vietnam and Indonesia, 1945–1950', in Goscha, C. E., and Ostermann, C. (Eds), *Connecting Histories: Decolonization and the Cold War in Southeast Asia, 1945–1962*, Stanford, 2009.

Thorne, C., 'Indochina and Anglo-American Relations 1942–5', *Pacific Historical Review*, vol. 45, 1976, pp. 73–96.

Thorne, C., *Allies of a Kind: The United States, Britain and the War Against Japan, 1941–1945*, London, 1979.

Tinker, H., 'The Contradiction of Empire in Asia 1945–48: The Military Dimension', *Journal of Imperial and Commonwealth History*, vol. 16, January 1988, pp. 218–33.

Ton That Thien., 'The Influence of Indo-China on the Evolution of the French Union', *India Quarterly*, vol. 10, part 4, 1954, pp. 295–313.

Tonnesson, S., 'The Longest Wars: Indochina 1945–75' *Journal of Peace Research*, vol. 22, no. 1, 1985, pp. 9–29.

Tonnesson, S., *The Vietnamese Revolution of 1945: Roosevelt, Ho Chi Minh and De Gaulle in a World at War*, London, 1991.

Tonnesson, S., 'Filling The Vacuum: 1945 in French Indochina, the Netherlands East Indies and British Malaya', in Antlov, H., and Tonnesson, S. (Eds), *Imperial Policy and Southeast Asian Nationalism 1930–1957*, Surrey, 1995.

Tonnesson, S., 'Franklin D. Roosevelt, Trusteeship and Indochina: A Reassessment', in Lawrence, Atwood, M., and Logevall, F. (Eds), *The First Vietnam War: Colonial Conflict and Cold War Crisis*, Massachusetts, 2007.

Tonnesson, S., *Vietnam 1946: How the War Began*, London, 2010.

Vickery, M., *Kampuchea: Politics, Economics and Society*, London, 1986.

Viorst, M, *Hostile Allies: FDR and Charles De Gaulle*, New York, 1965.

Watt, D. C., *Succeeding John Bull, America in Britain's Place, 1900–1975*, Cambridge, 1984.

Waugh, E., *Brideshead Revisited: The Sacred and Profane Memoirs of Captain Charles Ryder*, London, 2000.

Wheeler-Bennett, J. W., *KingGeorge VI: His Life and Reign*, London, 1958.

Windrow, M., *The Last Valley: Dien Bien Phu and the French Defeat in Vietnam*, London, 2004.

Ziegler, P., *Mountbatten*, Glasgow, 1985.

Index